Yank

Yank

The Memoir of a World War II Soldier (1941–1945)
From the Desert War of Africa
to the Allied Invasion of Europe,
from German POW Camp to Home Again

Ted Ellsworth

Thunder's Mouth Press
New York

Yank: The Memoir of a World War II Soldier (1941–1945)
From the Desert War of Africa to the Allied Invasion of Europe,
from German POW Camp to Home Again

Published by
Thunder's Mouth Press
An Imprint of Avalon Publishing Group, Inc.
245 West 17th St., 11th Floor
New York, NY 10011

Library of Congress Cataloging-in-Publication Data is available.

ISBN-10: 1-56025-834-9
ISBN-13: 978-1-56025-834-6

9 8 7 6 5 4 3 2 1

Book design by Susan Canavan
Printed in the United States of America
Distributed by Publishers Group West

To Barbara

Table of Contents

Publisher's Note

This book was written in 1945. Every effort has been made to retain its historical flavor and to remain as faithful as possible to the author's original prose. Certain phrases that may be unfamiliar to contemporary readers have not expanded upon within the text itself; however, the publisher has added an endnotes section to explain and expand upon any possibly unfamiliar references.

Foreword

It was sunny and warm on the Dartmouth College Campus in June 1940, and we seniors waiting for the graduation exercise known as Commencement had nothing to do but sit in the sun and talk. Ted Ellsworth was next to me. We discussed potential jobs and wondered what we would do next. We read the newspaper. Two stories in the *New York Times* that month had been galvanizing. The first was a wake-up call. It began, "Since dawn, the fate of France and perhaps of the Western world has been in the hands of God—and the French army. The sun rose at 5:02." The second came two weeks later: "Adolph Hitler's mighty men in armor—100,000 strong in the advance guard—turned westward last night on a new tangent: the English channel as their goal."

Quite suddenly talk about post-graduation jobs ceased. What was ahead? What should we do? We turned from the newspapers to the radios in our dorm rooms and there we listened to the voice of Winston Churchill:

> *. . . even if, which I do not for a moment believe, this island or any large part there of should become subjected*

and starving under the heel of the conqueror, then with the aid of the British fleet and from our empire beyond the seas, we shall carry on the struggle until in God's good time, the new world with all its power and might shall come forth to the aid and rescue of the old.

Both of us decided to join the British Army. Ted Ellsworth and I had been close friends and companions since the seventh grade in Dubuque, Iowa. He was and had always been a fascinating and charismatic figure, always at the center of things, from football games to escapades, always laughing, always the life of the party, always ready for new adventures. Together we climbed the bluffs along the Mississippi River, boasted about good-looking girls, rode our bikes through cornfields and together we decided to join the British Army.

After the war, we kept up with each other. Ted returned to the bluffs of Dubuque, Iowa, to raise his family and start a business. I went on to publish a newspaper in Oceanside, California, and begin a career as a syndicated columnist, author, and television news commentator. That was some time ago. I am eighty-eight now and my good friend Ted has been gone for twenty years.

I'd like to tell him, "Ted, you captured it, thank you!" In all the years of our friendship there was one thing I never knew about him: I never knew he could write. However, Ted Ellsworth, a hero in battle, writes about battle brilliantly, amusingly, and factually. You will find this out in the pages that follow.

Tom Braden, 2005

Prologue

Nov. 15, 1944
2712 Reynier Ave.
Los Angeles, Calif.

My darling Teddy,

This is the first opportunity I have had to write since that day—at least to write alone. And now I have the courage to do it. I feel sure that some day you will read this letter, and that is why I am writing it. Not just because I want to get something out of my system.

It was while I was talking on the phone to Aunt Alice about 8:30 that Tuesday morning that Watt started to bark. He was up in my bedroom. That is the day the laundry man comes, so I excused myself for a moment, thinking that it was he coming up the drive.

But, instead I saw Daddy and Uncle Clifford, and I started to shake. It could only mean bad news. But I went back to the phone and listened to Aunt Alice though I couldn't tell you to this day what she was talking about.

I was still shaking but I mustered enough strength to gaily say, "Well, what brings you two up here at this hour of the morning?", hoping against hope that my intuitions were wrong. "Missing-in-action"—they are agonizing words but at least there is hope in them. And that is what I am doing—hoping and counting and praying for your return from this mess some day. I know you will come back to me, darling. You must come back to me.

And so I cried on Daddy's shoulder, and your dear little Watt knew something was wrong, because I suddenly felt his paws on my shoulders and his nose in my neck. He has grown since you went away. I turned around to pet him and make him feel a little better. And, too, I felt sorry that Uncle Clifford had to go through this, after losing Bill. I had another cup of coffee and a cigarette and dried my tears. We phoned Mother who was in Grand Rapids. We got them out of bed, and they were stunned. Mother wanted to come home right away, but I persuaded her not to.

Then Daddy and I drove to your house. We walked in the front door because it was open and found Uncle Clark at breakfast. I left Daddy with him and went upstairs to see your Mother. She cried, but she was very brave, too, and after a while I went home. The word got around town and the phone rang continuously and Aunt Alice and Uncle Philo came over, and it was bedlam. I didn't get any of the housework done. I intended to write you that day, but I couldn't.

Carol and John urged me to go to Moline with them, when they took John down to catch his plane. I wanted to get away from the house, away from the phone, and away from the doorbell. So Watt and I went to Moline, and it was a beautiful day. Watt and I sat in the back and comforted each other. At the field he was amazed at the planes and kept his eyes on them every minute.

When I came home that night, Daddy wasn't there. I fed Watt and answered about a dozen phone calls, and then Daddy came home and he answered some more. We cleaned up and phoned Mary at Leiser's, ordered dinner, and went out there. We had time for one drink before dinner.

Afterwards, we took Watt for a walk, and he cried a little during the walk. I mean Daddy, not Watt. The children Halloweening wanted to pet Watt. That night I didn't realize how tired I was until my head hit the pillow. I ached in every bone in my body. I slept the sleep of the dead. But before that I prayed. Darling, I love you with all my mind and body.

The next day we called Mother and Aunt Marj again. They both told me that I had better continue with the plans to go to California with your Mother and see your Father for the first time. Everyone told me that, and so here I am. I guess it is better than sitting around Dubuque waiting. I miss Watt terribly, but Mother and Daddy are taking good care of him.

I am glad that I came to California, even though it has rained and rained. I love your Father. I think he is a wonderful person and he is so sweet and kind to me. He looks unhappy though, and that bothers me. He loves you so much.

I have seen your brother Ben several times and have grown very fond of him. We got along well from the moment we met. All of these things I will sometime talk to you about, but I just thought I would put them down here.

If only the word will come soon that you are all right. It will come, but the suspense is terrible. My sweetheart, you know that I could never love another man after knowing and loving you—and knowing your love for me. We were one, we are one, and we will always be that way. And now that you are home and have read this, won't you please take me in your arms and kiss me and hold me close forever and ever. It is hard for me to keep the tears away. I love you, I love you, Teddy.

Barbara

Chapter One

Dartmouth was playing Princeton in a rather dull affair early that autumn of 1941. Our minds weren't much on the game. Barbara and I had driven East on our honeymoon and were seeing old college mates for the first time since graduation in 1940, when France was falling, Italy was stabbing, and Britain was holding its breath. And not many of us were conscious of the war, because it was going to take the Battle of Britain to get us interested.

But this was more than a year later when Tom, sitting next to me, still wearing some of his college-day clothes, while I had bought new ones to show the boys I was doing all right in Chicago, asked, "What are you going to do about this war, and the draft and all that?"

"I don't know. It looks as though I won't be called for a year or more."

"Bolte and those guys have left for England to join the Army there. I'm thinking of going, too."

"What's the deal?"

"Well, it seems there is some sort of old American Regiment over there, and the State Department is letting twelve fellows from here join. Sort of an Eagle Squadron set-up, only you go in the Army."

We were on a honeymoon, and I didn't want to talk about such things just then, but I told Braden I would write him about it, because it sounded like a good trip. I had already made up my mind to go, but was too scared to admit it to myself. A few weeks later when Tom came back to Dubuque to say good-bye to his family, having quit his job in New York, I told him I was going along with him, if it was all right with Barb and the British Embassy in Washington. Barbara cried when I asked her, nodded her head slowly, and as far as I know, that was the first of two times she cried during the war. I immediately wished she had put her foot down. This thing was gathering momentum.

Not wishing to worry Mother any more than necessary, I didn't tell her until early in the morning of the day I was to leave. I awakened her, sat on the edge of the bed, and heard myself making words and I hoped some sense. Maybe it was because she was sleepy, but she seemed very calm, taking my hand, looking at the lifeline on the palm, studying it, and then patting my arm with the utmost confidence. "We Richards live a long time. You will be all right."

Mother gave me some help packing my suitcase, and the last thing I tossed into it was my uncle's .45 pistol. This gesture struck me as being cheap, melodramatic, an attempt to be glamorous. I had never fired a pistol, never wanted to, hoped I wouldn't have to, but Braden had said to bring a pistol. I was hurrying with the packing, though there was no rush, but I was trying to forget that perhaps I was playing the fool. My father-in-law had already spent fifteen minutes on the phone, trying to talk me out of it. I couldn't back out now. Tom seemed calm. I learned later he was in worse shape than I.

I kissed Mother good-bye, told her not to worry, and she cried, which she didn't do when I was reported missing-in-action nearly three years later. I spent the afternoon saying good-bye to friends. They asked me why I was joining the English, who hadn't paid their debts from the last war.

"This is our war, too," I said, trying to throw a skein of idealism about this move I was beginning to doubt.

Being a bridegroom, I couldn't say that the adventure appealed to me. Then followed the theme that we pulled England's chestnuts out once, and here we were about to do it again. This bewildered me. I was meeting for the first time the violent anti-British feeling of the Middle West. I hadn't realized it existed. I soon found myself agreeing, because I had never thought of the British much one way or another, and didn't know enough to argue. Four years later, I have passed through the agreeing stage, into the angered state, out of the habit of keeping quiet and letting the people rave, on to the cool plateau of discussing England pro and con. But this is many thousands of anti-British statements later.

My father merely said that he hoped I would play St. Andrews golf course in Edinburgh, which he had done in the last war, and to always remember, "It is the guy in the next tent who gets hit."

I used to tell Tom he was the guy in the next tent, and after a while, Tom didn't think it was very funny.

Barbara, Tom, and I drove to Chicago, and spent one night in our apartment there. The next morning Barbara made our double bed, as she had for four months, and put both our handkerchiefs under the pillows. Then she caught herself, pulled mine out, and said, "Look what I did!" I thought she was going to break down, and that would have been that for me. "Don't get silly now," I said defensively. She was only twenty and already her world was beginning to spin.

In Washington, Tom went in to see Colonel Rex Benson, the British military attaché, ahead of me, and while waiting in the reception room, I was offered the use of a castle in Scotland to do some grouse-shooting. I thought that maybe this trip would be all right after all. An effete clerk said to me, "You know, I love wars. They are so secret. No one knows anything except the Germans."

Later, when Colonel Benson told me to take tails, a run-about if I had one, some liquor, plenty of cigarettes, and several hundred dollars, I felt better. Maybe we would just be liaison officers around London, or guarding the King and Queen, one day on, three days off. Of course, Colonel Benson had not been in England since 1938, and was a bit out of touch with things. We had forgotten our tails, we had only three hundred dollars between us, and the only run-about we had was Tom's old station wagon that had just limped in to Washington and we sold for a hundred dollars. It would have been better if the Colonel had told us to take silk stockings, lipstick, lingerie, chocolate, and soap.

Our physical examination consisted of being asked if we were in good health, and being told that we both looked like fine boys. Later we learned that such things as our moral character had been checked, whether or not we could hold our liquor, if we would be apt to break up some English mess, and how we stood in the draft. They had turned down one boy who was obviously volunteering to avoid the draft, which might have been an attempt to cut off his nose to save his face.

The last I saw of Colonel Benson, he was complaining that he had to go to Kansas the following week and talk to an American Legion gathering. He laughed, "The Legion men always ask questions they shouldn't in war time."

As we went out the door, we were told we were joining a very fine Regiment, which didn't mean much to us, then.

Our stay in New York was expensive, but we didn't care, because we didn't know that for the next year we were to earn just fifty cents a day. We gathered about us all our Dartmouth classmates. Graduating from college, one is mentally set to meet many of life's disappointments. One has been told time and again that there are many things which will get one down. But the one we are not ready for is the flat feeling of seeing people in different situations than the old days. Usually these meetings are not too successful, surprise failures, which leave me with a guilty feeling, that maybe it is my fault and not the external surroundings. The carefree casualness of those college days is lacking.

The stay in New York became a delay. It was in the days when a lot of the boys were trying to line up Naval Intelligence work in Washington. When a man's position and salary remained static until the army took him, unless he had two children. When youth had that futile feeling, marking time at work. Couples were confused with each other regarding the war and what to do about it. We were resentful that a war had come to break up our lives, and we made visits to our draft boards to see how we stood. Pacifism and isolationism were going downhill fast. Staffs of peacetime pursuits were being cut. Life had become a series of choices again. We were beginning to realize that the war was only a phase of the next fifty years and not a crusade and an end in itself. Tom and I wanted to be dashing and laughing, but we were only sad. If we expressed an opinion and older men agreed, we were pleased with ourselves. Because we had the fear we had false ideals. We had the fear, too, that each generation would have to make up for the mistakes of the preceding one. We were unconsciously preparing for a new life to fight against a "new order." We were going to fight *for* nothing, only *against*.

All of us were realizing that the average life is the happiest, and why was it disappearing? When the war was over, we all vowed to live a normal, average, plain, family life and to be the happiest of men.

Like all the soldiers going away in those days, we got countless bottles of liquor for presents. We thought we'd be gone eighteen months and it would be all over, and we felt a bit guilty getting gifts of cigarette lighters, pipes, tobacco, leather cases, cookies, and vitamin pills. Because people showed more confidence in us than we had in ourselves, the presents made it obligatory to do a good job. Tom and I admired humans; that they went on cheerfully in the face of awful sadness. But we blamed humans for this war we didn't yet understand.

We spent some of our time writing to relatives and friends we had been putting off for years. We wanted to leave with a clean slate. We were getting enough criticism anyway for joining an army that burned our Capitol more than a hundred years ago.

Our starting date was postponed again. Shipping was in a bad way on the North Atlantic. But we had to get out of New York, to avoid prolonging good-byes, and so that Barbara and I could part slowly without a lot of phone calls. We were to start from Montreal, so Barbara, Tom, my Aunt Marj, and I took the train for Canada. Jerry, my mother-in-law, made a surprise trip from Dubuque and met us there.

The first few nights were gay, no doubt about that. Then followed a subdued calm feeling, the dawning of just why we were all gathered in Montreal. Those days, Barbara and I lingered in bed just a bit longer in the mornings.

She said to me, "I guess happiness is some sort of feeling that lots of times we don't recognize until it's over."

"I suppose. But I'll be back soon, and then we will live slowly. We will have earned that, by all this. Just the way we earned the right to sleep late Sundays, by getting up early the other six days."

I thought of some quote about parting being all we know of heaven and all we need of hell.

At last it came. We were to leave on a Free French boat; no convoy, fast, sailing from St. John, New Brunswick. Barbara did some last-minute shopping for me, Aunt Marj made arrangements for them to leave Montreal, Tom got us train tickets to St. John, and Jerry said she wanted to talk to me.

"Ted, your mother wonders if your love and Barbara's can outlast this separation. You are so young. I'm not sure you appreciate what Barbara is going through on all this."

I could see right away that Jerry had become confused and deep feeling, not the best combination for happiness at any time.

I heard her say, in our room of the Mount Royal, "It will be easy to grow away from each other, and I've been so anxious for this marriage to work out. Damn this Hitler! Try to write us as often as you can. Waiting back here will be no picnic, though I know you are not off on a sight-seeing trip. We will take care of Barbs, until you return. Be sure to take Father's watch for good luck. I've been pretty mad at you sometimes, but I will pray for you with all my heart, for I love you very much. I'm being vague, but I hope you know what I mean. One can never say what he means at such a time as this, which is unfortunate."

"Don't worry, Jerry," was all I could say, as the whole idea was beginning to frighten me.

They left that night.

Leaving their train, Tom and I walked through the snow a while, and hailed a horse-drawn sleigh which was for hire and looked very picturesque. We thought it might cheer us. When we got in, the driver wanted to take us to a French house of ill repute. Disappointed in this picturesque sleigh and driver done up in furs, we told him to take us back to the hotel, where with the help of many beers we became talkative again, ending in an argument on what years Herb Joesting played for Minnesota in the late twenties. We climaxed the heated talk by telegraphing the *Chicago Tribune*, and when the answer was slipped under our door the next day, pulling us out of a big sleep, we had quite a laugh.

Those hours had contained the first of many offers to go to houses, the first of many agonizing good-byes, the first of many drinks and big sleeps, and laughs and arguments on football players of the twenties in the following years.

The Free French boat sprung a leak, which meant more delay. When the family had gone, we were left with a terribly lost feeling. The more we hung around, the less heart we had for what we were doing. It is best to do things suddenly, continue fast, believing you are right, entertaining no qualms or misgivings about your decision. We talked about turning in the whole thing. In our gaudy overcoats, colored socks, high-water trousers, loud neckties, tan caps, and college suits we felt out of place among the Canadian soldiers filling the bars, lobbies, and stations. It looked, after America, like a country united in one belief, though the talk on the war effort under the camouflage of the uniforms was far from that.

We moved from the Mount Royal to a room that cost us

seventy-five cents a night, and one morning, the Ministry of War Transport phoned to tell us to move to St. John immediately to catch a Norwegian boat. We were told, "You'll find her nice, and worth your wait."

Off we went, and twenty-four hours later walked on the deck of a sleek, gray vessel that had made the run once a month since Hitler's invasion of Poland. The passenger list on the merchant ship included Tom and me, a Labrador explorer, and a drunken doctor who got it in his head some way or other that I believed the world was flat. We ate with the captain that night who apologized about the toilets and plumbing being frozen. He said they seldom stopped long enough for anything but vital repairs. Toward the end of the meal, he rubbed his hands, smiled, said in fair English, "Well, I hope you don't have to swim for it."

We were silent, and he added, "Of course, I won't have to."

Some of the crew told us after dinner he was rather serious about going down with the ship, when the time came. This tall, middle-aged, gray-haired lean Norseman was typical of the type who had kept the Battle of the Atlantic even to date.

With the reports of submarines operating off the mouth of the Bay of Fundy to cheer us, we left in a bad storm, to make a fast run alone. Tom immediately got seasick, after telling me several times that he had never been seasick. And I suppose he never did before, as this was his first sea voyage.

Ten hours on the way, fire broke out in the hold, and the sailors agreed it was sabotage. As far as I was concerned, it was the end. In a few hours, after we had headed for shore, and the vessel received a severe jolt, I knew it was the end. I got Tom out of his sickbed, threw a life preserver around his shoulders, and told him we had been torpedoed. The drunken doctor mumbling we hadn't been torpedoed made me feel sure it was time to play "Nearer My God To Thee." Tom and I stumbled out on deck to find water pouring into our ship and a fire tug tied to us. That was the jolt we had felt earlier.

Fire did not reach the ammunition and fuel that was on board as the crew with blackened faces fought the blaze all night—while the doctor slept, the Labrador explorer referred to it all as "bloody bad luck," and Tom and I shivered. Port was reached, with the starboard deck almost awash, and thick smoke pouring from the hull. Newspaper reporters met us, and the Captain told them it was a "faulty electric cable" that had caused the fire, one hour after he told us, in our cabin, that it was undoubtedly sabotage.

The British put us up at St. John's Admiral Beatty Hotel, with free room service, a nice bed, and good meals, telling us to hang on. More waiting followed, and we could have screamed, so tired were we of good-byes, hotel lobbies, phone calls from the Ministry of War Transport, seeing men in offices who didn't seem at all upset about the delay, talking ships, and thinking how badly the war was going for Britain. If we didn't get over there soon, we wouldn't be able to make the world safe for democracy.

Tom kept saying something about a poor start means a good ending.

One day, a Navy Officer took us to lunch. He had been torpedoed twice, was waiting for a third ship, and also wanted to get home to England as soon as possible, but not until the war was won. That talk seemed strange, then, but the sailors around St. John made us a bit more sure that we were doing the right thing by getting in Global Struggle Two.

The next boat was an old Irish tub, rusty and red. The crew was basic and good company, with a very gloomy outlook and low morale. Their boat was slow and ancient, and it was only a question of time. Tom and I were the only passengers, and Capt. Haddock invited us to his cabin the first night.

"I hope your passage isn't paid yet. I don't think we'll make it. You are to sleep in your clothes."

We said nothing, took the nip the captain offered us, and wished we were home.

Talk got around to boxing, books, and poetry, with Captain Haddock carrying the conversation. When it came to the war, as all conversations did, the Captain summed it up with, "All these 'isms' boil down to selfishism and that's why the world cracked up."

Answering a question from Tom, the Captain said that there would be none of this going down with the ship as far as he was concerned. "If I can make it back to port, I'm one more man to take out another ship."

That seemed to make good sense to us.

At breakfast, our first morning out, Tom and I were early, waited for Captain Haddock to come down. Without so much as a nod of good-morning, the Captain took his place at the head of the small table, and prayed in silence, with clasped hands. During this minute, we were embarrassed and scared. We were at the mouth of the Bay of Fundy.

Captain Haddock said, after prayer, "Well, America, submarines are reported twenty miles away. Two Greek ships have been sunk near here. The hold started taking on water during the night, and we have engine trouble that keeps us to five knots. We're headed for Halifax, but I still hope your passage hasn't been paid."

At this point, Tom and I had had all the worrying we could

handle for awhile, and it was many months before we became frightened again. Halifax was reached, and we got our luggage off the boat. The Eastern Canadian port was filled with sailors, soldiers, and whores; and the streets were embellished with drunks during the day and night. To us, the place looked colorful. The basin was loaded with ships, eight-nine alone laid up for lack of men to work on them.

We bothered the Ministry of War Transport.

Pearl Harbor had happened a few weeks before we got orders to join a Norwegian boat that had sailed out of Bergen nearly three years before. We had little time to make the ship, but managed to get a customs officer to contact an Irish steward on our old boat and break the ship's bond for a case of scotch—sold to us for two dollars a bottle. Tom carried this up the rope ladder on to the "Brant County," one half hour before the boat joined the convoy for the trip across.

Chapter Two

Twenty-two merchants and six corvettes made up our convoy.

At night I went to sleep hearing the clump-clump-clump of the boots worn by the watchman on the bridge, which was on the roof of our double cabin. The only voice was an occasional singing out of the degree of our course. There was no shave, wash, or change of clothing all the way over, because it was too cold. The plumbing was frozen, but we used the Captain's bath water to flush the toilets. Where his bath water was disappearing remained a mystery to him the entire voyage. He swore about it in broken English and none of us said a word. We felt guilty, but the toilets had to be flushed.

Pancake ice near Newfoundland. . . . A rough ocean and the Captain joking about those who did not show up for meals. . . . Broadcasts of Lord Haw-Haw. . . . Gloomy war news and the Captain saying we really shouldn't play the radio, but it would be all right just to get the news. . . . Time heavy on our hands. . . . Thinking of your past life. . . . And some memories making you feel cheap. . . . The realization that the banal, ostrich dreams of isolationism were wrong. . . . The signs on board, "Serve in Silence" or "A slip of the lip may sink a ship". . . . The zigzagging convoy. . . . Coats on cabin hooks being shined by the constant motion of the ship. . . . Rummy games with the First Mate. . . . Read, sleep, and smoke. . . . Exchanging of books with the other five passengers. . . .

Thinking how wrong the saying is about how they who go feel not the pain of parting. . . . Ack-ack machine-gun practice when in range of German bombers. . . . Six rapid depth charges, and we fumble for our life jackets and extra clothing. . . . Setting our clocks ahead six hours. . . . A speech by the President who says we must sacrifice our personal happiness for something larger, and Tom and I are not too sure what "larger" means. . . . Beautiful sunsets over the ocean toward America. . . . More depth charges and the game of hide and seek for keeps goes on. . . . Read, sleep, and smoke. . . . Calm nights in the Gulf Stream with stars or the moon's reflection on the North Atlantic. . . . The moon stares softly through the silhouette of the ship's funnels and ropes and you stand on deck and wish life could go on through eternity. . . . Learning the values in English currency from someone who has been over before. . . . Kites above the convoy to ward off dive bombers as we near Ireland. . . .

Captain Brevik had not seen his family in Norway for three years. Fat, with bushy, red eyebrows, aged fifty-seven, partly bald, short, he was another man who looked like Churchill. He never called the Germans anything but "swine" and was continually swearing about the "goddamn Dane" who was in command of the convoy. When Tom gave him some fudge we had received in Canada, he gave us whiskey in his cabin. This exchange continued for several evenings. Each morning he would come in to our double cabin and get us up with, "Good morning, America!"

"Good morning, Captain," one of us managed to say. "How's the weather today?" as we felt the ship standing on its ear doing things Nijinsky never thought of in his finest hour.

"Moderately rough, America. Moderately rough. Breakfast is ready."

"How's the news this morning, Captain?" Tom or I would ask as we lurched out of bed.

"With these Japs in it, the fight to put Britain, America, and Norway out of existence is really beginning. Really beginning. And I don't know what they are doing out in Libya. They chase one way, then another. Yes, moderately rough, today, America."

Reaching the Belfast ship-building yards, we were anxious to get off, yet afraid of the disappointment we might face. The debarkation officials had met no case like ours, and though our letter from the British Embassy kept us from the third degree, it was not good enough to keep us out of jail. We were thrown in with Irish Republican Army suspects. We were both slightly disappointed in this, as we thought at least the King and Queen would meet us.

Bill Channing, a Canadian officer who had gone to Harvard and came over on the boat with us, got us out of the mess, taking us to a colonel who made us sign a lot of things and gave us five shillings for our first army pay. We learned later that we had not signed the oath of allegiance to the King and his heirs. Which meant we remained American citizens but in the English Army.

The bombed-out blocks and gutted, charred shrapnel-pocked buildings of Northern Ireland gave us our first concrete evidence that there was a war on. Such sights became commonplace later on to millions of Americans, but at that time our eyes were bright as shoe buttons.

We took a boat across the Irish Sea, landed in Liverpool, traveled by train to London and notified Winchester of our impending arrival. In Winchester, a captain of the Kings Royal Rifle Corps met us, took us to dinner, and was enthusiastic that we would make good. He expressed great thanks to us in superlatives we had never heard before.

"It is absolutely magnificent for you two chaps to come over and help us like this. I say, it must have taken great courage. Marvelous! We've told everyone about you."

Braden and I were on the way to a hero complex after a bit of this. Until it dawned on us that superlatives to Englishmen are not what they are to Americans. The captain simply meant he was glad to see us, how did we like our coffee.

During dinner, we brought the conversation around to how soon we'd become officers.

"Well, all personnel have a rather good go of it through the ranks, now. There are no direct commissions or that sort of thing anymore. That is all out. But you should be commissioned in a year or so. We'll try to rush you through."

Our hearts went through the floor. A year! That was eternity. Invasions later, I thanked the War Office fervently that "that sort of thing" was out now.

Already I could see that England was not a country of cousins, but a foreign nation with the same tongue, though difficult to understand. Little things like hot milk with coffee at dinner that night made me realize that all this was going to be rather strange. When the captain took us to a Riflemen's dance in the evening, and we met everyone from a lance-jack to a baronet, and had to have a flat, tasteless beer with each one, I grew more apprehensive. When

I danced, which Barbara had been unsuccessfully trying to get me to do ever since we were married, I became downright worried. A sergeant who had come out of Dunkirk took us to our horse-blanket bunks that night. We felt like two college freshmen. We might have cried, I don't remember. I know the English weather was going through me like a razor, and the barracks weren't heated. The Tommies were training at this Depot without the benefit of hot water, phonographs, post exchange, sheets, and candy. But this sergeant did tell us we had seven cigarettes per day ration. I was used to only thirty a day, but I thought I might survive—just.

A few weeks later, the ration dropped to thirty cigarettes a week, and Tom and I solved the situation by getting some pipe tobacco, borrowing an old pipe, and exchanging drags, inhaling deeply. We confessed to each other we had a smoking habit and that it wasn't something that we could just take or leave alone.

Our first breakfast was tea, lukewarm porridge, and a slice of bread. We waited five minutes for the sugar and cream to appear, but it was six months before any came. Other mornings a bit of bacon or fried bread would supplement this. At noon we had our big meal. Things were tough in England in those days, and the main meal was something like potatoes, potato pie, turnips, and rice, with mutton every so often, and a bit of starch thrown in for dessert. Each meal an officer came to our table to ask for any complaints, and there were never complaints. Because we all knew the food situation and that England was doing its best, there was no sense in voicing a grief. But we had the privilege of saying, "There are no complaints, sir."

Tea late in the afternoon was the end of the day's eating, and for that we had a piece of cheese, a bit of butter, two slices of bread and some jam. In the evening we were able to buy tea and a blob at the Naffy. For a long time, we went to bed hungry every night.

Tom and I shared a double-decker bed. We received our first army haircuts and were terrible to behold. We half-heartedly put our mufti in the company stores, helped scrub the barracks room once a week with sand, wondered why the cockney recruits in our platoon had their teeth pulled instead of filled, attended weekly pay parades to receive three dollars a week, marched to church, looked at the casualty reports from our Regiment in Libya, slept in our underwear and cool shirts, constantly scrubbed our gaiters' webbing, kept our battle dress in press under our mattress, were miserable and tired.

A Welsh sergeant taught us the Bren gun, Lee-Enfield, two-inch mortar, respirator, military courtesy, judging distance, and camouflage. He drilled us two hours a day, six days a week, for three months at 140–180 steps a minute; we were the fastest Regiment in the world on square bashing. A corporal who had lost his wife and nipper while sleeping next to them in the London blitz taught us map reading, while Tom and I kidded each other about being comedy characters in *The Big Parade*.

We learned to call the bayonet the sword. I punched my thumbs full of holes sewing black buttons on my greatcoat, replacing the shiny ones. Our Regiment wore black buttons and was proud of it and we were, too, many months later. My fingers were torn from hours of arms drill. I always caught the bolt on presenting arms.

On the edge of the conflict, we were less interested in world affairs, and letters from home were best when they contained facts, not thoughts.

Once taken for granted, a piece of chocolate, an egg, or hot bath made us happy for the day. The toilet was the worst part. You waited in a long line, you finally got in, you hurried, you waited in line for a bucket to get some water to flush it, you flushed it, and you hurried out. And toilet paper was scarce in those days. A "Save Paper" campaign was serious, not something to make the people war-conscious. Mailing envelopes were used over and over again.

April 1942, we were ordered to stand-by for a Nazi invasion. It turned out to be a practice by the Germans along the French Coast. An air raid sounded as we entered church for Easter services that year. We played football, which turned out to be soccer, but Tom and I used football tactics, and that caused laughs and objections. The cockney boys asked us about America, and we told them. They examined our typewriter, played with our cigarette lighters, read the labels on our after-shave lotion, asked us for the stamps on our letters from home. They even wanted to look at the printing on our toothpaste tubes. We listened to their admiration for Russia and the hopes for a better England and discussions of the St. Nazaire raid and Cripps' mission to India.

My morning job was to clean the brass in the barracks room, and I hit the floor as soon as the orderly sergeant shouted, "Get out of them bloody beds." Tom appeared before the company commander for not cleaning a toilet for which he was daily responsible.

A sergeant said to me, "The British soldier and the French officer could lick hell out of any country."

The English spring came about this time, but what weather we had to go through to get it! Spring to Barbara meant just more nights of lonesomeness, while the pain of separation was leaving me and the core of love remained. She wrote me that Dartmouth lost to Stanford in the National basketball finals, and that didn't seem important anymore.

We listened to the faith, hope, praise, and cheer of Churchill's speeches. It was always a cold, rainy, dreary day when we fired on the range. There is no thunder and noise with the English rain, but it is steady, soft, and penetrating. If there was noise, it would be a few bombs, a bit of ack-ack, or the distant British channel guns. Occasional pilfering took place, and the thief was never caught. Sunday was the day we used to battle the venerable Home Guard in a twelve-hour scheme. Paddy Finucane, Fighter Command's twenty-one-year-old ace was shot down, and his last words were, "This is it, chaps." The British only feel—do not discuss—the death of a hero. Thirteen-mile forced marches were completed with forced laughs, in two hours and ten minutes, with rifles and battle dress and soft, bleeding feet, singing "Bless 'Em All" and "Bash Bash." But never "Roll Out the Barrel" or "We'll Hang Out Our Washing on the Siegfried Line." Those songs reminded England of the retreat from France.

We resented being trained as infantry. Aircraft and tanks were going to win this war, and a sergeant overheard us. "Now listen to me, you horrible people," he said. "The prime weapon of Jerry is his infantry, and he is accomplishing his stinking ends through good ways, democracy in his infantry. His poor bloody infantry is smashing. You'll find out. Whether they take us in by lorry, tanks, or plane, we're still the most important bunch in this show. In the meantime, that table and form wants moving, so get it over in the corner, out of the way, and we'll get on with the bloody next period, which is Bren."

Most of our thought, individual actions, and conversation came under three headings: stomach, bowels, and nerves. The last because of being constantly keyed up over things like lost cap badges or folding blankets, which irritations increased the desire for cigarettes. So we would talk about the brand cigarette we liked best, or how we wished we had one, or we looked for one, or we thought silently about one. We might hand in our blankets or underwear in the morning and be ordered to withdraw them in the afternoon. As such things happened in the American Army, so they did in the British, and it bothered us.

The English traditions and genteel talk and quiet laughter tried me some times, and in a polite gathering, I often wondered what effect one loud, short swear word would have. I feared it might start the church bells ringing for the invasion signal. But the thatched roofs in the villages, the sea of green which was the commons, the tinge that time has painted on the gray cathedrals, the small churches peppered about the well behaved hedge-rows and fields and streams, the old estates with coats of arms on the gates, and the still excellent statuary hacked and mutilated by Oliver Cromwell compensated for much.

It was in the days of tip-and-run bombing, lone enemy raiders, small groups of Wellingtons and Spitfires and Hurricanes making runs over France, barrage balloons over Southampton, the German reprisal raids on the three-star, "must see" towns of Canterbury, Poole, Bournemouth, Bath, Exeter, and Portsmouth. We were judged almost ready to be able to meet a General and know how to act. When an inspecting general did arrive complete with Rolls Royce, Tom and I were brought around for introductions. I forgot myself, stuck out my hand, and asked, "How are you, General?" Tom also failed to salute.

That delayed our entrance to officers' school exactly three months. The company commander, Captain Bering, had us down to office the next morning.

"You two are not smart enough. Your drill is the worst at this depot. You don't stand to attention when talking with a sergeant, and you fail to call the sergeant-major "sir." You'll have to brace yourselves up if you wish to become officers in this Regiment."

We were then wheeled out of the office, replaced our caps to show that humility had finished, and the company sergeant-major dismissed us. I asked Tom if the captain meant we were dumb when he said we were not smart enough. Tom didn't know, but we learned later that he meant we did not scrub our gaiters and webbing and packs as often as we should.

In the Winchester public houses we never tired of watching the continuous dart games; the players crawling from pub to pub, carrying their own darts, playing for ales. We visited Winchester College, one of England's public schools, and gawked at the young scholars, wearing gowns such as we wear only on graduation day. Inside its fourteenth-century walls we talked to a schoolmaster who was shocked by our accents coming out of British battle blouse. We kidded him about the British burning Washington during the War of 1812. He said, "We had a right to burn it, as our funds built it."

That was a viewpoint I hadn't considered. He felt that newspapers caused all the trouble in the world.

One morning in training our company attacked St. Catherine's Hill, an old Roman fortress for five hundred years. We ended the attack on the graves of hundreds of victims of the 1066 plague that swept England to the cries of, "Bring out your dead." Walks along the Itchen River and visits to St. Gile's Hill where the Bishops once had their annual fairs, receiving free beer and bread at Twelfth Century St. Cross where the tradition of the wayfarer's dole was carried on, looking at William the Conqueror's palace and chapel, and Alfred's castle, and King Arthur's round-table relieved the boredom of kit inspections, scrubbing, drill, and standing by our bunks for nightly roll call by sergeants.

Once a week we were on the fire team, to watch for incendiary bombs. Occasionally Southampton was bombed, while we listened to our ack-ack, the beating drone of the planes, rumble and noise, watching the long fingers of the searchlights and sudden great flashes of light that lit up the countryside. And we thought this while our families in America unnecessarily worried about us.

Our platoon had two Eton boys in it, on their way to cadet training. They were proud of having come from Eton and the rest of us were constantly aware of that pride.

A cockney said it reminded him of the boy who said, "I was brought up at Eton."

To which was replied, "Oh, I thought you were eaten and brought up."

We walked in to Winchester from our barracks to meet the Etonians for a high tea. A cockney, who had a bomb wound in his side and whose name I don't remember, though he was one of my best friends in those days, was with us. We took it for granted he would have tea with us when we told him we were meeting the Eton boys.

"Blimmey! I couldn't do that. You go on alone."

We protested.

"No, you Yanks don't understand. But it wouldn't work out if I had tea with you, with the other two there."

Over my bed were some patched shrapnel holes, and the only sign in the barracks room. It was red and white, with a picture of the crown on it, and "Freedom is in Peril. Defend it with all your Might." I read that sign at least four times a day, and gradually believed these words and hoped I would follow the advice.

Chapter Three

We forever received lectures from subalterns on Regimental history. We knew the names of our riflemen who won Victoria Crosses in the last war. We were proud that our regular battalions in Libya had been in constant contact with the enemy for two years. More and more we believed that we were in the world's best fighting unit. This sort of thing makes for better soldiers when the shooting starts. A company sergeant-major talked to a group of us one day, and it went something like this.

"This mob you're in started in America in 1755, and was known as the 60th Royal Americans. The settlers over there were the soldiers. They fought at Quebec and General Wolfe gave us the motto 'Celer et Audax,' because we were swift and bold against the Red Indians and French. There's been a lot of books written about our mob in North America. A certain Major Washington in our Regiment taught us to fight in the forests, and wear green uniforms and wear black buttons, for better camouflage. That's why we have green on our uniforms and wear black buttons today. The American colonies got discontented, and when the War of Independence broke out, the Royal Americans were shipped down to the West Indies so they wouldn't desert or have to fight against their own people.

"After America became independent, our name was changed to the Kings Royal Rifle Corps, and we have seven battalions, here and in the Middle East. We're the only Regiment in the British Army allowed to call ourselves a Corps. We've fought all over the world, and we have more battle honors than any other Regiment including the bloody Guards. The enemy used to call us the 'Regiment from Hell' and Wellington thought we were all right, in his second front against Napoleon. In the siege of Delhi we stormed the Moghul Emperor's Palace and drank to the Queen's health in the throne room. In Russia there's a village named after us. We march to the 'Huntsmen's Chorus' and the 'Wild Hunt,' and our cap badge is the Maltese Cross with a crown, and it reads like a map. Before this present battle dress our trousers were cut so as to force a quick step. The King himself is our colonel-in-chief. They call us the 60th Rifles for convenience. You can see what we did in the last war by going down to the Winchester Cathedral and looking at the names of our dead.

"This war, we held Calais, while the Guards held Boulogne. Only thirty came out of that show, but it kept Dunkirk open so that the rest of the bloody army could get back here. The Prime Minister talked about us in the House of Commons.

"So a lot of our mob has gone out, fought gloriously and died. We've got a jolly good record. It's up to you blokes to keep up our reputation and traditions and distinguished past.

"Now some of you have wondered what these Yanks are doing here. I don't know much about it, but as I get the story, Anthony Eden, who fought with us last time, and the American Ambassador Winant and our colonel-commandant, Sir John Davidson, cooked up the plan and twelve Yanks have come over here to fight with us, and that keeps alive the old traditions that we were once an American mob."

Traditions of the British Army sometimes give it a narrow mind, but they have never failed to make its soul very great.

Besides Tom Braden and me, there were Stewart Alsop, Avon, Connecticut; Harry Fowler, Katonah, New York; George Thomson, Long Island, New York; Deering Danielson, Groton, Connecticut; Charles Bolte, Greenwich, Connecticut; John Brister, Ambler, Pennsylvania; Robert Cox, New York, New York; Heyward Cutting, Far Hills, New Jersey; William Durkee, Balboa Island, California; and William Channing, Washington, D.C. We were all from Harvard, Dartmouth, or Yale, and had joined for various reasons of adventure, idealism, health, travel, twisted thought or romantic appeal.

We traveled in a pack, and we were good friends. We missed letters from home together, learned the English together, laughed and drank together until in terror, delight, and excitement. Bolte, Brister, Cox, Cutting, Durkee, and Channing, who received commissions months before the rest of us as they had been the first arrivals, went out to Egypt in the dark days and found death, wounds, and "the end of the beginning." They were brave and probably more idealistic than the rest of us.

Danielson was a wealthy, professional soldier, often in London brawls. Thomson was smooth, good-looking, and thought the reason America had gas rationing was because everybody drove to Maine for the summer and that took too much gas. His family did spend the summer in Maine. Fowler was ugly, friendly, rich, and probably the best-liked of our group. Alsop was quiet and unnoticed in a crowd, perhaps my best friend. We knew him six months before we learned he was President Roosevelt's cousin. Tom and I had the least money of the bunch, and I was the only married man. We argued and fought continuously and we would have done anything in the world to help each other. We liked to think of each other as being colorful.

Corporal Cragie called me in to his bunk room, after I had been training for several weeks. He slowly filled a matured pipe, while I sat petrified and rather proud that I was allowed in this corporal's hallowed room. I knew he had fought with the Black and Tans. I looked at his clothes, hung neatly, an old campaigner who had lived in a small room all his life.

"Yank," he said, "I like you, and the rest of you Yank blokes. I want to see you get along, I do. Now a bit of advice. I heard you calling a bloke a 'bastard' the other day. I know it was in play and all that. Don't call blokes 'bastards' even in mischief. That don't set so well with us, it don't. Now you can call me a 'bastard' all you bloody well want, and I know you don't mean it. But some time it might get you in deep."

I thanked Corporal Cragie, and never called a man a "bastard" again. Cragie from then on, after lights out, would bring me pieces of cake he had stolen from the cook house, explaining each time, "I know you Yanks are used to more food than we got here."

It was about the time I began "collecting" mailboxes, which are dated with the reigns of the ruler at the time they were made. Edward VIII's was scarce whereas I had as many as I wanted of Queen Victoria's. I never told the rest about this hobby of mine.

Tom and I used to visit Dr. Selwyn, the Dean of Winchester Cathedral. I asked him why God permitted war.

"God did not start the war. Why should he stop it? Through war we are perhaps punished. In war, too, we have an opportunity to study the basic foundations of our race."

In the Dean's drawing room was the coat of arms of Charles II, purchased by a former Dean for twenty-four pounds. Many Americans have become familiar with the motto on it, "Dieu et mon droit"(God and my right). Eleven days before the abdication of the present Duke of Windsor, King George, his brother, looked at the coat of arms, and told the Dean that the motto was originally "Dieu est mon droit" (God is my right), but that somehow a mistake had been made, and the present one is used.

Sometimes on Saturday afternoons we took the bus to nearby Southampton, and I always enjoyed walking along the quay, where allied soldiers had sailed for France in the last war. At this spot was the gate where the soldiers of England had passed through for the decisive battles of Crecy 1346, and Agincourt 1415. Near the gate was a monument that brought home a bit closer, an inscription on it reading "placed here in grateful memory of those Pilgrims of the Mayflower who left from this quay." I thought of all the soldiers who had sailed from this spot and wondered if I ever would. I was learning that people, friendship, family, and love were the most important things in life. To get this, I knew we had to beat the Axis. This is trite, but once learned and believed, it makes a better soldier.

David Hosington had been in a German prison camp, having been captured at Calais. He escaped after nearly two years of hunger and other atrocities. Hosington was not sent to the Middle East for more fighting. He remained in our depot to mingle with the recruits in our barracks, at the YMCA, during training, and in the pubs. He told us about the enemy, and how and why he hated the Germans.

We looked to David as a hero, and we believed what he said. So that when we did meet the Germans, we already hated them and we were better fighters for it. This avoided the talk about Jerry not being a bad bloke, "a lot like us really, he's just misguided."

Hosington said to me, "If you ever have to cross a street, or a railroad track, or any open place, go first. Our officers at Calais always went first, to show us, they did. And they didn't get picked off by Jerry. Jerry hadn't got them in the sights. But he was all ready and waiting for the blokes who followed the officer. So always go first, and it might help you out some time."

I never forgot this advice. It saved my life.

Of course, at this time the talk was that the Germans could not stand one more winter of war, so we didn't think we would have to fight anyway.

Then one night it happened. We had the party at the "Coach and Horses" we had all been looking forward to during the boredom and anxiety of our platoon's recruit training. Many of us would never meet again. Those who were not going to officer's school would leave the next day for advanced motor battalion training in another county of England. The next morning we stood together for the last time as a platoon, while our Welsh sergeant watched us anxiously. We were his babies, and he was proud of us, and we knew it. Though he had never let on that we were anything but the worst recruit platoon it had ever been his mortification to handle.

The regimental sergeant-major called all the passing platoons together with a voice that carried beyond the drill square. "Look to your front! Look to your front, RIFLES!" And we all came to attention. And a little later I remember marching behind Tom with our rifles and our neatly pressed battle dress past the reviewing stand, 160 steps to the minute, our free arms swinging parallel with our shoulder. This moment was the ultimate of army life. Recruit days were a thing of the past. We were soldiers.

A few days later, along with several rowing and reading public school boys, we became acting, unpaid lance-corporals, and proudly put up a red and black stripe. Recruits took orders from us, and the first few weeks of their arrival, they stood to attention when we talked to them. We helped sergeants run new platoons, and it was about the time England had dipped down in the man-power barrel as far as she could. We trained the thirty- to forty-year-old who had been deferred to early 1942. We took them on assault courses, and on physical training, either just before or just after breakfast. I don't know which was worse. We got them out for muster parade, church parade, taught barbed wire defenses, marched them on coal carrying fatigues, supervised gun cleaning after firing, and yelled "Jello" to make them hurry. We had them bring us tea in the morning, but as corporals, we had to sleep in our own room on the floor. There were not enough beds in wartime England for everybody, and recruits needed them before they were hardened.

We played cards in the sacred corporals' club. We read from a pamphlet to the recruits how to act if taken prisoner of war, to give the enemy only name, rank, and serial number, to combat Nazi interrogators with silence. We had the Jews in the squad sign papers that they would go in to combat: for they were not forced to, as the Germans were supposed to treat the Jews with no regard to the rules of international warfare. I never knew a Jew to refuse to sign the papers. The ones I talked to felt they had a bigger stake in the war than the rest of us. We smoked cigars and caused quite a sensation. It seemed that cigar smoking is done mostly by England's landed gentry.

When Barbara wrote me that termites had got in to our antique dresser that she and I had purchased with such glee, it all seemed inexpressibly remote. For in the few months in uniform, we had unconsciously changed. We weren't as afraid about seeing action. Some impelling force was dragging us on. We wanted to use what we had learned. Tom had lost his little WOR radio station man-about-town tummy, I was losing the soft, Chicago loop appearance, Alsop and the rest were looking better than they had since their early teens. We didn't yet know that discipline was the pay-off in action, but the discipline we were absorbing with a fierce pride that once would have made us hoot with sneering laughter. Discipline, thick and fast all the time, taking it in, handing it out, was the foundation of the British Army. With some individual adjustments.

When Barbara wrote me that she had bought a purse with her month's allotment she received from the British, I decided from then on, to keep the twenty-five dollars for myself in England where it would go further.

For us it was the weeding out process. If we made good as lance-corporals, we went on to officers' school. Once in officer's school, one usually got through. The trouble was getting in, as far as the English were concerned.

The beginning of summer, 1942, a whiskey ad British Army colonel with a distinguished World War I combat record, Eddie Campbell, gathered six of us Americans together and ninety English. "You are going off to your officer's training," he said. "When you become officers you will be only horses and dogs. You will work hard and you will get little consideration. Leading men in to battle is the greatest honor in the world. This camp has been overcrowded and you have been underfed. You have had to live on turnips, dumplings, boiled potatoes, and bread. This cannot be helped. As you know, Tobruk has just fallen in the Western Desert, but soon we will attack. You will be the officers for our attack, after it starts. It is a gloomy time to go to school, for we are losing the war. But when you meet the Boche, kill as many as possible, and teach your men to kill. The Bren and rifle will be your weapons, and they are lethal. The more Boche we kill, the less trouble we will have on our hands after the war."

And with a smile, he waved his baton at us, and said we were to go on a ten-day leave before reporting to the Officers Cadet Training Unit, known as OCTU, and pronounced "Oc-too."

Tom and I, with seven pounds each, decided on Scotland for our leave. We had four pounds each when we returned to England, which blew up the myth that the Scotch are stingy. They wouldn't let us pay for much and they showed us a good time. Sleeping on the floor of the train to Edinburgh, where we were guests of the English-Speaking Union at Green's Hotel, we spent the first day wandering around Princess Street and in Edinburgh Castle looming high on a rock. The view from there is supposed to be one of the three most beautiful in the world, according to Boswell. Holyrood Castle, home of Mary, Queen of Scots, where "even the walls have ears," quaint old closes, the Royal Mile, the Cathedral where John Knox preached, all fascinated us. Then Tom got in a jam, and we thought it best to leave Edinburgh early the next morning. Which browned me off, as I had promised my father I would play St. Andrews golf course.

A train to Stirling and Callender, gateway to the Trossachs and highlands of Scott's novels. . . . Loch Achrey and the long-haired sheep down from the hills for lambing. . . . Day-old lambs we held in our arms, too young to be frightened, as the excited mothers ran around us in circles on dainty, black legs, feminine in an overstuffed way. . . . Long-haired highland cattle. . . . The faint Scotch mist and the dark, somber haze over the land. . . . No darkness until after midnight. . . . Ammunition for war stored about the Lochs. . . . The Brig 'O Turk where the last Scot boar was killed. . . . Ben Ledi, Ben Enn. . . . Talks with Scots on the clan warfare of the Campbells and McDonalds. . . . Offers of biscuits and sweets, which are cookies and candy. . . . "Could ye stand some tea?", and we always accept. . . . A three-day hike straight over the hills of the McGregor country where Rob Roy lived by his sword. . . . Loch Katrine, Loch Drunkie, and Aberfoyle, where a Scottish priest shows us stone coffin locks, used for protection against grave-robbers and tells us that fairies and elves live in the hills back of his church. . . . The field where Rudolph Hess landed a year ago. . . . A hotel room in Bulloch on the south end of Loch Lomond, which is virgin, without hot dogs, screaming children, and box cameras. . . . The only tourists are ourselves. . . . No thought or reminder of war. . . . Sixteen eggs in forty-eight hours for what we think is a Great Britain war-time record. . . . Giving a boy two shillings to row us to the foot of Ben Lomond and climbing to the summit above the snow line to find icy winds and sheer cliffs and a view of the surrounding Lochs and Bens.

And on the way back to duty, a stop in Cambridge where the full power and meaning of education overwhelm us and we realize that co-eds in sweaters, the Yale Bowl, weekends at Smith, beer picnics, and cheer-boys-cheer are not absolutely necessary to study.

Cambridge iron fences gone to war. . . . Watching punting on the Cam. . . . A few small men in black horned-rimmed glasses and RAF students. . . . Beautiful walks along shaded university paths. . . . King's College Chapel where music dwells. . . . The chestnut court of Trinity College. . . . Trinity Cloisters. . . . Statues of Tennyson, Bacon, Hooper. . . . Paintings of Butler, Thackeray, Baldwin, Dryden. . . . Sir Isaac Newton's mathematical bridge. . . . Hobson's carriage stand of the seventeenth century where men were offered conveyance of a certain type to London, "that or nothing," and thus the modern phrase, "a Hobson's choice."

Cambridge that year reminded me we have to risk the finest things in life to keep things fine.

We came south to find the Americans had arrived.

Those men had not been in the army long, seven weeks and they were shipped over to prepare the way for millions to follow. The Southern boys resented being called "Yanks," but they were all "Yanks" to the British. And the British were to get used to being "Limeys," but never quite liking it. The difference in pay was the first thing to go wrong. Some of those first Americans to land in England were proud to be in a country that had once stood alone. Many were friendly but held in contempt the British Army, saying, "We won the last one for you, and we'll be in France three months from now."

The first few days, the Americans wore their steel helmets, for this was a war zone to them and they were taking no chances. The British and the Americans sniffed each other like dogs, exchanging differences in uniform, and sometimes there were fights.

British soldiers would say to me, "Dirty and scruffy lot, the Yanks."

American soldiers would say to me, "We're going to rebuild this England in a short while and show 'em how to run a country."

I saw the Americans hanging around the doors of shops, as they had all over America, and it made me homesick and smile wistfully. The British don't lean about doorways the way we do.

It all could have started better between the soldiers of America and Britain. But the outfits, which were in Britain more than eight months, were pro-British when the war ended. It took six months of living, sleeping, eating, and training with the British before we Americans in the 60th Rifles appreciated the great virtues of the English.

Watching a small convoy of my countrymen pass one day, I heard an old man say, "The Americans this war are much more quiet than they were last time. They seem to have settled down. Like the Australians. It was a lark to them in '18."

It wasn't long before the first United States court martial in England took place, a charge of rape in an air raid shelter on a sixteen-year-old girl by an American soldier.

"See here, Ted, look what you have in your army," I was kidded.

The soldier was acquitted promptly, as the girl was found "willing" and her actions were not of one entirely ignorant of the facts of life.

It was my turn to get even, and I told the English, "Your women are seducing our soldiers. A fine thing! And I suppose you still think Tommy Farr was robbed in his Louis fight!"

Those early Americans saw rusty barbed wire entanglements, no road signs, village names blanked out, pill boxes, pitiful tank and road blocks, and other hasty defenses, thrown up in 1940 to meet the German panzers. They wouldn't have halted a kindergarten much less Jerries. The Yanks laughed at these defenses, but not in a sneering way. They were beginning to see the spirit of Britain that had held alone against evil while the world waited for the third time in history for England to go under. And for the third time in history, somehow England didn't. The Spanish Armada, Napoleon, and Hitler muffed it.

I talked to a hero of the RAF's Battle of Britain, training American fliers. "We're both about the same in the air," he said, "except your Americans are so frightfully keen."

That first summer of Americans in London saw a small parade of GIs and officers. The English watched it with interest and appreciation. There was no shouting, cheering, or waving of flags. Some of the Americans wondered about these British. They didn't realize that actually London was tickled silly the New World had at last stepped forth. And I don't mean the shopkeepers, taxi drivers, and bottle club owners who later were to make such profits from homesick boys.

Chapter Four

Our OCTU in the walled city of York was small, commanded by an over-dressed major who knew war, was all soldier, and expected us to be the same. It lasted nearly six months, and the 180 cadets in it were the sons of the big names of England, preparing for duty in the Rifle Brigade or Kings Royal Rifles, two of the only three Regiments remaining where family connections and old school ties counted toward commissions. It was the most boring period of my life, and I learned more than I did in four years of Dartmouth.

We Americans were wide-eyed the first few days to hear such remarks as, "I don't want to be snobbish, but how does he speak?"

"His battle dress fits like a sack."

"Does she kiss well?"

"I don't think he'd do for an officer in the Regiment."

Half our platoon was made up of men who would have gone in to the Army if there had not been a war. The apples outnumbered the crabs. They were young, and the Englishman matures late. They were effeminate, we thought, but they could afford to be. Their courage was unquestioned. They never seemed to tire of hearing us talk about Hollywood, gangsters, and killings. Puppies, later magnificent in action, they believed America was like the films, and after the war they wanted to visit our country. Once I wore what I thought was a perfectly normal pair of underwear shorts, and an eighteen-year-old gasped, "You see things like that in the cinema."

A cadet wrote a poem about our major's opening lecture:

Henceforth I must prop up the proper bars,
I must be scrupulous with whom I eat,
I must salute all doubtful looking cars,
I must not dally in the public street,
(There is a spy at every window seat),
And I must cycle strictly at attention;
I must be quite unnaturally neat.
Then there are graver things that I could mention;
I am forbidden, in my present guise,
To look on women with admiring eyes—
I pass them by with an unseeing frown.
And one last thing on which the major's hot:
Lest I be shanghaied, I have promised NOT
To drink with any tailors in the town.

Mainly we were warned to avoid girls of husky voice, pale, white face, and a clumping walk.

Six months of river crossings on the Cuse. . . . Maneuvers in Northumberland and field firing on Blubberhouses grouse moor.

. . . Night compass marches. . . . Swimming tests. . . . Only two eggs that entire time. . . . White bread once. . . . All at one time nursing a burned leg from falling off my motorcycle, a sore heel from a draining ten-mile route march in one hour and forty-five minutes with full platoon equipment, and a smashed finger from putting a half-shaft in the axle of a Bren carrier. . . . Air-raids when the Jerries seemed right over the bed. . . . Battle drill in the open country, ditches, hills, moors, bogs, streams. . . . Pistol, light machine gun, Tommy gun and Stenn, mortar, heavy machine guns, anti-tank gun, rifle. . . . Village fighting. . . . Unarmed combat. . . . Teaching the English touch football.

Seeing the land army girls mowing hay. . . . Thinking the most beautiful spots in America are better than the best England has, but England offers constantly pretty scenes all over. . . . Weekends at the "Shoulder of Mutton" or the three-hundred year old "Roebuck" . . . pubs for half-crown a night, carrying our rifles, steel helmets, and gas masks in case of invasion. . . . Stops in villages on driving instruction where the people gave us tea and apples with remarks of, "I can always find some things for the soldiers". . . . Drill an hour every day, with such confusing commands as, "Move to the LEFT in threes, RIGHT turn". . . . Growing tired of expecting people have me say something funny because I am American, and Americans are supposed to have a good sense of humor. . . . Seeing a hunt at Gate Helmsley, like a picture on a calendar with forty beautiful hounds, ladies in side saddle, red coated gentlemen in riding hats and some in military costume, a hunting horn, well-kept horses, and even a fox, but no guns.

Pulling peanut butter out of a package from home and Tom saying, "Christ, let's get some bread!". . . . Smelling the sausage on breakfast plates because often it was bad. . . . Putting up and taking down blackout boards. . . . The slow, gray drizzle that was rain. . . . The bugle getting you out of cold blankets. . . . Cold porridge, flat beer, sleeping alone, feeling sad and proud about life. . . . Thinking there has forever been war and you have been in it always. . . . A Close where slop is still thrown out the windows to the cry of "Mind your heads". . . . Browned-off carriage expressions of service men who had ridden too many English war trains. . . . A weekend at Whitby, high on a cliff, near the ruins of an abbey in a room overlooking the North Sea.

Tom receiving a letter from his draft board saying the authorities were after him for evading military service. . . . White ribbons on our caps and epaulets to mark us as lowly cadets. . . . Laughing at Lady Astor in Parliament when she scorned Russia for not helping in the Battle of Britain. . . . Marching to church while the band played "Swanee River" and "Dixie". . . . More inspections than religion on Sundays. . . . Tactics at Stamford Bridge, where Harold beat the Danes in 1066 and then rushed to Hastings to be defeated and killed by William the Conqueror. . . . Discussing Gandhi's threatened civil strike. . . . And not understanding Britain in India any more than the English understanding the Negro in America. . . . "Pull back, mag off, press trigger". . . . Hours and hours of night training.

Scrubbing, polishing, and singing, "Russia bleeds while Britain [rule]" . . . . Plane rides to study camouflage from the air. . . . Disgusted with a girl who said to us, "Boys improve so much after they have seen action.". . . . Hearing a nineteen-year-old RAF flyer say, "I don't know why the Cologne Cathedral is still standing. I aimed right at it.". . . . Thinking of America in the days of wanting to stay put, the hell with the war, let Hitler make guns, we'll make refrigerators, they can't touch us. . . . Being amazed at the abundance of game for shooting, on such a small island. . . . Drinking bitters in the kitchen of a 1673 Yorkshire farmhouse. . . . Fish-paste haversack rations. . . . Beginning to appreciate the keen and dry sense of humor of the English, so subtle at times that the world thinks they have no humor in them. . . . And the Waa-Waa-Waa-Waa-Waa-Waa of German planes in the night.

They called me "Elmer" in the army. Now if an Englishman's name is Roger, he is called that by one and all. If his name is Rodney, everyone calls him Rodney, not Butch. If a man is from Devonshire, his appellation is not Devon. Parents who name their son Robert know he won't be called "Bob" even by the sports writers. They don't seem to have our passion for nicknames. It all started because Alsop read Trollope's "North America" which mentions an ancestor of mine, Colonel Elmer Ellsworth, Lincoln's side and first man killed in the Civil War, shot while dragging down the Confederate flag in Alexandria, Virginia.

Trollope writes, "A hot brained young man . . . a pity so brave a lad who had risen so high should fall so vainly, but they have made a hero of him in America, have inscribed his name on marble monuments and counted him among their great men. Ellsworth had shown himself to be brave and foolish. Let his folly be pardoned on the score of his courage."

It seems Trollope thought a corporal's guard should have been detailed to take down the Confederate flag, and that America's great men to 1862 were few if my ancestor is honored.

After being called "Elmer" three or four times, I objected. That was fatal. It might have been forgotten, otherwise. The Doom fell.

I was "Elmer." In addition, my hair always looked as though that should be my name.

Later, when a well-meaning Englishwoman asked why I was called that and George Thomson told her I was descended from a great American, she took Thomson seriously, and told all her friends I was a descendant of a famous American pioneer. The English assumed that any famous American must be a pioneer. The English admitted they couldn't quite place the name, but they thought they had heard of it, being too polite to say, "Hell, I never heard of the guy."

All's fair in love and war, they say. So I got my revenge, though it took six months to hang permanent names on the rest of the Americans. Fowler was "Plow Boy," Braden "Slack Jaw," Alsop "Al," with the nasal twang emphasized, and Thomas was named "Turk" after a Negro boxer.

They, too, objected at inopportune times, and as a result will be called that long after people have forgotten in this atom age there ever was a British Army.

Once I got influenza and tonsillitis at the OCTU, and was in bed for a week, sharing a double room with a physical training instructor. It is horrible enough to be sick and have to share a room, without sharing it with a physical training instructor.

Continuously he said, "I never felt more fit in all my life. Don't know why they got me in here, I don't."

When he slept twelve hours one night, he said that he had never slept so long in one time in his life, and I felt guilty about all my wasted mornings in bed. He dreamed two nights, and until he left, he was still in amazement over that. He had never had a dream prior to this, and I thought of all my nights filled with fitful images. When the sister wasn't around, he would do hand stands on the floor for me, a feat I couldn't do, even on the best day I ever had.

After he was discharged from the hospital, I recovered rapidly.

Captain Cohen, Sergeant Halliday, and Corporal Stidoff were in charge of our platoon. Halliday was an old regular Army man with tales of Rangoon, Egypt, and India, such as some forgotten 60th lance-jack knocking out thirty-six feet of Guardsmen in a Cairo brawl.

He shouted at us and kept us in a frenzy. "Hurry up. You've got only TWO minutes to get outside and on parade. Jello!"

It was impossible to get out in two minutes, but we might just make it by risking a nervous breakdown, and we never knew exactly how much time we did have. He once used "one minute" on us, but even cadets couldn't swallow that one. I don't think we were ever late for a class, and we were always early.

On instruction, we usually did things wrong the first time. He never failed to check us on some thing. The second time made certain we were correct, and he would say, then, "This and better'll do. This and worse won't."

Halliday gave himself away once, saying, sadly and seriously, "I'll never be happy until this war ends and I can get back to civviesstreet and my nippers. This is a bolo life."

We knew, then, that he was human, and did not revel in this existence of nervous prostration. Things were better after that.

Stidoff was quiet, well liked, a veteran of many raids on the Coast of France, and he didn't shag or chase us. He taught us many things that weren't in the book. Stidoff was killed later in the war.

Captain Cohen was a bit exuberant and young but we are very

good friends today. One time I was behind a stone wall, flat down. A section leader, I had just tossed a seven-second grenade on a field firing exercise. Cohen yelled at me, "Leadership, Ellsworth, leadership. Now is the time to show leadership."

If leadership meant something else beside being behind that stone wall at that particular time, it was a quality I lacked. After the grenade went off, and Cohen became aware that he might have had it, I didn't hear much more that day about "leadership."

It bothered me no end that the instructors thought all Americans were wonders when it came to mechanics. Somehow we were supposed to be born with the knowledge of how to fix engines or repair a radio. It became embarrassing, as I have always been about as mechanically inclined as a cow. We spent two months on wireless and motors.

When it came to throwing grenades for distance, Braden and I always won the six pence from the English. We used the baseball wind-up, learned on sandlots, and the others used the stiff overhand cricket bowl, learned on the grass pitch. We out-distanced even Stidoff by twenty yards. However, when it came to accuracy, the English could drop the grenade in a small circle, and we ended up even on the six pence.

Once a week we had to participate in recreational training. Tom and I selected cricket, and looked a bit astounded when we left the barracks seeing the English carrying books and magazines as part of their equipment. After standing around ninety minutes, we knew why. We didn't get a bat that day, but the following week we did. I was up first, and the first bowl knocked down my wicket. Tom laughed. That was funny to him, and I was slightly surprised, because the game looked easy.

Tom was up next. The first bowl came over so fast that Tom didn't have time to swing. Out he went! Revenge was sweet, and I carried on for ten minutes, until he told me to forget it.

Out in the field, I gave encouragement to our bowler. "Give him the ole dark one, now, Denis, boy, ole boy, ole boy! He looks like an old weak woman up there, Denny. He can't hit it! Let's go now kid! Git him out of there!"

Denis Lloyd stopped in the middle of his bowl, and said, "Elmer, you DON'T shout in this game!"

After that, Tom and I played golf once a week, on a course of tall grass, huge bunkers, fast greens, gorse, abandoned air-raid shelters, and sheep running all over the place. But we felt more at home, anyway.

I can remember only one argument I had with the English boys. Three of us were out on a night compass march, and I disagreed on what we were supposed to do. We were tired, bored with the OCTU, and we were still losing the war.

"Why you smug, complacent, damned Englishmen," I said.

"That's the trouble with you Americans. You never admit when you are wrong," I was told.

It might have ended in a fistfight, but they were gentlemen. One of them was later killed at Caen.

Sister of King George, great-granddaughter of Victoria, HRH Princess Royal visited our OCTU. Twenty of us were excused training for two days to polish ourselves for the Royal Guard of Honor. We practiced the Royal Salute and beefed about it, and Captain Cohen told us we were lucky it wasn't King George coming, as two weeks training had been dropped the previous year to prepare for his visit. She arrived in a crowned car, wearing the uniform of a General of ATS, Britain's women's service. She talked to a few of us, and we addressed her as "M'am." HRH looked quite as though she wished she were some place else, and in her questions and conversations she didn't seem to be in actual contact with us. Shy, with a distant look, hesitant in speech, pretty, though plain, she had perhaps made too many Royal Visits. Later, she came upon Tom reading Thomas Wolfe's *The Web and the Rock*, and she inquired about the author. She had never heard of Wolfe.

I asked one of the boys later what he would have done if during the inspection I had begun to rattle my sword. He looked at me with horror and said, "I'd have been petrified and stood stock still."

The British were keen about giving us lectures on salvage. A major returned from the desert fighting said the Germans had marked the old British four gallon petrol tins as the number one item to salvage whenever possible. This distressed the major, for the British didn't know what to do with them once drained, and lamented the fact the Germans wanted them for something or other and could use them. The civilian in charge of salvage at York was quite put out, he said, because he could not use cardboard boxes in his salvage pile, as the boxes were always re-used. If the boxes weren't re-used, he could get a huge pile for salvage to the Government. He was losing sight of things a bit, we thought.

In one of the OCTU buildings were some old recognition posters, discarded, showing British anti-tank guns firing at well-described Russian tanks, pointing out the most vulnerable spots on Stalin's armor. They were printed when the Soviet made the non-aggression pact with Germany, and it looked as though Britain might have trouble with the Russians.

The worst time in the army is just after waking up, when you feel as though you have slept in a hurry, and you face queuing up for a wash bowl, shaving, hurrying through room jobs, gobbling cold porridge, and the first parade, all before you have had time to collect yourself. And you can't afford to lie there very long thinking about things. It's up and out.

But the best time is the few minutes just after lights out, and all is quiet in the barracks. It is comfortable and even the rough blankets feel good. I would think of home, and cold cream and sugar on corn flakes, and horns honking in Times Square, and I remembered the many quiet afternoons spent on the Mississippi River. The hills sleep and at their feet the River flows, and not a ripple mars its bland, brown face. A heron, like a gray ghost, flits silently to hide itself in the fluffy green of the willows. The sudden, clear whistle of a blue jay, like a valiant boy's, cuts the still air. In the meadow, studded with the purple spires of vervain, a cowbell tinkles. And I go to sleep, in England.

Some of our wireless schemes were carried out in Bishops Hilton, where the children would push and chase each other, showing off for the soldiers. I liked the moat and ruins of a Norman castle there, with a haystack placed in the space, open to the air, that was once the huge banquet hall where people ate, drank, slept, and loved centuries ago. In the earth on the floor of what might have been the kitchen, a Yorkshireman was hoeing a garden. I asked him to tell me a bit about the castle's history.

"Oh, it's old, I guess. It's been here ever since I can remember. I don't know much about it or who owned it."

Thus, fame and splendor.

It was the summer before El Alamein, and the training of the

Army of the Empire of Great Britain was suddenly changed from defensive tactics to the attack. Up to then, Britain was trying to hold, and that not very well.

Our major told us that the weakness of the British war effort was getting the man-power and production to carry out glamorous schemes of the planning staff, often necessarily modified by political necessity. Such as the time Wavell could have gone on to Tripoli, but his soldiers were taken for the first campaign in France. So it is that as officers in the army, we would find the people suspicious of the army, as they have been since Cromwell. The army would be blamed for reverses, never the RAF or Royal Navy. England still believed the stupid son was put in khaki. The army was often misrepresented in the press. Dunkirk, Norway, Greece, Crete, Singapore, and Tobruk had not been pleasant things to write about. But he made us believe that we were in a good army, and soon we and the world would be shown.

Toward the end of OCTU days, the English were like young debutantes, discussing what sort of uniforms they were going to get, where, how many fittings, how much money, and the cheap grade of leather in Sam Browne belts during the war. I shall never forget how impressed I was, receiving a letter from my tailor in Saville Row, which ended,

> *We beg to acknowledge with sincere thanks the favor of your remittance and have much pleasure in enclosing receipt. Soliciting the continuance of your esteemed commands, are, Sir, your most obedient servants.*

Not, "Paid, Thank You," and the date.

English tailors cash your checks, do your shopping, handle your kit, lend you money, and they are obedient servants.

At last the band, and the passing out parade, and the reviewing stand. We were officially welcomed in to the Regiment by two great men and soldiers, Sir John Davidson and Sir Harewood Wake, who had seen a generation of Englishmen killed in the last war. There was much shaking of hands, bags of tea, new, stiff Sam Brownes and battered, brightly polished ones. Smiles, pink cheeks, smart mustaches, rows of ribbons, and we were yet to earn ours.

It was all over, and Tom and I received two of the six As awarded to our class of ninety. The other four Americans were jealous. They got Bs. When Bill Durkee of our Yank group graduated with the top honors a few months before, and Anthony Eden heard about it, the Foreign Secretary said, "It would never have happened in my day."

Off we went for a two-week commission leave in London. None of us remembers much about it. We had the world by the tail. The first night I lost my new cap and swagger stick.

Chapter Five

The Old Lady was a mélange of races and tongues. Czechs; tough Canadians; swank Free French; quiet Poles who knew more about Hitler than any of us; English; sightseeing New Zealanders; hard-drinking Aussie flyers; a dash of Scotch kilt here and there; American staff officers; Belgians; and Norwegians. An olio of everything.

And the women of all types who had some things in common. Generally, they had a fresh and innocent look, all possessing a quiet nerve and spirit in the face of strict rationing and bombs and invasion jitters. The streetwalkers thought as much of England as the women who attended the dances at Windsor. If they were pretty, it was genuine beauty because cosmetics were scarce.

London, comparatively speaking, was not crowded in those days. Scott's, the Dorchester, Hyde Park Club, Bristol Bar, Shepherd's Market, The Mayfair, Embassy Club, Claridge's, Les Ambassadeurs, Bag of Nails, Berkeley Buttery, and the Turkish Baths of the West End were our haunts.

The Cavendish Hotel was our main magnet, and Rosa Lewis, once the favorite of Lord Ribbendale and King Edward VII, was the proprietress, age eighty-four. A dozen books have been written about Rosa, the Cavendish, Miss Edith, and Kippy, the dog. All have failed to catch the atmosphere of the place. One has to live and be liked there to appreciate it. We Americans in the KRR uniform were pets, which meant our bills were small, and Rosa charged what she thought we could pay, putting the rest on somebody else's account. If we were particularly witty, our settlement was small. If we did not take Rosa about and spent too much time outside the hotel, we had to pay more.

For decades, Rosa never slept outside the Cavendish until the blitz put her in the hospital for a few weeks. When we first wandered into the hotel, thinking it was a fairly normal place on London standards, there were more than a hundred rooms. At the end of the war, bombs reduced the vacancies to a couple of dozen, but the Alice-in-Wonderland qualities remained about the same.

Bennett dropped his duties as general handy man when we arrived, and became our servant. Tinkling gin and limes appeared from nowhere. He brought French champagne on our breakfast trays, and photographed us. Rosa would send barbers to our room, because she thought we were looking shaggy. We accepted quite normally the fact that strangers appeared in our rooms and waited for haircuts while we struggled out of bed after Rosa would send word, "No more drinks for the KRR boys until they are on their feet."

Betty helped Bennett bring drinks. About forty years old, she had worked in a department store across the street, dropped in to the Cavendish for a beer and sandwich one noon, liked the atmosphere so much that she stayed right on through the day and started work that night. Betty's husband visited her at the hotel, and Rosa called him the "Pregnant Parson." No one ever knew Rosa's reasons for calling people what she did.

We left our clothing and gear in the rooms for months—nay, years—and it was never disturbed, except by bombs. Telegrams, messages, and phone calls were usually ignored, and this was sometimes disconcerting but had to be accepted.

If the phone would ring, Edith might say, "Do you think we should answer it, dear?"

Some Guards officer might reply, "Come, come, Edith, it is a bit early for that sort of thing. Let them ring later."

Five of us returned to the Cavendish rather early one morning, and Rosa brought us a tray of milk, champagne, sandwiches, and laxatives. Why the latter, I don't know. But she thought it might be good for us. The Germans were overhead, and we could hear the hollow, harpy voice of the ack-ack, echoing about the London buildings.

And then she broke into the Yale Bulldog song.

Once Alsop introduced her to a baroness. Rosa at that time was down on dukes and barons, for some reason, and generally crowned off. With a cute, wicked look, she turned to Thomson and said, "Too bad her mother wasn't barren."

We often asked Rosa when she was going to visit America again. Her answer was always the same. "Never. You cannot repeat a beautiful experience twice over."

We knew that she meant her visit had been made so wonderful by the hypocrisy of prohibition and those halcyon days. Colonel Harold Fowler of the London Embassy received a million-dollar check from Rosa, to atone for her failure to contact him on her visit to the States. Fowler was forever threatening to cash the check.

We were taken aback a bit one afternoon when Rosa wandered in to our rooms, took a sip from Fowler's glass, remarked, "I'm so sorry to see that young J. P. Morgan has died," and wandered out of the room.

I suppose to Rosa that seventy-five was a bit young.

She believed the world's troubles began when women were given the right to vote. When a duchess carried on like a tart, she mumbled all day about "these bloody modern women."

Her system of accounts and the register was always good for a laugh. Off-hand, I remember glancing at these:

There's a girl in 42.
KRR boys had 8 double gin and limes.
The Commander had two breakfasts in his room today.
Old Frog Face had a double brandy.

Only once did I see a fight in the Cavendish. That was when an American Lieutenant from the South said that after the war he was going to lead a troop of Texas cavalry across the George Washington Bridge and shoot up New York. Danielson flattened him the third time he said it.

Sometimes Rosa would talk about the last war, and the English who spent their leaves at the Cavendish. Her rooms were packed every night, and every morning at five she would open the rooms, and call brightly, "Who's for France? Who's for France this morning?"

And the soldiers would shake themselves, make for Waterloo station, Southampton, and death in the trenches.

Rosa liked the First World War better. She said to me once, "The difference between this war and the last is mechanics. Everyone is so mechanical, and it's not nearly the fun."

Occasionally she would try to sponsor the last war atmosphere, and when we brought a cab driver in to the hotel for a glass of champagne, she asked Moon, the night-man, and Ernshaw, the Hollywood-type butler, to bring the cab in, also. Which they didn't.

Things were not always in a state of clairvoyance around Rosa. I was trying to read a newspaper in my room one day and in she came. "They took all her clothes off and covered her with toothpaste."

"Who did that, Rosa, dear?"

"All of them did it. Every single one of them."

"I wonder why."

"Because she wouldn't let him drink or smoke or come in here anymore." I never found out who "she" was because Rosa got started on something else. But I gave it one or two thoughts because toothpaste was not easy to buy.

"I'm so old I ought to be burnt," Rosa said to me. And I thought when Rosa dies, London will be a little bit less London, and she will leave thousands of friends. Which isn't often the case of people in their eighties.

In those days, the London blackout was just that. There was no light at all. Later, restrictions were gradually lifted. Flashlights were permitted, a few dim lights appeared, and people did not constantly bump into each other. The women of Piccadilly could see their quarry. Smoking was permitted, and we no longer heard, "Mind that bloody fag."

But when we first arrived, London remembered the blitz days. Even the Cavendish got after us on one instance. I was in bed. There was a small air raid on, and during it, Alsop and Fowler returned from the Queen Charlotte's ball. Alsop turned on the light, threw open the window and said the light would attract the Dorniers in to our room. Fowler suggested closing the door so they would be trapped in the room, and not buzz about in the hall. When the ack-ack opened, Al said, "Oh, they're going to do it that way."

And closed the blackouts.

Rosa and Edith did not think that was funny, and we never did it again. We were new to war then.

A few days after that open-air slaughter house on the beach of Dieppe, some Canadian officers who were there staged a party in the Cavendish. Anyone in the hotel always attended the parties.

I talked to a Canadian officer who said, "I guess it was reconnaissance in force. If we had succeeded, it still wouldn't have been the invasion. You can't get surprise with such a large force. We should have bombed them first instead of trying for surprise. We really got the hell beat out of us, but we showed the bastards we could fight and take it."

The Town's war society was complicated and the flesh was frail. I remember a lunch we had with a baroness and a captain of the Northumberland Fusiliers. They wished to marry, but she was engaged to a prisoner of war captured at Dunkirk. Before dessert, they left, saying, "If you'll excuse us, we're going to bed and play phonograph records."

The American Eagle Club on Charing Cross was started by Londoners who appreciated the volunteers from United States. There we were able to get unobtainable items—hamburgers, peanut butter, ice cream, doughnuts, waffles, and toasted cheese sandwiches. The Eagle Squadron, volunteers in Canadian uniform, Americans in the Polish Air Force, Marines guarding the American Embassy, and Yanks in the KRR's all received mail there. Packages from home came in duty free. I remember orchestra leader Freddy Martin sent many cartons of cigarettes to the Club. It was a little bit of America for us, and several times we made broadcasts home from there. Mrs. Frances E. Dexter was our guardian at the Club and one of the best friends I had overseas. The Eagle Club later became the first Red Cross Club in Europe. It never had much swank, but few who knew it when freedom was in peril will ever forget it or the people who worked there for us.

Tom and I met Sir Samuel and Lady Gurney-Dixon in Winchester, soon after our enlistment. We were invited to tea, and I made the best of the opportunity. Toward the end of the third cup, I asked a few questions about rationing, for odds and ends to write my family.

"For example, how much butter does each person get a week, Lady Gurney-Dixon?"

"For example, you have just eaten my week's supply," she replied.

After that rather shaky start, we became friends, and I spent many happy weekends there. The Gurney-Dixons lived in the Cathedral Close in a home once owned by Isaac Walton, who fished in the Itchen. Like all houses built before 1600 in England, this one supposedly had ghosts. Sir Samuel never quite recovered from his heroic work as the doctor on duty when the Germans first used gas on unprepared British troops during the First World War. Previously, he had been mentioned in dispatches for great efforts on the prevalent tuberculosis in the early trenches. Sir Samuel would always see us to the door when we departed, ask us to come again, and until we were out of sight, hold up two fingers in the victory sign. Often I looked back on the little figure in the doorway, and thought how typical he was of the British, who were amused when their country's life was held by a string because they knew the string would not break. The string was made of guts. And upon it depended the survival of Christian civilization.

It was in their drawing-room that I heard the evening BBC begin with, "Last night it was Cologne."

Somehow, that lead made me realize we were over the hump. We were sure to win. It was becoming routine, these great raids over occupied Europe. I was sure in the end all would come right.

Sir Samuel was not a fatalist. He did not believe "if you're gonna get it, you're gonna get it, and there's nothing you can do." He used common sense, and for many long years, whenever there was an alert, he and all his family went to the concrete air-raid shelter carrying gas masks. I have sat in there with them many times, even though we knew it was perhaps a single raider. "Why take even that thousand-in-one chance?" he said.

A lot of people lost their lives unnecessarily in this war, because they were fatalists.

Sir Samuel's favorite story on the blackout amused me. A man was walking down Piccadilly, and in the dark he heard a small voice from the pavement, "Don't step on me, please sir. Don't step on me."

The man asked, "Why, who are you?'

"I was once a luscious beautiful blonde and a wicked old witch turned me into a frog. The only way I can become myself again is to sleep on a man's pillow."

So the kind man picked up the frog, took it home, put it on his pillow, and went to sleep.

But when his wife returned unexpectedly from her factory job, she didn't believe the man.

Out on the 250-year-old lawn at one end of the garden, surrounded by a wall built before the Conqueror, we played endless hours of croquet with Lady Gurney-Dixon and two of her six children. She was once women's champion of England, and I usually lost. Under the lawn were the remains of a second-century Roman villa. One of Lady Gurney-Dixon's daughters was the only woman in England at that time who flew in torpedo attacks on German shipping.

Sometimes we took two of the daughters to the dances at the Guildhall. But the English are not good dancers, and Tom and I are worse. So we passed up one of the dances on a weekend by saying we had nothing for dancing shoes. It meant wearing our hobnail army boots all weekend, but it was worth it, until Lady Gurney-Dixon brought us tea and biscuits to wake up on the next morning, and saw our low street shoes sticking out of our haversacks like red lights. The embarrassment was worse than the dance would have been.

I used to sit in the four-hundred-year-old nave in the Winchester Cathedral on Sundays, near the coffin of King William Rufus, killed by an arrow in the New Forest during the eleventh century. Shortly after I was commissioned, I was there next to Sir Edward Breyer, a full admiral and Fifth Lord of the Admiralty. We didn't start off too well together. First I had my cap on his seat and he told me to remove it. Then he seemed to blame me when we were told to turn to the eighty-fifth Psalm instead of the seventeenth as the program read. I had a bad cold he didn't enjoy. As the service progressed, Sir Edward became more purple in the face. He is a big man, and I was about ready to leave any minute. Both the Admiral and I kept our offerings well hidden in our palms when the collection box was passed. Each of us for a different reason, I fear.

During the First World War, after the Battle of Jutland, he discovered why the work of one German shell equaled the results of three British naval shots. Whereupon he had to disarm the entire Navy for several months, keeping this fact a secret from the enemy, who could have wiped out the British Navy at that point if they had known.

Alsop and I were standing in front of the Cathedral one day, talking to the pretty Dean's daughter, putting on our best 60th subaltern airs. I think we were making quite a hit. Just as I was thinking how pretty she was, I was struck on the head, and the Dean's daughter had to do a tap dance to get out of the way of the overflow. Though I was bareheaded, it looked as though I had on a hat.

Al said, "Shrapnel!"

I was groggy and thought it was a brick.

When we came to, we realized it was from a huge rook, a direct hit. And as I cleaned up, Al and I laughed. Laughed hard. As the Dean's daughter backed slowly away, blushing.

We were standing under nothing except the clear sky, and it was a beautiful flying shot. I had always heard of things like that but never believed they happened. And a rook is a big bird.

Afterward, Lady Gurney-Dixon told me this was a sign of good luck, to be hit by a rook. But the Dean's daughter always avoided us after that. I guess she didn't like the giggles we had.

The people of Winchester were always doing something for us. Usually it was a game of charades, with limeade and sausage rolls for refreshments. Al, Tom, and I staged an enigma where Al was his cousin, Eleanor Roosevelt, and Tom and I were a bull, with the hind-end being Tom. The polite English congratulated us each time we did the riddle. Tom's stock remark was, "Shucks, I wasn't the brains of the bull."

We shook them, occasionally. Not on purpose.

I was posted to the Queen's Westminsters, 12th field battalion, Kings Royal Rifle Corps, and I took over 12 Motor Platoon. The sergeant was Lawrence, two decades in the regulars, an Irish red-head, dependable, had fought in Palestine. We had the cleanest weapons, vehicles, billets, and the best discipline in the whole ruddy army. As well as being the most fun. If happiness is possible in a wartime army, we had it there.

Knights was my batman, wireless operator, personal servant, protector, friend. The English friendship, once given, is for life. Especially in the case of a batman.

I was a bit awed by him at first. Several years older than I, with two children in Nottinghamshire, he did my laundry, put flowers by my wife's picture, arranged for haircuts, awakened me gently each morning with a hot half pint of tea in a chipped enamel mug, cleaned my boots, laid out my clothes for the day, made the bed, kept me fairly smart in appearance with such things as, "Excuse me, sir, but there is a button off your blouse. I wouldn't wear it again until I get at it."

He even cleaned my safety razor after shaving. If he didn't do another stroke all day, that alone was worth excusing him platoon duties.

Knights sent telegrams for me, and if things were rushed, he occasionally wrote Barbara to explain the situation. My American knick-knacks were new to him, and he spent endless time sorting out my things, which I had always kept in a heap. On bivouac, he brought me bully, beans, biscuits, and tea. My sleeping bag was always ready. When we slept out, he carefully explained to me how to pull the canvas over my head in case of rain.

He loaned me his only pair of pajamas for weekends in town.

Best of all, he loved to polish my Sam Browne. I had Knights stop drawing my bath, as he never could hit on the proper temperature for satisfaction. One has to gauge one's own bathwater heat, just as one must adjust one's own hat for complete comfort.

The only argument we ever had was over my socks, which he refused to darn. Every morning, I put on socks with holes in the toes. I ticked him off a few times, and finally he said, "Darning socks drives me crackers, sir."

"Well, holes in my socks drive me to drink, and there isn't much of that around."

Our solution was to send the socks to his wife to darn, and that was that. She had only two children and a war job, so I knew she had plenty of time for my mending.

The other ranks did not resent the officers having batmen. Because they knew that when the time came, in the face of the greatest odds, without hesitation, the British officer taught the men how to die with courage. A fact that bothered me a bit, though I decided to enjoy Knights while I could.

When things were dull, I would badger him unmercifully about a book I caught him reading, *Modern Ball Room Dancing*. When he learned I was a poor dancer, this ceased.

I promised him faithfully that if I went overseas, I would take him along.

My first time in our mess was not too successful. I forgot to take off my Sam Browne and was politely reminded that an old custom was still in effect, to leave the belt in the lobby, as officers of old did with their swords to show that all was well within. I was overwhelmed by the leather chairs one melted in, the officers in civilian clothes, the sherry, the perpetual kettle of cocoa, and the accents as crisp as a bowl of mush.

The subalterns and field officers paid no attention to me, and I knew that if I soldiered with these men for months—or years—I could never get next to them . . . and yet, in a few days, I had made lifelong friends. Shy and frigid, the English break down easily with a spot of encouragement.

I read two articles over the fireplace. One, a letter from Wellington, in Spain, in 1810, to the Secretary of State:

> *My Lord,*
>
> *If I attempted to answer the mass of futile correspondence that surrounds me, I should be debarred from all serious business of campaigning.*
>
> *I must remind your Lordship for the last time—that so long as I retain an independent position, I shall see that no officer under my command is debarred by attending to the futile driveling of mere quill driving in your Lordship's office—from attending to his first duty, which is, and always has been, so to train the private men under his command that they may, without question, beat any force opposed to them in the field.*
>
> *I am, My Lord,*
> *Your obedient servant,*
> *SIR WELLINGTON*

The other was rules for dinner night, which we had once a week:

1. Officers will be assembled in the ante room five minutes before the Commanding Officers.

2. On entering the anteroom before dinner, Officers will say "good evening" to the Senior Officer present. When a Commanding Officer enters the room, Officers will stand up and say, "Good evening."
3. On being informed by the Mess Sergeant that dinner is served, the Dinner President will inform the Senior Officer present.
4. Before sitting down, the Chaplain will say Grace.
5. The President will circulate the port when this is placed before him, and when all glasses are filled, he will ask the Vice President to propose the Loyal Toast in the following manner: "Mr. Vice, the King." The band will then play the opening bars of the National Anthem.
6. The Vice President will then rise and say, "Gentlemen, the King."
7. After the Loyal Toast, cigarettes or cigars will be handed round but not smoked until the President has lit up. The pipes will then play in the dining room, the Pipe Corporal receiving a glass of whiskey from the Senior Officer.
8. Officers will not leave the table until the port has been round twice.
9. The President and Vice President will not leave the table after dinner until everyone else has done so.

The English seldom shake hands, yet deep, sincere, honest, comradeship means everything to them. They just aren't demonstrative. I remember watching two brothers say good-bye to each other in our mess. One had just come back from Libya with the Military Cross, and the other was on his way out. I realized they were fond of each other, but there was no pumping of hands.

As one left, the other said, "Cheerio!"

The one remaining replied, "Best of everything," showing no emotions I knew he felt.

Even their introductions are casual. No carnival about them, no fuss and feathers. It is too often taken for granted that everybody knows everybody else. Half the time, when they do get around to introductions, they leave out names. But maybe it couldn't matter less.

Many pleasant evenings I spent playing bridge in that mess with John Holdsworth, Jimmy James, both killed in France, and Ronny Kershaw, taken prisoner in Italy. Henry Crookenden was perhaps my best English friend, and we constantly ragged each other on Anglo-American relations with jolly camaraderie. He always claimed it was bloody of me to be so bloody when I told him the legs of American girls were the prettiest in the world, how vague he was, and how the great, strong, generous, simple American is invariably done down by the sly, smooth, corrupt, and deceptively effete-looking Anglo. Henry was very badly shot up leading his company in Italy.

Chapter Six

Tom tooled all over the United Kingdom while I was with 12 Platoon. He was in and out of hospitals with a trick knee and was sent on several war courses. I visited him when he was recuperating from an operation in Princess Royal's Harewood House, peaceful, serene, constant—one of the three authentic things to see in England and most tourists miss it. It is in Yorkshire, and HRH had rooms throughout the war for about twenty-five sick and wounded service men.

George, the Viscount Lascelles, nephew of the King-Emperor, ninth in line for the throne, was a friend of Tom's in his mother's home. He was later captured in Italy. Tom told me of visits he had with him.

"I go down a long corridor lined with pictures of the Coldstream Guards in dress uniform to a heavily-carpeted room, in one corner of which is a phonograph with a huge horn, the kind you see on the Victor trademark.

"George is a tall boy and gives you his hand quickly and gently, a thrust like his mother's. He is extremely bashful, and blushes red when we shake. We talk pretty stiffly about the war and stuff while he plays the 'Eton Boating Song,' and then some John McCormick and Lotte Lehman. I have never met anyone who knows so much about music or talks as critically and intelligently as he does about it.

"There is a picture of his grandmother, Queen Mary, on one of the tables, and he tells me that he spent all his vacations with her in the London palace. Then he asks me how it feels to be thousands of miles from home, as he has never been more than two hundred miles away. The fact that he has led such a hell of a sheltered life makes me feel sorry for him. And yet, I'm not so sure after talking to a guy like that whether or not all the travel and different kinds of experiences you and I have always had makes a man any better. Sitting at home, he has learned more about music and books and art than you and I ever dreamed of —enough to make me feel illiterate.

"I went to the movie here the other night with his mother, and I remembered to say, 'How do you do, your Royal Highness?'

"But the sisters tell me afterwards that my bow is not so good. We make the usual kind of polite small talk during the movie, and it is hard to understand her. I have to keep saying, 'What?' all the time.

"So that she has to repeat some silly remark, and it is all very foolish. The reason she is hard to understand is that she never turns her head to look at you when she talks. Her son is like that, too. It must be shyness.

"However, the old Earl of Harewood is sitting on the other side of me, and he and I get along fine. When Alsop and Plow Boy and Turk were here to see me, we walked down to the lake past all the black cattle, and Al hobbles on a cane, gesturing, and mumbling about the estate, pretending to be the old Earl. Fowler almost kills himself laughing at Al, and Thomson gets sore because Plow is making so much noise."

Tom slept in George V's old quarters, using the King's bathroom in the eighteenth-century home. There was an electric lock on the door, operated from where His Majesty had had his bed, over which was a Rembrandt painting. Downstairs, the windows were Chippendale, as well as the furniture. I saw a ceiling in one of the rooms that is the most beautiful and valuable in England. Paintings of the German ancestors hung on the walls, including the old Kaiser's father and mother. The billiard table was made of wood from a famous Man o' War, and the butler's dining-room alone would house a Dubuque Elks' picnic. Many of the books in the huge library were from Victoria.

Harewood was quite an experience for a couple of soldiers from Iowa. But not as amazing as the visit we paid to Simon Worsthorne's. Simon was in OCTU with us, and a few months after we were commissioned, asked us to Cliviger, Yorkshire, for a weekend.

We got off the local bus in which most of the people traveling were wearing shawls and wooden shoes. In a little store, we asked where a guy named Worsthorne lived. No sooner had we said that than the man took his cap off to us, showing us the way to Simon's grandmother's house, named "Dyarnley," twice as large as Harewood House estate. They gave us a valet. We had two shaving kits and two pair of socks between us, no dressing gowns. The valet caused us untold anguish, but cleaned out our shaving kits that contained muck from Montreal, the North Atlantic, Winchester, and the OCTU. Simon and his grandmother refrained from dressing for dinner after the valet discovered we forgot our dinner jackets.

On Sunday, Simon took us to Townley, the ancestral home, and he put on clogs that he wore "to encourage the tenants to wear theirs because shoes are so expensive." Children and old men tipped their hats to Simon. If they didn't, Simon would say, "Things are changing. Half of them don't tip their hats anymore."

Townley was built in the tenth century, had dungeons in the cellar, secret panels, and holes where the priests who administered mass to this old Catholic family could hide if Protestants of Elizabeth or Cromwell were on the loose. We pressed a button and the wall opened, showing a small room for the priest and a trapdoor leading to the hidden staircase and the outside. Simon's grandmother lived in Townley when she was a child with more than one hundred other people, most of who were servants. It is now vacant, but a caretaker told us about kings who had visited there and showed us a desk insured for forty thousand pounds. Watching Simon, the direct inheritor of all this, Tom said he understood for the first time aristocracy's attitude toward socialism and public ownership, as well as why things like this must pass.

Townley is now more or less of a museum piece. It was once lived in, by people who fought and were killed and were loved and used the dungeons and ate the huge meats that came off the gigantic spit in the gigantic kitchen and threw bones to dogs in the corners. As a museum piece, it was vapid.

The estate was really moorland, and one can see where the moor encroaches as soon as the reseeding stops. The tenants have a constant battle against nature, and though they can always keep ahead, they can never win. In three years, once reseeding stops, the land becomes a moor.

Sunday afternoon, the butler came in to tell Simon's grandmother that So and So had purchased a nearby castle.

She replied, "Oh, he's a manufacturer," saying it with all the scorn that goes with reference to a practicing pimp. "Rather strange to buy a castle just now when so many people are trying to get rid of them."

To which the butler said, "Yes, M'Lady, but think how strange he will look in a castle."

The year was early 1943, but not that weekend.

Cumberland was Tom's destination for a driving and maintenance course. Back at the Battalion I received this letter from him, after seeing him on the train.

I'm not writing this on the typewriter because I naturally lost that on the train, as well as my two suitcases.

It was a close call, and I nearly got here with everything. In fact, by the time I reached Penrith, only forty miles away, a person who didn't know the English railroad system through and through as you and I do would have given me odds. I was jumping out at every change, rushing to the luggage van and making sure that my stuff got off one train and on the next, a consistently grand effort. Particularly as I was suffering from a hangover and feeling lonely and nervous.

But they got me on the last lap with an old trick—like the Statue of Liberty play or hidden ball—which fooled me completely. They pulled the train in to Penrith with the baggage van on the platform, so that the passengers couldn't get out. Then they took the baggage off and shoved it on a train for Glasgow—naturally, because it was all marked "Keswick"—and only after the Glasgow train pulled out did they let the passengers off the Keswick train.

It worked perfectly, and besides myself they caught four other officers and three NCO's going on the course-caught them flat-footed. The fans cheered. We were whipped fairly.

As I write this, they are still holding out. I have telephoned Glasgow, Penrith, Carlisle, and been to the station here four times. The adjutant has done the same. But the person who answers the phone at any of these places either says she will look and then goes off and doesn't come back to even tell me to go to hell, or says she doesn't know and there's nobody else in the office just now and I'd better call later —at some time when she secretly hopes she'll be off duty, and won't have to handle it.

In addition, of course, when you call up a railroad station, you have to first deal with that definition of insanity, the English telephone system, so you are caught before you start. Any self-respecting English telephone operator will cut you off just as you have almost persuaded the railroad girl to at least take a look and see if the bags are there.

I will tell you, Elmer, as I told two frightened old station agents in a speech I delivered at the Keswick station today: There is not a single ordinary public service corporation in England today with a smattering of efficiency attached to it. If there is anything efficient left in England, it is the army—and there are two schools of thought there.

I didn't tell them what I think of the Army Pay Corps. I'll do that tomorrow. And while I'm at it, the income tax people got out of going to the asylums providing they volunteered to work for the Government. They are after me again and my eighteen dollars a week salary.

Otherwise, things are great up here. I was booked to room with our old friend McAlpine, but I got out of that because I was so heated over the baggage business on arrival that I told the officer I couldn't room with McAlpine because he has fleas—a statement that astonished him so much that he let me out of it.

There are a couple of Canadians here—good for plenty of gags. It's a change to meet someone who says, "My name is Rocky Smith," instead of, "James Ebenfield-Watking," or something like that.

I'm rooming with a captain in the Rifle Brigade, an effete-looking ultra-England with a long cigarette holder. He is one of the weakest characters I have ever met, a degenerate noble, but quite honest about it, and I find him amusing. He is the type who fails courses.

The scenery is magnificent, the best since our Scotland trip. We're on a lake, with high mountains all around, and few soldiers.

Keep in touch with me. Give my best to Crookenden, and if by any slight chance my laundry might have appeared, which I doubt, of course, send it up to me."

Yours ever,
Slack Jaw

I bought a black and silver Alsatian Wolfhound puppy in Berkshire, son of a long line of international champions. He was to travel to the front with me, but he didn't know that in the days when he hid behind my kit bags, jumped with fright as I opened a window, chewed my clothes, slept on my bed, or in a wine basket, stole paper out of the waste basket, and bit at the broom when Knights swept my room. I called him "Watling Street," after Lord Derby's English Derby winner, which in turn was named after the Pilgrim's Way to Canterbury. My platoon called him "Watt," and I eventually brought him to my wife many shells later.

Around England he rode on motorcycles, in London taxis, Bren carriers, trucks, and tanks; entered pubs and brigade dance, was known all over the West End, chased the pigeons in front of Buckingham, and had a passion for barking at the statues in Green Park.

Plow Boy Fowler taught him to shake hands, and anything else he learned, he learned the hard way. The only time Watt nearly got me in trouble was when he stole the adjutant's pipe on bivouac in Exmoor. And I was threatened with a six weeks' bayonet assault course if it happened again.

He had a bed of his own at the Cavendish, and would cock his head from side to side at the weird wail of the air rail sirens.

Knights and I nursed him through distemper with whisky, milk, sugar, and vapor rub, the colonel giving us two days excused duty during the crisis.

Our Battalion colonel had served in Burma. After a grueling maneuver against the Guards and Canadians, he gave us a talk.

"The exercise just concluded shows quite clearly what the Germans may expect when we get our chance to get at them. We are now fit and hard, tough in the proper sense of the word. We must not get soft, and that means even if you have an indoor job. The Officers and Other Ranks who lost weight in the last few weeks will not regain it. This is an order.

"Get realism into our training. The more realism, the fewer casualties in the long run. The War Office has allowed us a certain percentage of casualties before the real shooting begins. But you must use common sense, both now and overseas. I am keen on common sense. Let me tell you a story on common sense.

"A farmer I saw was working in a field with no trousers on, and I asked him why, as it was a very cold day. He told me that it was his wife's idea. The day before he had plowed twelve hours in the sun without a collar, and at night he had a stiff neck."

The English sense of humor got it right away.

It was eighteen months before Normandy. . . . That sort of happiness which hurts in the stomach comes in waves. . . . Buying a banana at an auction for sixteen shillings. . . . Fishing beats on "Broadland," home of Mountbatten. . . . The first American to sign the guest book at Beckford's "Font Hill Abbey," the tower that fell like Babel, where Nelson and Lady Hamilton attended parties, which started the imitation Gothic architecture craze in England.

. . . A letter from the pastor who married us, "How come you could just up and leave a girl like that?". . . . Trading sardines to Yank soldiers for cigarettes. . . . Sleeping under the stars, on the ground in Sherwood Forest, and getting that trite, insignificant feeling when life is not as important as at noon.

Watching black Halifaxes circling and circling to gain altitude like huge, constipated birds, and seeing them come back from the Continent at dawn, relieved and light. . . . On a motor cycle, darting in and out of an armored column of tanks, Whites, Fordsons, anti-tank guns, shouting to the drivers, "Keep your distance". . . . Stonehenge, built nearly four thousand years ago, by whom no one really knows. . . . Ruins of ancient Britain on Salisbury Plain. . . . Solid, still gray stone eighteenth century villages, made to last, "Stow-on-the-Wold," "Bourton-on-the-Water," "Moreton-in-Marsh," "Hinton-in-the-Hedges," "Shipston-on-Stour," "Napton-on-the-Hill". . . . A judge passing sentence on a man who wrote a thirty-three page love letter when paper was so scarce. . . . The King disgruntled with the Queen because she filled her plate three times at a Windsor buffet party.

"Sulgrave Manor," George Washington's ancestral home, and the family's coat of arms with the five-pointed star. . . . Signs "Bed and Breakfast. No Hawkers". . . . Sleeping in the bitter cold of farm-yards and watching the antics of ducks and chickens, the rooster being fierce and quick, the drake cozy and coy. . . . Sometimes pretending I am a peace-time tourist that eases army life. . . . Amazed at the basic, integral, intrinsic honesty of the English who seek out train conductors to give them tickets if in the rush they have been overlooked.

Three wonderful days of picking apples and hazel nuts in Sussex with the direct descendant of Robin Hood, who I thought was a fictitious character, but was an Earl named Fitzooth, born 1160, and died a natural death at the age of eighty-seven. . . . Astonished that England looks like England, with wild ponies, dark and light green patches of landscape. . . . Stone walls, hedges. . . . Hills and bridges and streams and cows all in perfect co-ordination to blend in to a soft, pretty picture. . . . Small, gray-green graveyards, so restful they invite death. . . . The North in the winter, white as a wedding cake. . . . So much room because one-fifth of the people huddle in London.

Near the spot in the water off Scarborough, where Captain John Paul Jones lost his ship *Bonhomme Richard* is the recently discovered small house of the man who wanted to trade his kingdom for a horse, King Richard III. It is overlooked by St. Mary's Church where Anne Bronte is buried and which Cromwell used for a citadel.

John Armitage, killed in Greece later in the war, and I, took time from a maneuver to investigate the shambles of low, old yellow dwellings, sharp corners, and narrow passages. The pub where Captain Jones did his drinking is still operating, featuring fish and chips. A 1691 brewery next to it continues to make beer.

A chimney sweep, who might have stepped out of the nineteenth century, took us to the King's house, built in 1350. The stone mullion windows, heavy wooden rafters, stone doorway, fireplace, and sundial are the same ones used in 1483, by Richard. His red-room was painted in bullock's blood and is in good condition after five hundred years. In the middle of the ceiling are three stone rabbits, each with one ear, but so placed that it looks as though they have the normal number.

The Hunchback King who lived there was slain by the Earl of Richmond at Bosworth. Richard had murdered his wife, Queen Ann; King Henry VI, his brother; the Duke of Clarence; Lord Hastings; and King Edward V. To top it off, he had intimacies with his niece, Elizabeth. All in all a fairly full life for a man who lived only thirty-two years.

In the house, John and I saw the spurs of Cromwell, a pillion upon which Milady rode behind Milord on a horse, battle souvenirs of Waterloo, John Wesley's spectacles, a knee-breaker used on captured poachers, devils' drumsticks to frighten any demons who might be about, a cock-fighting chair on which the spectator sat backwards, complete with a drawer for bet money, above the fireplace a dog wheel in which the family pet was placed and as it walked, the spit turned.

A friend of ours was Dr. C. F. Garbett, Archbishop of York, a bachelor whose sister kept house for him. Tom and I first met him when he was Bishop of Winchester. Invited to tea, we acted as well-bred as possible, all things considered. Afterwards, Dr. Garbett mentioned to an acquaintance of ours about the visit, "Yes, one was educated and the other was not."

For two years we each claimed the other was the uneducated one.

We called on the Archbishop, eleventh since America declared its independence and ninety-first in an unbroken line from 627, a few times in his palace at Bishopsthorpe, built seven hundred years ago, scene of many battles, complete with secret passages. The great hall was the site of the treason trial of Archbishop Scroop, condemned to death by the King and beheaded in the yard. Shakespeare writes of this, describing the hall, and the frantic efforts of Canterbury to save York's life.

Dr. Garbett always had rabbit and good conversation for us. He said that he was in full accord with the Beveridge Plan. For a time he was protesting our actions toward Vichy France, but after sitting in on a secret session of Parliament, he was satisfied with the Darlan arrangement.

The man had courage and said what he believed. I remember one of his statements, "The Germans, both civilians and soldiers, should pay head for head for the millions of Jews they have killed in Europe."

The last time I saw him was by the huge gate, waving good-bye. He had sent us off a few miles in his automobile with the chauffeur. We were without transportation and had to catch a bus to return to duty. The trip was illegal under gas rationing, and he was worried about it.

Turk Thomson would get us invitations. He took me to three of London's famous clubs, White's, Boodles', and the Conservative. They were unbelievable places, straight out of the Victorian age. In the Conservative, I was politely but firmly reprimanded for smoking in the dining room before dessert. Quite vulgar, you know. After sherry, we retired to a separate room for coffee and smokes.

During evening meals, there was no holding back on the amount of liquor our hosts provided. No matter how much liquor the English consumed, they rarely wandered about, shouted, sang, or fought. They remained drinking at their own table in good control of themselves. At one dinner, Turk and I had cocktails, champagne, port, and whisky. When it came to the brandy, an industrialist asked me to speak sometime to his factory workers, as he felt an American in British uniform would show the close cooperation of the Allies. I took a sip of brandy and asked how many employees would be present.

"More than three hundred," he said rather proudly.

"Well, I'll be glad to see them on my next leave. Though I'm used to speaking to at least two thousand at a time."

I had never seen the inside of a war factory, much less talked in one. But then, I had never had so much to drink before, either.

In Dr. Johnson's days, these were coffee-houses. Now they are loaded with fussy, retired generals, widowers, bachelors, Colonel Blimps, *Punch* magazine characters, rich dark walls, great paintings, high ceilings, correct dress and change for dinner. The members give a severe darkening of brows if any undue noise is made at the half-hour before a meal allocated for newspaper digesting. Guttural, short comments of disgust on some outlandish error in journalism, such as a Latin quotation not being used in its exact sense, may break the silence.

The aristocrats are loyal to their kind. The newspapers were panning a Club member for allegedly misappropriating army funds for a personal political tour. A brigadier of the Boer war said, "Even if true, things like that shouldn't be mentioned. Bad, you know."

At another time, over port in the Yorkshire Club where I had been invited by Montague Norman's son as the first American to be within the portals, I was trying to explain our electoral college.

A white-haired gentleman with a very red face said, "Surprising you people can ever elect a President out of that muddle. Never heard of such a thing."

And then he paid me what he thought was the highest compliment possible. Turning to the group, he smiled, "If it weren't for this chap's rather sharp accent, you'd think him an English boy."

Chapter Seven

Hanging about London for a time, while I was off with my platoon, Tom was invited to have cocktails with Anthony Eden, who lived at the Foreign Office with his wife.

Tom gave me all the griff at our next meeting.

"Mrs. Eden is good-looking, too. Their apartment is small. Eden talks easily, fluently, and with all the old English idiosyncrasies we are accustomed to and get a bang out of—like 'He's a cavalry officer; of course, not that I have anything against cavalry officers.' Or 'You know, after Dunkirk I was attached to our 2nd 60th, and Winston told me he wanted me back in the Cabinet. I said, 'Look here, old boy, I'm in the army.'

" 'Winston said, 'Oh, we'll fix that.' "

" 'But you know, it wasn't so damned easy. Winston had the devil of a time, and I finally had to be seconded to the Foreign Office, but I'm still in the 60th.'

"Then we talked about the fuss which was created when our 7th Battalion was disbanded and the Riflemen sent all over creation.

"Eden said, 'You know, we had an awful racket about breaking up the 7th 60th. One day, just as I was going in to see the King, Jimmy Grigg stopped me and said His Majesty was all upset about the 7th and for heaven's sakes not to say anything about it to him.'

" 'Well, I hadn't known about the 7th and the fuss, so I asked Jimmy what it was all about. He said your people are raising a terrific amount of feathers. I said that I hadn't known about it, but now that I did, I would certainly mention it. Can't understand why they would want to break up a 60th Battalion.'

" 'So when I finished the audience, I said, 'Look, here, Your Majesty, what about the 60th?'

" 'Well, His Majesty was in a frightful stew, but we decided to leave it to Winston, and Winston decided to let the War Office handle it and so there you are. It might have set a precedent if His Majesty stepped in and all that.'

"Mr. Eden is not a great man telling a story. He has no airs, not even the unconscious ones of very successful businessmen who demand silence and eager listeners while they talk. He's just a very natural, rapid-speaking OCTU boy grown up to a man, looking in morning dress exactly like an *Esquire* model. Beautiful figure, long legs, curly black hair just getting gray at the edges, and with an interest in everyone in the 60th as great as yours or mine. He knew all the officers' names in the 60th. And he thinks Mr. Winant is a great man.

"Through these cocktails and a viscount who dropped in, I got a chance to hear Churchill's speech the next day. There is no sense in trying to describe a Churchill speech, because you've heard them, Elmer. I will only say that he looks like an ancient turtle, and that he speaks almost without manuscript. I sat close enough to see his notes, and they were like chapter-headings: one huge scrawl defining a subject on each page. The subject matter and the phrases are ad lib."

John G. Winant, America's Ambassador to the Court of St.

James, who did such a magnificent job through the war, was always on the lookout for our welfare. All twelve of us had the highest regard for him, as did the thousands of other Americans who knew of his efforts in England from the "we stood alone" days until the other side had had enough of it.

Whenever we would leave his office, his last words were, "Now are you sure you boys have enough money? I can let you have some any time you wish. Drop in next door to the apartment when you are in London again and stay there."

On one of our early visits, he was getting a great slow, chuckle out of the first American to land in Ireland to begin the slog through Europe. In his shy, quiet, naive voice, behind which is a great amount of confidence in himself and the world, he said, "When the soldier came down the gang-way, all the reporters and camera men were waiting for him to say something historic, like 'Lafayette, we are here.' But he looked around forlornly and mumbled, 'Gee, I wish I was home.' As a result, the second combatman to arrive got all the publicity back home."

If any of our group would mention a mutual friend to Mr. Winant, his reply was always, "Gee, isn't he a nice fellow!" Everybody was a sincere, honest man to the Ambassador, until he found out otherwise.

The antidote to Joe Kennedy, Winant was concerned about American airmen who were taking a poor view of Britain. "They don't get around enough. On leave, they are with other Americans and stay at our American clubs. While working and flying, they are always with their own countrymen. The little contact they do have with the English is usually something about a huge cab or bottle club bill. And our men judge the English on that alone."

A man who had fought with distinction in the last war, he told us that any boys who sincerely wanted to see action in this war would be able to do so. Opportunities would arise for transfer to combat units.

Overseas a year, we wanted to phone home and asked the Ambassador about this. “Gee, I’d sure like to let you do it. But we can’t take any chances. The Germans have wireless recording machines operating all the time. And you might say something in your excitement.”

Long, black hair shot through with gray, brown, deep-set, twinkling eyes, not quite as tall and gaunt as Lincoln, wearing dark suits and high, brown shoes, friendly but not in the politician way, a New England accent, Winant knows the difference between right and wrong. And he stands for what is right—a champion of humanity, too idealistic, perhaps, to become well known.

We were worried about transferring to the American Army, and we asked his advice. “Maybe later on you should transfer, but not now. You fellows are doing the best job for the war where you are.”

His ADC, Major Manning Jacob who always could find cigarettes and entertainment for us, said, “Stick it out where you are for the present. Don’t transfer.”

Mr. Winant’s housekeeper next door to the Embassy told us about the Prime Minister and the Ambassador waiting for the news of the African surprise landing by Allied troops. “For several hours those two men paced up and down in this apartment. The word of success came just in time. The carpet was about to go. I suggested several times they sit down, as I was worried about the carpet. They did after the flash.”

When the set back came to the Americans in the Kasserine Pass, there was no gloating in Britain. The British Eighth Army was doing brilliantly while Yanks were retreating. The way of Allies is of mutual understanding. Here a bit done by one today, yonder a bit by another tomorrow. When I heard the terrific American criticism of the British, stalled before Caen many months later while Patton was sweeping France, I was hurt. We outnumbered the British on the Continent, just as the British outnumbered us in Africa. It is a stupid policy to offset one against the other in peace or war.

The most terrifying experience of my life is the time I had to walk the plank every day for a week in Chelsea. I was on a village fighting school in a bombed-out area. Part of the assault course, wearing everything ever issued, was climbing to a roof by a drain pipe, going on all fours across the smashed-in roof to the edge, and then lightly skipping across a plank three stories high to another roof where you might stand up if your grandfather was a thorough-bred baboon. All that was necessary then was to jump down a story and swing out a window into another window across a passage via a rope and walk down some stairs and jump over a wall. The general idea was to act like something out of the *Hunchback of Notre Dame*. I couldn't even walk down the stairs well, as by that time I was more dead than alive.

But the plank was the worst. I crossed it like Father Time looking for a needle in a haystack. No net, not anything below—just some bricks. The plank was not secure and jumped about like an Olympic diving board. And I continually felt the urge to ignore the plank and simply jump into space. My imagination worked at a rate of knots. If I was terrified, the people watching me were more so. I seemed to be the only one in the school who didn't think the plank was fun.

If I am bothered with nightmares about the war in a few years, It won't be some fat Hun with a machine pistol chasing me around the bed. It will be that plank.

One day our company marched to the gymnasium for an experience that has yet to be explained. Two old knights complete with maps and a motion picture machine that didn't work told us about "In-Ja," which I found out was India.

They were directly out of Wodehouse, the Hollywood films, or the popular imagination. Harrow, Cambridge, army, retired, they had evidently bubbled over one night in their club and decided to tell the modern army about India as they knew it forty years ago. England humors its men of title who in the long past have served their country well, and the tour was no doubt easily arranged. The climax was a little argument they had between themselves on a certain bit of Indian culture. It was a touch of the old England that I wouldn't have missed for the world.

As a British officer, I had very little money. But I was compensated with privileges. England makes up to a degree in its lack of wealth by understood privileges. The British officer could go where he pleased. Those without that prerogative go where they can.

In maturation, the English make little to-do about death when it comes. They have none of our elaborate mortuaries, the best houses in town. Often a man is a combination of carpenter, wheelwright, furniture repairer, and undertaker.

My cockney platoon was in raptures the day I received a copy of the *Chicago Tribune* from my mother. The front page was devoted to the vivid escape and capture of the Touhy gang. The great

Russian war drive was secondary. Underworld names such as "The Owl" and FBI quotes like, "Come out backwards with your hands in the air," were flung about.

Boys who had been at Dunkirk and endured the blitz clamored about me.

"Let me see!"

"Then it's all true about America!"

"How wonderful!"

"What do they mean when they say 'Parole stinks in Illinois'?"

"Can I send this home to my wife, sir?"

We spent many hours talking together about America. The questions I was most often asked by the English riflemen were: Why are you called Yanks? Why do you have skyscrapers? Why do they pay the Yanks so high? What's the New Deal? Can you get me a Peter Arno book? How does America feel about the Irish being neutral? What do you think of Russia? Will it be easy to get a job in the States after the war? What's your equivalent of our Victoria Cross? How many Negroes do you have? How many Jews? What is Tammany? How do you elect a President? What's the difference between a Republican and a Democrat? How come America waited so long before getting in the war?

In our consciousness, there is one interval of time that stands alone. It is removed from all that preceded it or anything that may follow. A period set apart for remote memory, called forth by a smell, an accent, a face, a frame of mind. My period like that was following my commission in England, and it ended suddenly.

Alsop cornered us in the Fishermen's Arms, Brendon, Exmoor. "You fellows have got to help me. They are sending me on a month's battle course in the mountains in Wales. You know what that means. But if we go overseas, I can avoid it. This England act is running out. Let's pull up our roots and go."

"You mean, Al, go to Africa, just to get you out of a battle course?" Braden asked.

"Sure, and we can march gloriously at the tail of the Eighth Army. Besides, when I have a son and he asks me what I did in the Great War, I don't want to have to tell him that I told my batman to put a nice press in my pants. The first six went down to the Eighth, and we ought to follow them."

I parried. "Yes, and look what happened to them at Alamein. Also, I've been getting a lot of griff in the platoon about the terrains in Holland. So there might be an invasion soon. It is top secret. And what about my dog, Al?"

"We'll take the dog along, and you know you are just dreaming if you think we'll invade Holland or France this year. In addition, I might be able to get Tish to say she'll marry me on our embarkation leave. Think of the embarkation leave, and the laugh parade."

Fowler said, "I can't understand you, Alsop. To you, every wave will be a sub and every seagull a German plane, on the boat trip. Little brothers, most women, telephones, and snap orders frighten you. Yet you want us to go to Africa, and you want to get engaged. But I'm for it. This company commander of mine makes me cut my hair, do thirty-mile marches, and stand at attention in office. If we go overseas, I can avoid all that."

Braden thought there ought to be a little bit of idealism in the decision, and said, "We can't, Elmer, have the type of world the pacifists want unless we do something about the present world. Maybe we ought to go."

"I'm not parsimonious when it comes to laughs. If you think

we'll have a lot of fun on embarkation leave, suits me. Off we go, if it's all right with Turk," I said.

It was all right with Turk.

Sir John Davidson fixed it with Whitehall.

I had a nervous and tight feeling when I said good-bye to my platoon. I hadn't realized how much I loved them. We had planned on going in to action together. They later did great work on the Continent.

Proudest moment of my life was when I said good-bye to Company Sergeant-Major Young, cynical, unsmiling, tough, smart: the finest soldier I met during the war. He had spent thirteen years overseas and was a member of Wavell's Army of the Nile, which formed the nucleus of Montgomery's Eighth Army. We shook hands in the Sergeant's mess. "You were the best officer in the company. I am sorry to see you go. If you do as well out there as you did here, you will have no worries. Give them my best out there, and write me. Will you have an ale, sir?"

CSM Young was the impeccable martinet who kept the junior officers in line with such counsel as, "Excuse me, sir, but it might be better for the men if you would put on a little neater appearance in your dress."

Lady Gurney-Dixon and I went shopping in Winchester, and I mailed Barbara a Georgian diamond spray and an eighteenth-century bracelet. Then to London for two weeks that were gay, sad, glorious, rushed, pleasant, blurred, dazed, and happy. We spent pounds like dollars. Refreshing civilian clothes were allowed on leave. Rosa in the Cavendish beamed, saying, "This is just like the last war."

Colonel Tom Joyce, World War I veteran, took time off from his American Air Force desk job, and paid our way in the best of places. He had a passion for "stingers" and thought everyone else did, too.

Some afternoons we walked around London, saying good-bye slowly. The Duke of York's column, Guards monument, statues of Edward VII, Field Marshall Burgoyne, Lincoln, Washington, the hideous Albert Memorial, India House, 10 Downing Street, Westminster Abbey, Big Ben, Parliament, the Tower, Buckingham, and St. Paul's, alone in its symbolical glory.

There were only two detracting situations that arose. One, we had Queen Elizabeth's nephew sing "The Eton Boating Song." Tim had had more than his share that afternoon, and Tom was having a laugh at him. An unidentified girl suddenly slapped Tom's face, claiming we were making fun of England. Which definitely was not the case.

The other, Corey Ford, a slick paper magazine writer, appeared from the States and asked us to the Savoy for a drink. With a huge expense account and a direct commission as a major, he told us how wonderful it was of him to have forsaken an 80 percent cut in his income to go around the world in planes to write about "the boys."

In his soft racket, he seemed to think he was heaven's adjutant. We asked him if he had seen any of the historical things in London. "No, and I'm not going to. I've been here two days, and every time I step out of the hotel the English make me so damned mad, I go right back in the hotel again. The captain here and I had a good dinner last night. I thought they were starving over here. What kind of stuff has England been handing us in America? And as far as the blitz goes, London looks okay to me along that line.

"Tom, what are you going down there to Africa for? You have your future to think about. There's no sense in getting killed.

There's plenty of jobs around where the bullets aren't, you know. Get out of this war what you can. Don't be a sheep."

We thought the war was past the stage of handing out commissions to men who liked to strut in highly-tailored uniforms and knock allies. So we left in the middle of the second drink.

Knights was ordered to London by his company commander to say good-bye and help us with our packing. We had decided that it might be best for Knights to remain in England, all things considered, though he wanted to come with me.

It was a pathetic little scene I caught on the steps of the Cavendish when he said good-bye to Watt, *sotto voce*. Then we shook hands, and it was one of the most difficult things I ever did. He said, "Sir, I'm going to take over a Bren gun. I stack in. I'm not going to be a batman anymore. I wish you'd leave Watt with me, at least, I do. Good luck. Keep your head down. You're the best friend I ever had."

We never saw each other again.

Al became engaged, Winant gave us cigarettes, the Eagle Club came forth with sweaters and socks, we managed to buy our tropical kit, and the Cavendish gave us a send-off, with more than thirty people in front of the hotel as we drove away. In the middle was Rosa, in a dressing gown, a handkerchief lightly placed on her head, a glass of wine in her hand, saying, "Don't get snipped off! Don't get snipped off! Come back soon!"

Bennett piled us on the train at Kings Cross, five of us and a dog.

Chapter Eight

Getting Watling Street aboard the Dutch ship *Volendam* was no problem. I marched up the gangplank in the middle of the other Yanks with Watt in my arms covered by two trench coats. We had a cabin among the five of us, and the steward brought Watt better food than we had in the dining room. All would have gone smoothly, but we had to wait five days near Glasgow while the convoy formed.

The second day on board the RAF ship bound for Cairo the adjutant discovered Watt asleep on Turk's bunk.

"Oh, a dog. Whose is it?"

"He's sort of our mascot, sir," I replied.

"What nationality are you?"

"We're American volunteers, and the dog is sort of our mascot."

"Well, no dogs are allowed on troop ships. Even if dogs were allowed, embarkation papers are needed by the dog. I've seen no papers on all this. I guess the dog'll have to be destroyed."

"We can't destroy him. He's our mascot," Braden said.

"Now there's no time for argument. Don't be contumacious about this thing. Too many convoys in this war have been given away by the bark of a dog."

If the adjutant hadn't made that statement which was obviously false, we might have arranged to send Watt to Knights for the duration.

Nothing could stop Turk. When the adjutant left, Turk went to the captain of the ship. It turned out the Dutchman liked dogs, giving his permission for Watt to remain aboard.

This stopped the RAF temporarily, but soon a forty-eight-hour running pitched battle ensued. The troops on board were laying bets on whether the dog would sail or remain behind. The betting was against us.

A Dutch ensign spotted Watt on top deck and signaled shore. The embarkation officials replied that the dog must be taken off, destroyed, or have London's consent to go with the troops. The RAF beamed. They knew we couldn't get London's permission from our isolated position. But they didn't know Turk.

He flagged a small vessel playing around the ship, sending a telegram with it to shore. The telegram was direct to the War Office. We hid the dog with the ship's carpenter when the Ministry of War Transport united with the RAF and embarkation officials. On the ship's final inspection, Watt was discovered—at the same time permission for Watt's embarkation was granted by the War Office. An hour later we sailed.

But the RAF had the last word. "That dog can't go on top deck."

On the first submarine attack that amounted to no more than an alert, Watt and Al landed in a protected bunk at the same time in a mad scramble. Al got out sheepishly when we laughed, but Watt remained in bed.

Our convoy was fast, sleek, comfortable, safe, and orderly, exuding the power and production of the United Nations. The sea was calm and the air warm. Looking about us, I could see concrete evidence that we were going to win, that we couldn't possibly lose.

So different from our trip over in the early days on a rough and wild North Atlantic in a convoy of rusty, old, badly controlled ships on a hit, miss, and pray proposition. When there was no time for maintenance except on the voyage.

Going to Africa was dull compared to that first exhilarating trip. We wondered when the war was going to be like "What Price Glory," "Journey's End," or "Hell's Angels."

We amused ourselves by listening to old tunes on the piano, arguing, discussing how the female entertainers grew prettier as the days dragged on, having a few cocktails, sitting in the sun, debunking, or living in a fantasy. We pretended we were on a drunken yacht trip, and Al was "Sir Anthony Allopp," the owner, steering us to the war zone by mistake. Or we put on a post-war reunion in which we were stolid, self-important characters, no longer interested in the men we knew as soldiers.

The British on board were taking for granted this strange trip to a distant port. Each generation protected the heritage given them by their ancestors. Their fathers and grandfathers had gone on missions to Africa and India and the Orient. But we five Americans were the boys who liked to play golf on Labor Day, visit the Grand Canyon, and ski in New England. Mentally, we were out of place on the *Volendam*. We did not come from a country that to exist at all must be in some sort of form of empire.

When I lost my Zippo lighter, the trip was ruined.

"As both of you probably know, the main role we have is to assist the tanks forward. Sometimes we can get out of our vehicles and knock out obstacles holding up the armor. Again, we maintain ground until the infantry comes to relieve us. The tanks can take the ground but can't keep it. We protect the tankers in their static night positions."

"Tom and I have often wondered in England whether the 60th goes in front of the tanks, or the tanks in front of us."

"It's one or the other, or we might move right along with them. But we must keep the tanks mobile, by attacking infantry dug in, knocking out field pieces, and generally going here and there. It's all quite simple."

Commanding officer of the 2nd Battalion, Kings Royal Rifles, Colonel Bill was taking Tom and me for a stroll shortly after joining the outfit that was resting and poised in the sand, heat, flies, and our bushes of Libya. An officer for twenty years, William Amory had won the DSO for the battalion's attack at Alamein.

"I know you two would like to be together, so I'm putting you in the same company. You will have platoons of six pounder anti-tank guns, frightfully important. Of course, everything is. You should have no trouble. Play along with the sergeants for a time. They are experienced.

"We are all terribly frightened sometimes when we get steep or sticky assignments. But it is nothing. Queer what one does in action sometimes. I was blowing up a German tank with a sticky bomb. I walked a few yards and explosions took place before I anticipated. The noise and fuss was awful. So unconsciously I put my handkerchief over my head. Perhaps you will be called upon to do some patrolling. We get information for the armor. If you can do a good patrol, you can handle anything."

When I met my platoon, it went something like this. "I am very pleased to be with you out here. I know you men have been in Libya and Egypt for a long time and want to go home. We'll go through this thing together, and I will stay with you until the end of the war. If I can help you at any time, don't hesitate to see me."

The platoon laughed, and I didn't know why. Later, I asked my sergeant, Bill Cook, what it was all about. "Mr. Ellsworth, we have lost so many officers that the boys were a bit surprised that you thought you would be with us long. Also, there seems to be a jinx on you Americans. The first six of you went out rather rapidly."

I felt a bit giddy but smiled cheerfully. Too, I had my first touch of Gyppy Tummy, which means you have dysentery and are feverish, weak, and your bones ache. Sand, sand-fleas, and flies had broken open my skin. Healing of a simple scratch took months in Libya. I had "desert-sores" along with everyone else. Ugly, pus-edged sores, which gave the Eighth Army more trouble than had Rommel in his hey-day and left permanent scars. The bandages we had were used over and over again. They were not expendable.

To top it all off, for the first and last time in my remembrance, I was homesick. Being homesick is all and more than I had ever heard about it. It lasted four days, the most lonely and sad period of my life.

When it passed, I became proud that I had joined the 7th Armoured Division, the original desert rats, the only division to wear the jerboa as a shoulder patch, exploiters of the Alamein breakthrough, Britain's crack unit. Tough, small, cocky, friendly men who wore shorts, knee-length stockings, desert boots, whose bodies were black from the sun, their hair bleached. Their mail came addressed "M.E.F.," for Middle East Forces. But they said to me, "Gorblimmey, it means 'Men England Forgot!' Are we ever going to get out of this bloody desert?"

Six pints of tea a day we had, an almost sacred ritual. Bully beef three times daily, and an occasional small egg from a Wog for a shilling. In the evenings we played bridge by candlelight in a tent, drinking warm gin and lime juice out of glasses made from beer bottles. Twice a day we swam in the Mediterranean, and Watt learned to jump and ride the waves.

In the heat of noon we saw perfect mirages—lakes with sail boats, hills with lovely green trees. They were in the same places every day, reflections from somewhere, I was told.

The nights were cold and comfortable, during which time Watt played, chasing small lizards and romping with Arab dogs. During the day, he snapped at flies and slept. I never knew whether Watt was an asset or liability when it came to flies. He attracted them, but he also destroyed them.

The 1943 Eighth Army, perhaps the greatest single fighting unit, man for man, the world has ever seen. . . . Five months Tom and I are without mail. . . . We are allowed to send one airmail letter a week. . . . Men who haven't seen a white woman for months talking sex. . . . Sergeant Ted Osborne of my platoon who came out of Dunkirk, Greece, Crete, chased up and down the desert with Wavell, Auchinlek, Montgomery and hasn't a single piece of ribbon he can show for it. . . . Osborne later decorated posthumously in Normandy. . . . Camel caravans, picturesque at two hundred yards, dirty and smelly at ten. . . . Roman ruins, Arab ruins, gaudy colors and bare brown feet. . . . Censoring browned-off cockney letters which say little, because it is all sand, but recall the original green of England, or a simple, pleasant incident like a walk, a swim, a dance, or a night in a pub before Munich. . . . Water wells used for fifteen hundred years.

A sudden Middle East check-up, unearthing thirty-five hundred deserters. . . . Wogs stealing Tom's kit. . . . Cooks, bakers, ground crews, and the rear echelon worrying and writing about death, but not these victors of Alamein, jealous of their reputation. . . . Welfare officers handling four hundred divorce and separation cases each week. . . . Litter of the Afrika Korps retreat, ammunition boxes, empty food tins, pot helmets, Jerry cans, leather cartridge belts, shovels, shell cases, trucks, grenades, charred tanks, hasty graves. . . . Tasteless cigarettes from India, smoked by hot, sticky, dirty, sandy men who had kept Germany from linking with Japan via the Suez. . . . Mohammedans, alone on their knees in the evening, facing the Kaaba. . . . Always someone with jaundice. . . . A squeaky phonograph, good for memories, but not music. . . . Joy in the company over sunken oil barrels for toilets instead of four-gallon petrol tins which cut the seat.

Watt climbing about in a crashed Junkers 52. . . . A rifleman in my company receiving ten shillings in the mail from an Allied serviceman in England who had spent the night with his wife. . . . Cheery Italian prisoners, the ice-cream man, hoping the war ends soon and asking for a cigarette, making the cutting of the throat sign when Mussolini's name is mentioned. . . . Sullen, tough, well-built, highly trained Germans waiting shipment to North America. . . . Twilight on the desert, cool, with a purple glow on the sand in the distance, a stillness over everything. . . . The desert moon, best in the world, when night falls suddenly. . . . The dry, hot sirocco sweeping from the North, filling our shaving kits, shoes, socks, ears, and suitcases with a fine sand. . . . The Army of the Empire of Great Britain, two-thirds of its personnel and three-fourths of its casualties from the United Kingdom.

Eighth Army humor was not the best, but it was an attempt. The men had no special services of shows, concerts, vaudeville, or magazines to keep them posted on the latest laughs. Shipping space was used for guns, replacements, tanks, and bullets. The popular desert joke of 1943 was, "What did the top hat say to the brassier?"

"I don't know," naturally.

"You give those two a lift and I'll go on a head."

It was better than nothing.

The Tommy swears more often than the American, but the latter wins in blasphemy.

Tom and I decided it was high time the Eighth Army learned baseball. We contacted a medical major of the American 79th Fighter Group to get a bat and ball. He phoned special service in Tripoli, making arrangements for us to drive the twenty-five miles from Clivatto and secure the equipment. We complimented him on the efficiency and lack of red tape, and how different it would have been in the British Army.

He smiled, "I'm surprised myself. It's the first time it has ever happened this way."

We substituted baseball practice for training. There were difficulties among the English on confusing the game with cricket, but we brought them to a standard we felt necessary to challenge the 79th Fighter Group to a game. They beat us by one run, though it could have been by fifty. Two more weeks practice, and we arranged a game with the American Field Service, the volunteers who drove ambulances for Montgomery's Army. It was for blood, and we won 8–6, watched silently by a large crowd which had never seen a baseball game before. I guess it was Tom's greatest thrill in his British Army stretch.

We started "desert basketball," a mixture of American basketball, rugger, and boxing because a sergeant used our bat to pound tent poles and Watt stole the baseball.

The American Field Service men were favorites of the Eighth Army. They did great work for no pay. But a more miscellaneous collection I have never met. Communists, Jews, wife dodgers, draft dodgers, conscientious objectors, college flops, drunks, poor little rich boys, interventionists who thought England's war was our war when we were still debating compulsory military service, and men who had been rejected for active duty. Quite a story could be written about their heroic work and play.

Tripoli was a symbol to me of the hypocrisy of Mussolini's African Empire. Along the Corso Italo Balbo, where we bought sherbets of mushy, colored water, were the cheap, pockmarked, artificially colored buildings built in the thirties and already crumbling. Roman columns and monuments had been built by the Duce, dissimulating the Italians with their past glory. In the evenings I expected to see above this third-rate World's Fair a paper, lacquered moon with a naked, painted woman in the center. Even Marshal Badoglio's palace with separate houses for his mistresses showed that the Governor of Libya had many things on his mind besides advancing the Empire for the Italians. Only the ancient, original, gray seawall looked real.

Outside Tripoli was the Foreign Legion of short, untidy, unimpressive men who could fight but were a far cry from the Hollywood version. They were stationed in a red, white, dirty, crowded village dominated by a mosque. Outside the walls and gates were beggars, while inside were women in veils and dirty, bright shawls and skirts, tattle-tale gray swathed men riding small donkeys and carrying sticks, groups of men and boys lying silently in front of low one-room dwellings beneath palm trees, camels chewing cuds, camels carrying bags slung over their scruffy bodies. The Arabs had no interest in conquerors, having seen them come and go in this birthplace of civilization.

To relieve the boredom of waiting to sail for Sicily, I drove to Sabratha, on the Sea, founded by Phoenicians from Carthage, 500 B.C., and off the tourist route. Vandals, Berbers, and Romans overran it, and finally the Arabs wiped out the city, and sands drifted over it for fourteen centuries. Mussolini began excavations. A massive amphitheater where games and wild beast shows were held is in excellent condition, looming for miles in the desolate desert. The fine mosaics, made for sandals and not army boots, have been scratched and mutilated by Nazis, British, and Italian hobnails.

The Sabratha senate house is very small, situated near a fine thirty-seater with running water laid on and marble statuary of Romans with double chins. In the streets outside are the graves of the former inhabitants. My driver and I were the only two people within five miles of Sabratha that day. Sightseeing in wartime is not a rush and a crowd and a guide.

As Sicily developed into a foot race of artillery and infantry, Montgomery decided to save our armor for Italy, ordering us to act as enemy against the Black Cat 56th Division. The Black Cats were making their last preparations for the Salerno landing with the Guards and Americans, and they were most gloomy about the combined operation. At Zuara, planes, the navy, and waves of an assaulting infantrymen overran our battalion position, with a small number of training casualties.

I placed my six-pounders near a graveyard in the sand along the sea, putting my bed roll between the last resting place of Hans Klein of a German flak regiment, killed on his twenty-first birthday and one less present day problem, and the slab of an unknown Italian aviator shot down in 1941. My jeep driver used the stone marker for a table to make a brew and bully sandwiches.

Waiting for the Black Cats to attack, I set up platoon headquarters in a small, musty mausoleum. It was the logical spot but not the most pleasant. Four or five yellow skulls were scattered about on the floor. The walls were packed with skeletons folded neatly in to tight compartments. I looked down in the cellar through a large trap door. More than one hundred skulls were tossed about like melons. Thigh bones were neatly stacked along one wall, the arms piled like wood along another, and pelvis bones fitting on top of each other lined a third wall. This collection of sorted ex-humanity was once a battalion of Italians that had been wiped out thirty years before. In all the desolation, this was just one more thing, that's all.

In Libya, German graves were always the neatest and best situated. British graves were temporary, exhumed months later by South Africans and the bodies taken to a permanent cemetery. The Italian graves were scruffy and marked with anything handy at the time of burial. Over the German places of interment were well-made issue Nazi crosses, which the Jerries methodically carried with their mobile equipment. When we buried a German, we had to mark his grave, "Unknown German Soldier" and the army serial number. For the Germans did not have names on their identification tags.

Thomson, Fowler, and Alsop joined Danielson, who had preceded us to the Middle East, at the 11th Battalion, KRRC, harboring in Alexandria. Our first letter from them stated that Al had lost all three of his hats and was parading around in a sun helmet, which embarrassed him because only rookies in their initial overseas days wore the pith headgear. In addition, he was immediately sent on a battle and special hardening course that he had trooped all of us out of England to avoid.

Chapter Nine

My anti-tankers and I talk for hours on anything and everything. The desert rats are hungry for information, gnawing on scraps for news, digesting the thought that the army presents for orientation. Close to Hitler's Europe, they know what they are fighting against.

Some know what they are fighting *for*. Once conversation opens, they are like Gatling guns.

"If Rommel were in the KRRs, he'd probably have three stripes, bust."

"If he'd have bloody that. Why don't we pick our generals like Jerry does, instead of old school ties?"

"Old Monty says he is a better general than Rommel. I think he is, I do."

"Wait 'til old Monty is wrong some time. His head will fall, just like the rest of them."

"The Russians are the ones," says Hutchinson. "They do all the fighting. Stalin has only one uniform, just like us blokes with no rank at all. He isn't like our officers. Where would we be if it weren't for the Russians?"

Topper Brown answers, "Don't forget all the lend-lease America and Britain have been sending Joe. Who's been doing all the bombing of Europe? We have. Who held bloody Hitler off for a year before Joe was in it? We did."

With fourteen German vehicles to his credit, Sergeant Brown is my crack gunner and he tells his men they are in a good army. Because he knows that a soldier is not at his best if he thinks an ally is carrying the brunt. He wants his crew good, because he wants to get home alive to his wife.

"You should have known Richard Wood who had this platoon once, Mr. Ellsworth. He was just like us, a decent bloke, he was. Even if his Father is Lord Halifax. He met his lot in a funny way. He was in an old bomb hole, with his legs crossed, and Jerry come over. Jerry dropped his load, and one bomb landed right on Mr. Wood's crossed legs but didn't explode. He lost his legs. He's in America now. Right sort, he was."

"Did you hear about Monty when he first came out here? He wanted a KRR cap badge. And this officer said that it wasn't everyone who could wear a KRR cap badge. This officer was going to be sacked anyway, but he was given a bowler twenty-four hours earlier."

"Here's a cartoon I drew for you sir," Gibbs says. "It's about Watt. It's not an original idea, but I thought of it when I saw him playing with that Wog tart in the sand."

It shows two people going down the street on a tandem, with my dog saying to his girlfriend, "If we did that on the street, they would throw water on us."

"My old Mum is not getting the sixpence a day I allotted her. How come that? What are we out here bloody fighting for? I'm out here and because I'm out here, they think I won't know about the sixpence."

"What a flap that Alamein was, sir. Billett of 'Desert Mice's Jungle' even had some pups born in his lorry during the worst part. Billett has had his portee blown up three times now, and not a scratch has he got. Some people have all the luck. Remember the officer who came up to us, and didn't even get out his bed-roll before he met his lot? He had everything in his bed-roll, too. We opened it later. What a lot of gear, he had."

Then follows reminiscing of friends killed and how. Rehashing of old mistakes in battle. Recruit days. The trip out on the boat. The blitz. The army. And I think that it is a myth that soldiers, if they have been in the thick of it, do not like to talk about death and shells. They will talk way long after their children are grown up, to anyone who will listen.

"Ja know Mr. Cox, sir? 'E was one of your Yank group. 'E was in our company when a Jerry Tommy-gunner got 'im. We all liked Mr. Cox. And 'e used to give us books 'is family sent 'im from 'Merica. I was sorry to see 'im go."

"Was the papers carrying much news about us when we was chasing old Rommel? It was just a lot of dust and brews and we didn't know where we was going. We just kept going."

"Him? That corporal! He let us down at Alamein and I haven't given a Sweet Fanny Adams for him since. We were all ballsed up enough as it was without him taking off."

Cockney rhyming-slang. North-and-South means mouth. Plates-of-Meat means feet. Wog words. Indian words. Language of South Africa, Egypt, Syria, Greece and the Orient. Pukka, griff, wad, kip, muchin, buckshee, alakeefio, tiffin, connor, maleesh, whack. Colorful, but it takes time to understand what these Englishmen are talking about in the dialect they have inherited. But soon you are a part of the Eighth Army and using the tongue yourself, and you sing the songs that are peculiar to the desert troops.

"Did you hear about Major Gibbs and Captain Walker the other night? They stepped out of the tent for a short trot and forgot a compass. They wandered about for three hours when they finished. They couldn't find their tent again. So they slept on the ground, and in the morning they were only a hundred yards or so from the rest of the tents.

A hygienic mission in Libya requires all the kit of a reconnaissance patrol. In the dark, and sameness one gets lost easily.

"The trouble was," I said, "between the two wars you British wanted the wrong things and you got them. In America, we didn't know what we wanted, so we got nothing. The result is that we're here in the desert with a lot of fighting and whatnot ahead. Our people back home worry about your trained diplomats getting the best of us. But our two countries are frank about what we like and don't like about each other. I tell you fellows you can't make coffee and you tell me I'm a ruddy bad hand at making tea. We can clear up misunderstandings if we forget the chicanery of diplomatic maneuver. We don't understand a lot of things in the States because you Englishmen take it for granted that we know how good your cause is, and it needs no advertising. After the war, we will howl when you ask for a loan. That will be about the time we are arguing who won the war, Britain, America, Russia, China, or Brazil."

"I've seen a Yank outfit," says a chesty little rifleman named Broadhurst. "They throw their stuff around, and if they lose something, they pay for it and that's all there is to it. The Yanks have the stuff. If we lose a cap or a mess tin or gaiter we are charged for it first thing next morning on a charge in company office. We aren't supposed to lose our gear, but sometimes we can't bloody help it. Look at our platoon. Not more than eight tin hats and respirators in the lot."

"I wouldn't give no Jerry a cigarette if he was my best friend. He can fight, though, old Jerry can," says Billy Gallagher, my batman-driver.

"Me, I don't like Tory dictators. Churchill is all right as long as there's a war on, but we'll soon get him out of there when the shooting is packed up. Too many funny things are going on up there in England. The army is thinking about economics and all that. You always hear blokes talking about it. And when we get demobed, things are going to change. If they'll ever bloody demobe us. About which I have me doubts."

"Know any nice American girls we can write to, sir? Me and my mate are always writing girls. We've never met none of them, but it gives us something to do. We have pictures of some of them. Smashing, they are."

I censor these letters, and they are simple, longing, pitiful, homesick, abstract efforts. After the war, two or three end in marriage, which surprises everyone.

"Now we receive the sprayer. Then three months later we get the juice to shoot on the flies. By that time we've lost the sprayer. Jerry gets his in one package, both juice and sprayer. Jerry has us beat in a lot of ways. His tanks are better than the Sherman, too."

"There's a graveyard up the road where every Grenadier lieutenant in a battalion is buried. They attacked a hill. Jerry got hold of the Guards success signal. They gave it, and then proceeded to cut 'em to pieces. But the Guards stayed there. Who says the Guards officers are a heap? They're no more of a shower than any other mob, their officers."

Soldiers need a personal world. They can't live and fight on the crusade-for-humanity slogans alone. They need people back home worrying about them and writing to them and loving them. One of the worst experiences an officer has is talking to a sobbing, brave man—tortured, groping, dazed, his personal world shattered—because he has learned that his wife has been unfaithful, and he is far away and can't combat it, except by time.

It happened to me twice in Libya. One man who had been fighting for two years in the desert received a newspaper clipping from his mother. It described his six-year-old son playing in the street at midnight and the police taking him home to find the mother in the arms of a man. The case was publicized because a Member of Parliament wanted the allotment to the soldier's wife stopped immediately because the government should not subsidize adultery.

The other man showed me a letter from his wife, saying she was going to have a baby by the soldier's cousin. But that it was not her fault as she spent only one night with the man and to please forgive her. His eyes were a blank. I told him that one day he would be happy again.

He said, "Do you really think so, sir?"

We tried to get these two men home, but Cairo needed every soldier for the underbelly of Europe.

Both these men today are living contentedly in England. Time has passed. They forgave their wives, taking up where war stepped in. That was the desert rat.

"These boys look like they been in the sand for years and years," drawled an American Negro to me in the harbor of Catania, Sicily. We were on a United States tank landing ship. The American transport was new, having left America a few weeks before. Mt. Etna was above us. The radio was inappropriately playing "Ole Man River." Around the British boats in the harbor, men were swimming. American regulations were against swimming, so we sat in the sun on an oily deck, jammed with vehicles, 60th Riflemen in dirty shorts, and sixty battalion pets ranging from a rabbit to a goat peeking from underneath camouflage nets.

The invasion of Italy had begun a few days before. We were going in soon, to open the Mediterranean, capture the Foggia airfields, suck down Nazi troops from the North, relieve Europe of fear, help the Russians, beat Germany. It was the opening of the most tedious front in the war—the Italian.

Churchill told us the bloodiest part of the fighting was ahead. But that didn't bother us, because stepping on European soil meant the beginning of the end.

It was the start of the fifth year of war, a war that was supposed to be short because men, cities, and civilization could not stand a long fight. Our orders to move had come suddenly, but not unexpectedly. Toward the end of August that year we had been warned that Italian planes might fly over us soon and not to fire upon them. We did see many of them arrive under the secret surrender terms. When it was announced officially that Italy had turned it in, Colonel Bill gave the order to splice the main brace, and the battalion had rum.

Then we started the six hundred-mile trek to Bizerta—Gallagher, Watt and I in our jeep in the battalion column. I carried an emergency haversack slung on the jeep, filled with cigarettes, bullets, a quart of gin, peanut butter, sugar, malted milk tablets, and a can of bully for Watt. I chose those articles carefully in order to meet any situation across the Med.

The Mareth Line, used by the Germans against the British, built by the French in case of trouble with the Italians. Ben Gardane. Gabes. Wadi Akarit. Sousse. El Djeb. Sfax. Tunis. Carthage. The route thick with dusty rubble, tree stumps, crashed planes, minefields, knocked out ships peppered along the coast, plenty of cigarettes at last. Sights of women in dresses instead of gunny sacking. Bizerta. Malta. Catania. And on the way again in T.L.S. 21.

The boat was a cracker box and bobbed around like a cork. We were crowded, dirty, and hot. Our yellow-colored desert vehicles and the men's brown bodies looked out of place on the water. The riflemen sold Lugers and souvenirs to the Americans. From sleeping under the vehicles, Watt picked up a coat of grease that sealed the sand on his body. I tried not to be too affectionate with him.

One of my platoon said to me, breathlessly, "You ought to see them, sir! You ought to see them!"

"See what?" I thought it was at least a German wolf pack.

"The plates the Yanks are eating off. They are all partitioned, with places for different foods. I never seen plates made like that."

Our Riflemen were fed cheese, bully, biscuits, and tea. They didn't mind this too much in the desert. But when they saw the American crew eating food the like of which they hadn't seen for four years, it was bad. First the Americans would line up for their meal, and the British mouths would water. Then the desert rats got their ration, eating it any place they could find to stand. Some ate in the latrine.

The American commander watched this for two days. His men had been out of the States for a short time and in the service about seven months. Most of the British on board had been in the army four years, overseas fighting for two, and soon would be in action again. He told

Colonel Bill he had extra food, that the British would get American rations, use the Americans' tables when they had finished eating, and the British could buy supplies at the canteen. We literally had not seen a piece of soap for two months. The men bought cigarettes, candy, soap, toothbrushes, lotions, matches, and stationery.

George Lyon, our intelligence officer, asked for a toilet roll in the canteen. He was handed a large tootsie-roll, which he took, thinking it was a very compact, handy American toilet roll.

Good feeling was everywhere. I wish I knew the name of that American commander. He sent our battalion in to the Italian campaign well-heeled.

The old campaigners look on each new city with suspicion. They see them not through the eyes of a Cook's pamphlet but as a place where they will be ordered about, bored, fleeced out of money, homesick, without mail, standing in line, sniped at, hot, uncomfortable, their kit stolen, and stuck for no one knows how long.

That was the way we approached Taranto, where already the Italians were washing out the "Dux, a noi!," "Duce," and "Dux" signs that had been painted everywhere. Our landing was simple. The Germans had left the day before. We took off North after them. Our 4th Armoured Brigade was independent. The 7th Armoured Division had been rushed to the Salerno area under Bobby Erskine. We never joined them afterward. In our Brigade were the 44th and 50th Tank Battalions, a battalion of County of London Yeomenry tanks, and our infantry motor battalion. As we chased Jerry, we noticed the freshness of Italy, untouched by war.

But that was long ago. It will never be the same again.

If the people back home were disappointed by the slow advance in Italy, those of us who were there were more so. Especially the desert force which had been weaned on a fluid, mobile, swift advance with left hooks to lighten the load.

Our first objective was Foggia, and our Brigade tanks took that after we lobbed in a few shells. The American Air Force had leveled the city, which we found evacuated except for a few who had cringed in cellars. They were dazed and uncomprehending as they vacantly stared on their spilled homes. A stray cat or dog wandered about looking for food. The streets were choked with rubble, the dust gradually settling in the deathly stillness.

Montgomery halted us a few miles North on the Foggia Plain and came to spend the afternoon with the battalion in a large farmyard.

We were dressed in khaki shorts, as Monty liked us best. Giving a wide, slow salute, he gathered us about his big, low-slung yellow roadster, presented three medals, told us to sit down, smoke, and listen.

"We are going up the road. Rome and those places. There are some mighty good billets in Rome. I will see you there soon. You have made this army a household word all over the world. In all the battles we have fought together, you and I, we have not had one single failure. Indeed, a fine and wonderful record. We are a great family, the Eighth Army."

He didn't actually beat his chest when he said "Eighth Army" but it seemed that way, as his narrow, piercing eyes swept us.

"I suggest you name your children after our great victories. What about Mareth, Agheila, or Matruh for a girl? Of course, I don't recommend Radi Zem Zem for a boy.

"I'm going to some mighty queer places in this war, and wherever I go, you will be with me. I might go to China."

At this we groaned and Monty laughed.

"But—I might go to England."

The riflemen went wild.

The short man with the lined, deeply tanned face continued, while slowly flicking at flies with a horse-hair swatter: "The Sicily show was a perfect example on a small scale of the modern army in victory. It will be studied years hence when all the other battles are forgotten. It was well finished off. We killed and captured a lot of them. Not bad. We can and will do better, but still, not bad.

"All is well, Mussolini is in Rome shooting up people who kicked him out. An Italian general was in my headquarters yesterday. He told me we are now allies, and in that he was senior to me, he would take command of Eighth Army. But he doesn't know the form. He doesn't know the form.

"The Poles and New Zealanders are coming to join us here. Then we attack. I will use my gunners well. I can't win without my gunners, just as we can't win battles without the chaplains.

"We'll settle down for the winter north of Rome. And you know the Russians are not so very far now. Not so very far. We will do saturation bombing from Foggia. It will be great fun."

Continuing for a half hour in laconic, dictatorial, humorous, cocky sentences, he ended with his famous, "Together, you and I, we will see this thing through to the end."

Montgomery never captured the imagination of British officers as he captured the imagination of the rank and file. They respected him, but there was no love lost.

Then the rains came, and they were to last on and off for two years. With them they brought the end of decisive victories. Gradually we realized this was going to be a foot sloggers battle in clay and mud where the finest fighting machine of all time, the infantry soldier, would have to go in and die ingloriously in a puddle.

We worked our way slowly north from the plain, and Italy lost its freshness. The same old display was there. The brewed-up and charred vehicles, bayonets with a helmet on top stuck over the loose graves, mines marked with a body to show who discovered them and how, abandoned guns, and the families slowly wandering back to their villages to claim belongings and relatives stiff and fragrant on church floors.

Bewildered Italian soldiers washed our pots, pans, and clothes, dug our latrines, worked idly on roads, brought us wine and grapes for cigarettes and food, sold us pigs they had stolen, excitedly complained to us about Fascism and their officers.

As Jerry retreated, he was shelled in the homes. Then we moved in to the homes, and we weren't too careful about the furniture and dishes, while Jerry shelled us. We moved on and the Italians returned to their homes and saw they had received quite a sacking.

Little pictures remain in my mind. I was sleeping in a field just off the road, the jeep and dog by my side. Shermans were advancing to engage the 16th Panzers a mile ahead. The intermittent artillery flashes were lighting the night sky behind me. On the road were the black silhouettes and clang of the tanks. As each one passed, the silhouette changed to a row of dark crosses, graves of freshly killed Canadians on the other side of the road. Then the silhouette of the next tank. There was a low half-moon. I seemed detached from it all.

Or the first group of British prisoners of war, dressed in Italian civilian clothes, captured in Libya two years before, having made a break when Italy called it all off. One asked me for the commanding officer to show him the map he had of German gun positions in the direction we were moving.

Rodwell, revving up in the mud, saying, "Give me the sand to this bleeding muck."

And Italians sowing by hand in a field torn by tanks and shells. Four airmen bailing out of a Boston in to the Adriatic near the coast road. German flame-throwers shot at Ghurkas attacking a hill half-mile away. Awakening in a small room I had moved in at midnight and looking at eighteen pictures on the wall, all of Christ and the Virgin Mary.

Chapter Ten

John Hunt was too keen, hearty, and enthusiastic to be a rifleman's dream. A martinet, fitness figure, mountain climber, intolerant of drinking, he was the only man I knew who could make his chocolates issue last seven days. A major for seven years, he came directly from England to command our company. He was always sincerely anxious to tangle with the Germans and apologized to us if we were left out of a skirmish. The desert troops were accustomed to a casual, easy existence when out of action. But he gave us no time for personal maintenance, insisting on training when we weren't fighting.

The second morning he was with us, we had a short and sharp run before breakfast and from then on the riflemen marched to meals if not engaged with Jerry. But he had our interests at heart and was a thorough gentleman. On a river crossing we were making in trucks under light shellfire, he sent orders over the wireless to have the men sit straight, stop smoking and look like soldiers. Disciplined, they cribbed and obeyed. In a year he was a brigadier, but while he commanded our company we were turned upside-down and inside-out. We were not even allowed to thieve in vineyards.

Well-dressed troops straight out of England often marked us as a labor battalion or gazed at us in wild amazement. We had few steel helmets left. Some of our men wore blue, abbreviated athletic pants, others desert shorts or khaki, long trousers. Civilian caps and straw hats became the rage for a time. Officers invariably wore fleece jackets, silk scarves, corduroy slacks, and the light blue, wool well-made shirt of the Afrika Korps was popular. We rolled up the sleeves of our shaggy, pocket-festooned pullovers. Each man had his wash-basin. Large mirrors were on most of the lorries, along with tables, chairs, musical instruments, and a few beds. Pets peeked out of strange places in our column. In action, desert troops were like a Rose Bowl team. But their outward appearance was that of a sandlot eleven.

The variety and eccentricity of Eighth Army dress was not intentional. It was stark, common sense that brought about the departures from the War Office patterns. Sheepskin coats kept out the bitter cold of the night and were more serviceable than the army issue. Scarves were protection from the choking clouds of sand and dust, and corduroys were not stained by the sand and mud. Our clothes were a throw-back to the days when supplying the Western Desert was a three months' trip from England—and in Italy, replacements of equipment had not yet reached us. Overseas a long time, the Desert Rats had learned the little tricks of making themselves comfortable, and the pets were substitutes for the civilization for which they longed.

John Hunt changed all this as much as possible—put us on a tense, rigid, European standard. Which was just as well for we were entering a new phase of war in a populated country. I have a feeling John never did quite approve of the ubiquitous Monty in his sheepskin coat, old sweater, corduroys, and black beret with the tank and general's badges, waving at the men as he went up and down the roads in his car, throwing packs of cigarettes here and there. But the men approved. Seeing him two or three times a week, they knew the Army Commander understood our particular problems of battle, food, weather, and homesickness.

Forlorn under a leaking tarpaulin that had put in too long a stretch in the African sun, I heard John shout one night, "Platoon Commanders!"

I joined John and the company officers under another sieve.

"Chaps, tonight, we can get at them hand-to-hand."

Our hearts sank.

"Intelligence has just intercepted a German message. Parachutists and sea forces are to attack the entire Fifth Corps ammunition and petrol dump at Termoli. We are to go there armed to the teeth and fight. Our battalion is the only available unit. Our job is to patrol until he comes. Then it will be quite a party."

We moved in a rush in the mud and rain. Halfway to Termoli, driving a Roman road, I asked Gallagher if we had remembered to bring the seven live turkeys we had exchanged with Ities for bully beef.

Silence. Then, "We forgot them. They are still tied to that bush. The boys will do their pieces when they find out. This move is bad enough without losing the turkeys. Bloody browning."

We never got back to Serricapriola to look for the birds. I suppose they are gone now. In fact, I suppose the Italians waited no longer than five minutes after we left to gather them in and trade to the next unit for bully.

For two days and nights we patrolled and waited in a heavy rain, teeth chattering, shoulders hunched, chilled to the bone, soaked through. We almost wanted Jerry to come so we could forget the weather. Hunt was magnificent, bringing us tea, rum, and stew regularly.

Bill Cook, Watt, and I stayed by the seashore, inspecting the guards. Once planes machine-gunned the area. I lost my father's trench knife from World War I.

One of the corporals got dead drunk in a hayrick and fell asleep on his guard. He told me he couldn't stand the rain. He was courageous in the desert, but we sent him to the rear the next morning, and I don't know what happened to him after that.

The third day, Monty came by, handed out some Old Golds from an admirer in Ohio, and asked what we were doing. He ordered us to rest immediately, that information had come through that the Germans had intercepted our message that we had intercepted theirs, and the attack on the supply dump was cancelled.

He drove to Colonel Bill in a farmhouse, said we were to be used in an impending attack, to get all possible sleep, and then named four of our company commanders, saying he did not know the fifth.

"Alan Holmes is the man you haven't met, sir."

"Have him come to dinner at my headquarters tonight. I want to see him."

Monty stayed with Alan, until 9:30 that night, a half-hour longer than he had since we invaded Italy. He gave Alan cigarette lighters for each of his platoon commanders. Alan was killed a month later.

Eighth Army was a family and Montgomery its commander.

It was always the same. German rearguards, and few casualties. We went down a hill, crossed a small river, were counter-attacked and then fanned out, the Germans withdrew. We went up a hill to look north at the ridges until it was time to go down again. It was methodical, boring, and we had few pitched battles. Occasionally we took prisoners who told us the 16th Panzers and the Adolph Hitler SS Regiment and some odds and sods from Stalingrad we were facing wanted to surrender and their morale was low. They knew the war was lost, they said while in our custody.

But the fighting denied this, as well as letters we took from dead bodies. But we passed on the prisoners' words for our own morale. It was a gentlemen's war in those days, and if we came across unmailed letters to Germany, we gave them to the Red Cross for dispatching. We treated all prisoners strictly in accordance with international law. The story changed in France, creating unnecessary gold stars in America.

On our right was the 78th Division, on our left the very fine solemn and disciplined Indian troops who carried bouquets of flowers on their vehicles, and farther over, the New Zealanders, best soldiery in the world. Polite, brave, well-trained, humorous, big, handling liquor well, they raised our spirits if we knew they were near. In both wars, if a poll were taken among all the Allied troops, I believe the New Zealanders would win the popularity contest. My only criticism is that there are not enough of them.

After the barrage, our 4th Armoured Brigade crossed the Sinello in jeeps, Brens, trucks, and Shermans while the engineers were calmly making a bridge under shelling and enemy observation. Whether clearing mines, putting up bridges, or brewing tea, the sappers were always the same, and they had few headlines or medals. But they were the lifeblood of our move all over the world.

Gallagher, Watt, and I had a wild ride in the jeep up the hill on the other side of the Sinello, following Tom's platoon with my four six-pounders behind me. I was ticking Gallagher for not having put down the windshield of the jeep that might have splintered us. We passed the tanks, placing our guns in firing positions in an olive orchard. The Germans were supposed to be four hundred yards distant. The shelling had stopped. When Tom and I had coordinated our eight guns, and Sergeant Cook had set up our headquarters in a badly mauled house, I sat on the stone well with Braden.

"Tom, these Jerries aren't within miles. I don't know what the flap and rush was getting us here."

"I guess you're right, Elmer. Here's Gallagher with a couple of teas for us."

I never had that tea, nor did Tom. For two hours in that orchard, shrapnel was singing about us. Jeeps and haystacks burned. Having watched us move in to position, Jerry waited until we were comfortable. Then he had his say.

I visited Brown's gun first. Topper was laughing and grinning and making cheese sandwiches as though he were back in his old job at the Mayfair bar. His crew was crouched in a lightly dug gun pit.

Watt's sensitive ears would get the whistle of a shell a split second before I did, and when he flattened those long, black pointed ears, I ducked. It was difficult for me to judge how "brave" to act. If one is unconcerned, he gets hit, and it is worse on the men to see their officer go out than if he had not put on a false display that the shells were no more than flies. So when the desert rats became moles. So did I.

"This is no game," Osborne's crew kept saying to me.

I crawled and ran through the orchard to Sergeant Crane's crew that was getting plastered but was unhurt. Crane was singing a song about, "There may be trouble ahead," and I helped dig his gun pit from the prone position.

About this time, Watt had had enough. He sensed our fear, and there was a disorderly look in his eye. Bill Cook came up, and I had him remove Watt to our house in the rear. It was the only time I saw Cook wear a steel helmet. He claimed he didn't have one, but he had found one in a hurry. I hoped that outwardly I would not show fright. Inside, I knew I was scared.

Small arms like rifles and machine guns can be located in a fair fight. In a bombing, you know when it is finished because you hear no planes, and sometimes you can see the bomb dropping. You have a chance of avoiding a suspected mine field, or even mines scattered along road shoulders. But shelling is what each soldier dreads the most. Half the time you can't hear them coming. The gunner is hidden. He doesn't see you. You don't see him. You don't know when the shelling has stopped, or when it might start. And you have seen the ugly wounds it causes, not clean and blue like a bullet. Artillery was the cause of most of our casualties in Italy, and it was behind practically all the battle fatigue cases throughout the world.

Brian Gunn came sauntering through the orchard to inspect our positions, eating an apple and carrying a fly swatter. "This isn't bad, Elmer," he said.

I replied, "It's bad enough," and continued digging. Gunn led away two petrified jeep drivers from battalion headquarters that were shaking on the ground.

Crane said, "Those two were like that at Beni Ulid." He commented sympathetically, not with disgust.

Alone, Colonel Bill walked slowly up the road to our right, talking on a "38" set strapped to his throat, his hands in his long, white trench coat, paying no attention to the occasional rifle crack or quick burst of Spandau bullets shot in his general direction and hissing over our heads. He turned around and waved a come-on. He walked a few yards father, and waved once more. And one by one our tanks started forward with him, the Colonel leading them like puppies, enticing them on.

They had balked at going on to our objective but if a man on foot could go up the road like that, the tanks could, too. Our motor platoons on foot went with them, five paces between each man. I saw three surprised Germans near the village, Scerni, come out with hands up. A 60th sergeant shot one with a stammer of Bren because he didn't raise his hands fast enough.

In the orchard, ready for a German counter-attack, we lost sight of the advance three hundred yards to our front. We heard occasional MGs and the tank's guns. We started to make a brew. John Hunt came back to us. He had been forward.

"It's all over. The Germans have withdrawn. We got one German tank. They destroyed four of ours, and knocked out sixteen. Very costly but worth it. Our own 60th casualties were only three killed. You will be interested to know that the observer who was shelling us in this orchard was a Fascist in civilian clothes and has been dispatched."

We were shaky, happy it was over. Especially when word came through that we would be relieved in a day or two. Sergeant Cook went back to draw rations, brought me thirty-nine letters, my first mail in Italy. Tom came to see me in the dark to exchange laughs, frights, news, and views.

"I guess we were wrong about the Jerries not being within miles, Tom."

"I guess so. What do you hear from home? I got a flock of letters, too. Most of them old."

"Everybody's well. But I'm rather browned off. Barbara says she is so glad I am in Italy where it's pleasant and not in the Pacific fighting."

It was to be some time the following year that people in America learned the fighting in Italy was not a piece of cake.

We dug in outside Scerni for the night. Our vehicles came to us at first light, and we drove in to the village to rest while the tanks leaguered in the surrounding fields. I shall never forget the welcome, perhaps the most humbling experience of my life. Italians lined the curbs, cheering, waving, singing, shaking us by the hands, pulling at our arms, tears of gratitude in their eyes. The celebration was broken up for three or four minutes when three American fighters swept the street with machine guns, causing no casualties. We fired back, thinking they were German until we saw the stars. Some place in rear headquarters an officer had failed to notify the air force that Scerni was ours.

Several grizzly Italians dressed immediately in their tight World War I uniforms and came around to grin and look, children clustering about them. They, too, were heroes for a day.

We moved in to the homes, the families giving us their best rooms and beds. Women did our laundry and sewing. I set up Barbara's picture, and Julie, the daughter of the family I was with, brought flowers to place by my wife's picture. They explained to us that anything they had was ours, but they had little left. The Germans had cleaned them out. We watched families, however, dig up things in their back yards that had been buried while Jerry had the upper hand. Periodical shells would smash in the village, but no one cared. It was the day of liberation. That is, no one cared except the 60th Rifles. Scerni was just one more village to us, and we didn't like the shells. When we told the Italians this, they laughed, and brought out more cheap, red wine. They cooked chickens over the open fireplaces in the kitchens for us—not through fear, but in sheer thankfulness. A soldier can tell the difference.

An Italian handed me a letter to deliver to his family in Philadelphia some day, having written that he was alive, the house was not destroyed, but the Germans took his clothes and furniture.

Writing a letter home by candlelight that night, while an Italian woman in the next room was doing my laundry and the husband polishing my boots, I thought how amazing it was that the books, newspapers, allied leaders, army pamphlets, and propaganda machines had been right in what they had been telling us for ten years. I only half-believed it until that evening, somehow. Some soldiers never believed it. Our armies were treated as liberators. The first troops were, at least. Europe was in chains. German soldiers did rape women. Fascists and Nazis had plundered Europe and murdered those who objected. Jews had been brutally tortured. Evil was loose, and war was not an enforced bore. It was vital to our very existence. Even if the war would last ten years and be one hundred times as bad on all of us as it was in 1943, it would be worth it—not for what we might gain, but in order to set right the suffering, unhappiness, and conditions of Europe brought on by Mussolini and Hitler and their ardent lieutenants. People in America and Britain cannot imagine in their wildest dreams what the peoples on the Continent have been through and what we narrowly escaped.

Because America and England have been subjected to only a minute fraction of this wrong deed of mankind, they should pay the most in rehabilitating Europe. I thought our job was not finished when the guns and jeeps rumbled through the villages as we had in Scerni that day. It was just beginning and may last for years. I wrote home I was solidly behind the war. I wrote from the front, with occasional shells dropping near, having been overseas two years, with no hope of home for a long time, facing more fighting shortly. I wrote as a former isolationist, whatever that is.

I was not carried away by bands, speeches, or a pamphlet. I was in a small room, with a stone floor and dirty whitewashed walls. I knew there was no glamour to war. War was ragged, half-starved people and lying nose down in some mud, scared. It wasn't a Broadway celebration, and a notice in the paper about getting a medal, and uniforms in a night club.

That night I didn't care how much money the people back home were making or what soft jobs were to be had, or how much dirty work was afoot in America or England, just as long as the replacements and material reached us so we could advance. Whatever was going on at home, there was more dirty work afoot in Europe.

I knew I was no hero, that I loathed shelling and longed for America and didn't want to be killed, but I knew it was necessary to be at the front for the larger benefits and that the war was worth any price to pay, short of total extinction of the human race. America and England were putting up with a limited amount of heartaches, deaths, separations, and rationing; a small price to pay for the eventual good. The eventual good, of course, would not come immediately with the armistice or for some time after.

Long after August 14, 1945, I still believe what I wrote that night in Scerni.

After sealing the letter, I slept in the noise of the few shells and Italian singing. A soldier can sleep any place any time. He gets used to things, like the people who live near the railroad tracks.

It was in Scerni the next day that Tom decided to eat all his good things every morning. A shell landed across the street, demolishing a house, decapitating two white-haired women in black coats, and wounding Billy Whitbred, Hunt's driver. He thought if he saved things until the evening meal, he might not be around to eat them.

Often I watched him eat his evening meal first thing in the morning.

"Never know when an 88 might drop in," he would say.

Tom was living in a tattered house numbered 77, on the main muddy street. I walked over for a chat. We were tired, and our humor wasn't too good, but this sort of thing kept us going:

"I see your house is Number 77, Red Grange's old jersey number."

'Yeah, he and I are running a night club here, and we call it 'The 77'."

"Get much business?"

"Yeah, an awful lot. These Ities flock to it. Red is rarely here, but I pack in the suckers on Red's name. They all think he might be here, and they can see him."

It was simple little laughs like that which kept us on our toes.

Waiting in Scerni, we became thoroughly familiar with Italy's pail system and lack of sanitation, falling in with their method of cultivating vegetable gardens with human excreta.

There, as in other villages, civilians gave us a great deal of our information on Jerry, most of it accurate. Gun emplacements, defenses, and mine locations were pointed out to us on our maps by families who made their way south through German lines to remain with relatives until the fighting passed on. They made mental notes, and it all helped to save lives. Little muddy parties of them would stop in my platoon headquarters and I would pass on the intelligence to the I. O.

I suppose this worked both ways.

Chapter Eleven

On my fourth afternoon in the village I started to take a nap. As I had a last cigarette before going to sleep, I was thinking about after the war. I wanted a job where Barbara and I did not have to use an alarm clock, where I could appear for work anytime between 8:30 and 9:00 in the morning, where I did not have to be punctual to show how keen I was, where I was not working at an alarm clock job for people who didn't have an alarm clock job in a firm with signs for its employees, "Time Is Money."

Through subconscious effort, Barbara and I could wake up without the awful din preceded by one minute warning tick. I then would not have to carry on like a demented hen from 7 to 10, when I finally managed the second after-breakfast cigarette, the first one being left someplace in a rush. I would avoid the sudden panic at the opening clang. My heart would remain in my chest. I would not be lonely first thing in the day, thinking the alarm clock and myself were the only two awake in the world, followed by hearing traffic and noises and voices in the street and cursing myself for not being an early bird like the rest, pushing to get ahead. My job would not rush in on me while eating breakfast, which had ceased to be the most glorious meal in the world. By having a non-alarm clock job,

I would not have to sway my way to work with my breakfast in my throat, hating the man standing next to me because of his overcoat or hatband. Yes, I thought, as I happily dozed, after the war I will get a job in which the first waking hours are pleasant, and the day ahead descends gently.

I should have known better than to have tried a nap and happily thought about my future. The door was flung open, and John stood there breathless. "The Indians are attacking Atessa. The 6th Indian Lancers. Make a reconnaissance immediately of Monte Calvo. You've very little daylight left. Take your sergeants. I will bring the guns after you. You will have to use bullochs to get you to the top because of the frightful mud. Terribly important. A German tank attack is expected at first light tomorrow. Your platoon will fill in the gap between the Indians and the 78th Division. Last man, last round, of course."

I fumbled for my boots and gaiters. "Well, John they taught me how to drive a train in officer's school, but I didn't hear a thing about bullochs."

"Brigade is arranging for the bullochs to meet you at the bottom of Monte Calvo. Simply attach the guns to the bullochs. Italians will help you."

Sergeant Cook had gathered the four gun commanders, maps, Gallagher, my jeep and the dog by the time I had groped for the door, and off we sailed. The war's best weapon, the jeep, slithered us all to the high ground of Calvo and we looked across a valley to the German positions. In two hours, we had finished a difficult reconnaissance and returned to the bottom of the height to find the platoon, six Ities, Hunt, and twelve bullochs—huge, stolid, powerful, white, slow beasts with dainty legs and great eyes.

By midnight we had two guns in position. It was slow going,

with three bullochs to a gun and the jeep hitched to the front of the beasts, their broad backs shining in the moonlight.

Hunt said, "It is impossible to get the other guns up. I'll tell the colonel. Go up to the top and get some sleep. We've something up there, anyway. If we can't get the guns up, German tanks can't make it either."

That's what I thought, too. But Jerry often does the impossible, I remembered.

When John left, one crew moaned about the fact we had chocolate and cigarettes that had been issued to Sergeant Cook just before we left Scerni and the men hadn't received the issue. We intended to distribute it when the job was finished and there was time for dividing the ration. I calmed them down, said we would split the issue when we got the other two guns up. But the moaning went on, and then one of the Ities got after Watt with a bulloch whip. I was tired, covered with mud, anxious, and it was beginning to rain. I grabbed the Itie boy by the throat and shook him. I was shaking him for all the times in the past I had seen Italians treating animals as rats. I was swearing a blue streak, and the platoons laughed. It relieved the tension.

The Ities started work in earnest, and John Hunt didn't know the desert rats if he thought we couldn't get those guns up. At first light we were in position, just before John appeared with five gallons of wine for the men.

Unconcerned and clean in all the muck, with his close-cropped mustache and boyish face, Colonel Bill came and was very interested in a calm, detached, comforting way, wondering if the Jerries would attack. They didn't, and we went to sleep on the ground in that tired, light, happy, foggy feeling.

Our orders were to sit tight and hold. Monty had his attack planned for the Sangro River and cracking the German winter line. But he was waiting for forty-eight hours of dry weather. Monty was not hurrying. He was going to make sure of success. Hundreds of guns and bombing every half-hour would prepare the way. After the breakthrough, we would take Pescara, wheel left on the lateral across Italy to Rome, meeting the Fifth Army there. We knew we could do our 1943 Christmas shopping in the Capitol. The Fifth and Eighth synchronizing their offensives, it would be the biggest battle in Italy. Until the attack, we were to maintain silence, except for reconnaissance patrols.

I moved platoon headquarters to a farm cellar, and we lived there ten days; every few hours air-bursts being shot at us, causing no casualties. Casual Messerschmitts took whistlingspeeks at Monte Calvo. In the Indian sector, we could hear our sluggish, accurate Vickers and the fast chatter of the German MG 34s. Our view was beautiful. We could see high mountains covered with snow. Villages piled like an old gray hat on peaks that were once Roman forts. The Appennines are not fierce like the Canadian Rockies or Atlas Range, but undulating and soft, surrounded by an agricultural region. Ahead was the silver streak of the swollen Sangro.

The Italian farmer brought me an egg each morning. We had moved his family to the barn. He killed a sheep and gave it to us. Like most Ities, he had a four days' growth of beard. He never apparently shaved, yet his beard did not get longer. None of us could ever fathom the secret.

Watt chased the clucking, fussing scampering chickens if things were too dull. He was covered in mud and insisted on being friendly. With noise, gusto, and glee, he rounded up a flock of sheep and drove it toward the Sangro. In the cellar, he ate off the same plate with a kitten named Mish and let it sleep between his huge paws. When I thought I was unobserved, I played a game with Watt. I would hide from him, but he would always find me, his ears flat, his hind quarters wagging, his eyes sparkling in a general expression of my-you're-silly-and-I'll-play-your-game-with-you-but-I'm-awfully-glad-you-can't-hide-from-me.

For the first of seven times during the war, I caught lice in that cellar.

Every two days I went on a reconnaissance patrol with some of the platoon. It was browning us off. Arguments flared up among the men. It wasn't the Germans that were getting us down, because none of us believed that the Hun was built with a square-head, and we avoided him as much as possible. Italians in that exaggerated no-man's-land asked us in for wine and eggs on our patrols, as we were the first of the "liberators" they had seen. That part was pleasant. But it was the chill, mud, wet, and returning from the patrols looking and feeling like sludge out of an old motor.

On two nights John brought small, dark Yugoslav espionage agents to my headquarters, and Topper Brown and I took them toward the Sangro, leaving them in the dark after a quick handshake and pat on the back. Neither spoke English. Both wore striped, gray coats and gaudy scarves.

We watched the RAF drop pamphlets on the German lines, reminding the enemy he had no air force.

The rain continued, and Monty waited. We could always see the Sangro ahead of us. It was worse than sitting in a dentist's reception room. The men talked about their childhood, remembering things they hadn't thought of for years. Or they discussed the kind of house they would like after the war and how many children they would like to have. That was their defense mechanism.

Monty could wait no longer, and in appalling weather, we started.

There were no brilliant, awful fireworks followed by tanks and infantry as originally planned. Our troops, in small numbers night after night, made their way quietly across the river, among scattered mines, establishing themselves in the swamps, while the Germans shelled us from the high ground. Some Tommies were drowned in the strong Sangro current.

During darkness of piercing cold and rain, bridges were built and washed away time and again. Montgomery relieved the general in command of building the bridges.

With almost no warning, our battalion—less my platoon—was ordered to attack the first night. Our guns were bogged on Calvo, and wheels and tracks could not be used. It meant going in on feet. Our intelligence and air photos showed three German machine guns on an escarpment commanded by a pink castle four hundred yards across the river, and Colonel Bill was to take this. My platoon watched the men slip toward the start-line and three hours later we heard the machine guns. All that day we waited for results, watching shells drop on the Sangro, perfectly zeroed in by the Germans.

My men, happy they had been left out, repeated, "This is just the ticket for us."

The second night a runner brought me orders to report to Major Hunt immediately.

"Ted, I have a job for you. The battalion is down there in the river mud, without food and very little ammunition. They have no signal cable. The escarpment is held in force by the Germans. Our intelligence was wrong. This will be a methodical push, and the Rome show is probably out. The Colonel is going to try again tonight. He's just on the other side. Take your platoon by foot across country to Paglieta, and wait for me there. You will carry the supplies by hand to the battalion. Denis Wright will get them to the river in a jeep convoy after dark."

"I thought we were bloody anti-tankers. But looks as though we're just supply blokes. Why doesn't the bloody quartermaster get up here and get the supplies over the river?" So ran the remarks when I briefed the men. Like old campaigners, they never received an assignment without voicing disapproval. Like old campaigners, they were ready to carry out any orders.

I left six of the men with Sergeant Cook to guard the guns. We dribbled to the river in twos and threes, Hunt leading the way. Colonel Bill made the attack on the escarpment, but the Jerries had faded back, and there was no fight. Nor could we get supplies across. The river had flooded to such a stage that wading was no longer possible. In the darkness, Indian engineers built a footbridge, while we returned to Paglieta at dawn.

First the men shaved. The desert rats were clean, and seldom a day passed that they did not scrape their faces. Through experience they realized that a shave was worth two or three hours sleep in refreshment value.

With Brown, I went to the best house in Paglieta. Most of the civilians had evacuated the village, but a well-dressed group was in front of the house we had selected. I tried the door. It was locked. The Italians objected. I drew my pistol, as I had seen done in the movies, and pointed it at the lock. I felt very foolish, hoping to get out of the embarrassing situation. Evidently the Italians were film fans, for they immediately brought out keys to open the house. The entire platoon slept until noon.

I watched the escarpment from Paglieta and saw German mortars landing on the position, as well as 88s trying to knock out the Indians' footbridge. German planes strafed the battalion. Hunt and I took the platoon to the river in the afternoon, each man loaded with as much as he could carry.

Whack–whack–crump. Whack–crump. Crump–crump.

We waited for the shelling to stop, and then we were going to make a run for it across the bridge in full view of Jerry. We watched four C Company men carrying one of our wounded along the river bank to the bridge. It was only a question of time before they were hit, and the time wasn't long. A shell landed, and shrill cries of "Help! Help!" reached us. One arm in a sling from a rugger game, showing more courage than a country has a right to expect of its soldiers, Topper Brown dashed across suspected scattered mines, over the bridge under severe shelling. Hunt moved next, followed by Denis Wright and Osborne. I grabbed Wood, a truck driver, and the two of us took off to meet Brown, who was smiling, in the middle of the bridge carrying a man pumping blood.

We joined the others on the far bank and dropped our supplies in the mud. The shelling continued. Wood and I went to the bodies to carry them back across, but they were all dead. Minutes before, Brown had sorted out the only live man and taken him away.

All of us made a dash back with no casualties and Hunt suspended operations until darkness. The battalion was still out of food and ammunition. I told Brown that Hunt was recommending him for the Military Medal, and Topper said, "I hope it does't go through. The boys would disown me."

There were some more soldiers killed that afternoon while we waited. I wasn't scared, just anxious. That deep, hidden inner courage had come to me in time of violence. We surprise ourselves the way we can surmount troubles. Some front-line soldiers, now that the war is over, claim you get used to death and seeing men killed. I don't think a person ever gets accustomed to watching men die.

On our bellies in the mud, Captain Denis Wright and I were talking it over along the Sangro, just after two Tommies received a direct hit.

"That sort of thing makes me distressed and angry and repentant in the peculiar way a guy gets when very good, perhaps great men die in action."

"Yes, Elmer. But no matter how long this war lasts nor how many men we lose, it's worth it."

"Funny how you remember the last thing a guy said before he was killed. Things that didn't seem important at the time. Perhaps seeing a man killed like this afternoon is drama. It is supposed to be. Killed in action, defending his country. Sounds good, but that's all. There's nothing dramatic about it. Seeing a football player make an eighty-yard winning touchdown run seems a lot more dramatic than this Sangro stuff."

"I'm all for fighting this war," Denis said, "but I hope this Sangro packs up soon. Our string of luck on these shells is about running out."

Denis Wright, a London insurance agent and father of two children, while under fire was not cursing the war and death. He was killed in Normandy, long after the Sangro had been forgotten.

When night fell, I led my platoon across the footbridge. Artillery was lighting up the men's faces. Waiting on the far side for us was

Hunt, a patch over one eye from a bad spill on some rocks, no socks, low canvas slippers, full red beard, shirt tail out, trousers rolled up to his knees, no grin. I had to laugh at him, and he called me a "Brick" when I gave him his army boots Jimmy Stowe had pushed at me near the footbridge.

We carried the lead and food a mile, leaving it in the cellar of the castle with Colonel Bill. We had a cigarette and listened to the men.

"We're goddamn lucky to be here at all. They waited until we were forty yards away, and they opened with everything."

"One Jerry in his tin hat rose right out of a slit trench in front of me, pointed his arm straight out, saying "*Achtung*! English!', and his machine gunner let go."

"They kept yelling at us to surrender. 'Surrender, English! Surrender!' they would say. We just lay there in the mud and yelled back at them. 'Surrender yourselves, you bastards!' we said. That was when we were pulling back. I thought there was three machine guns over here."

"There was a whole bloody nest of them. No three. Three couldn't have made that much racket. Baker Company got the worst. Major Holmes is gone."

"Our artillery didn't land anywhere near Jerry. He was dug way in anyway."

"I don't like it here. Any rumors about getting relieved?"

I wanted that cigarette to last forever. It seemed safe in the castle and I could hear the shells landing near the bridge.

We wound our way back, stepping carefully where the bodies of soldiers lay half-curled on the ground, blown up on mines. Phil Curtis and his sergeant followed fifteen minutes after us, to bury three of their platoon lost during the day. Both were killed instantly when they moved the dead which had not exploded all the mines. That made two of General Curtis' three sons gone.

Two hundred yards from the footbridge we waited until twenty rounds had landed. Then we crossed, without casualties. Relieved, relaxed, thankful, I took my platoon back to Paglieta where we split a gallon of rum and moved in to houses for the night. We had to make another crossing with more supplies the next day, Hunt had informed us. But I thought I would worry about that later. The main thing was to get some sleep.

The door opened. "Anybody in here know the river road?"

"I'll say we know the bloody thing. And you know where you can shove it."

"Well, Mr. Wyndham is half way down the hill with sixteen mules loaded with rations and ammo for the battalion. Brigade sent them. We've brought them ten bloody miles tonight."

I told the man I would drive him there. Down we went on the winding road, to find David with twelve mules, and six men from the London Irish Rifles.

"Hello, Elmer. Do you know the way to the battalion? I have these bloody mules and a lot of kit. Four of the mules just wandered off."

"You get the other four mules. I'll take these twelve to the bridge and you meet me there." I didn't see Wyndham again that night. He was killed in France months later.

The mules had enough compo rations and bullets for three days. If we could get them across, my platoon would not have to take more chances the next day. Our luck was running out.

I stopped off to see John who was sleeping in a culvert near the bridge and told him I would take the mules across. Then I waited for Wyndham by the bridge. An Indian engineer told me I had better not stop long at the footbridge, because the Germans shelled each time there was noise.

"Okay, fellows. Start the mules across the bridge."

The mules refused to walk on to the wood. We kicked, pulled, and shoved. I decided to tell John we couldn't make it. I wanted to get away from that bridge. Then the shelling started. I got in the gravel and looked at my watch. It was ten minutes to midnight. I though by midnight I would be dead. When the air-breaking rush of the 88s stopped, five unconcerned Indians offered to get the mules over. I started to protest, thinking I had done my best and that it would be much better to go back to Paglieta.

Kicking them in the tendons near the heels the Indians got the first two on the bridge. And the other ten followed. I thought the noise of these animals could be heard in Berlin. In a way, I was disappointed the mules were obliging.

Still no shells. On the other side were dead men. The mules stopped at these. We kicked the mules in the tendons, and they started again. Three hundred yards away, we heard the shelling begin. All the way to the castle the mules stopped at the dead soldiers, and each time we kicked them where the Indians had shown us.

On the way back, we bumped into an Indian patrol looking for the observation post they thought was near the river. The German guns were too far back to hear noise on the bridge, yet each time they opened when someone scraped or coughed in the night. Toward dawn, the Indians killed an Italian civilian operating a wireless set one hundred yards from the footbridge.

Reaching the bridge, I was tempted to leave the mules and get the six men and myself back without all the racket. But over we went, the mules willingly. At the other end, shells started in a concentrated barrage with red bangs and hot iron whistling about us. I heard the short wet whistle of an 88 and thought it was for me. Then down I fell in a hole I hadn't seen, an old German gun pit.

MmmmmmeeeeeeeeeeeeaaaaaaaaooooOOOO. KARUP!

I stayed there, holding the guide on the mule, which waited patiently. Too patiently, because it was hit by shrapnel. Crawling out of the pit when things were quiet, I tried to move the mule. Bleeding, it refused to budge. I left it there, and not long after a shell killed it outright. I sent those six London Irish Rifles off, never seeing them again. Reporting to Hunt, he told me to get some sleep in Paglieta and in the afternoon take the men back to Monte Calvo.

"Tell your platoon they worked very well and that we all appreciate it."

The Sangro was all over for me. I knew it. Driving back, I had to stop the jeep three times. I was throwing up. I guess it was because I relaxed. Then I started to shake, for all the times I wanted to shake along the river and couldn't afford the luxury. I imagined I could hear the whistle of shells. I even ducked my head.

I was glad I was alone.

Chapter Twelve

At noon, I awakened in a master bedroom with eight Italians gibbering at me. I gathered they wanted us to move out. I called Simmons.

"Chase these Italians out of here. Tell them to clear out of Paglieta and come back in three days. Now that we have the Sangro, they are getting a bit thick."

"You ought to see in the living room, sir. These people were the big shots of the town. There's a scroll hanging there about a bloke named Angelo. He's one of the fifteen in this place who was in the March on Rome. A pukka Fascist. Look at the way these people are dressed. Well dressed."

"Get them to hell out of here, Simmons." I always felt guilty ordering people out of their own homes. Our instructions were to keep civilians clear of the villages and roads near the battle zone. Britain had learned its lesson on the crowded refugee roads in France on the way to Dunkirk. An army could not operate hampered by civilians. In addition, Eighth Army, the machine of steel, averaged one vehicle for every four soldiers. Road space was limited.

Getting out of bed, I could see the platoon had done a bit of looting. Catsup, flour, a few rings, some pictures, tablecloths, spoons. It was difficult to prevent homesick men who had lived on nothing in the desert, who saw that their enemies had scrounged bags of loot in their retreat, who were living from day to day, from taking souvenirs and comforts of life, especially in a pukka Fascist's house. Though our orders were to stop soldiers from appropriating property. In addition, the desert rats had never quite forgotten about fighting the Italians a few months previously.

That afternoon they brought David Jackson to the medical aid station in a Paglieta garage. His eyes were staring straight ahead. I put a cigarette in his hand, and he grasped it, without smoking. There was shrapnel in David's head, and I knew he wouldn't live. I thought of the bridge games and laughs we had together, what the newspapers would say when they learned of his death, that his company commander would write about the tragic loss and David's great-hearted courage. And I wondered who in his company would inherit David's squeaky phonograph that he had carted from those thirty miles of Alamein sand to the Sangro.

"Gorgeous," George Lyon's effeminate, courageous, humorous, kind batman arrived on a stretcher, ugly shrapnel wounds in his back. "Just look at me," he lisped. "Now I won't be able to wear my lovely backless evening gown. Really! This is no war for women."

"Give her a drink of this brandy," a medic smiled.

Gorgeous was the one who had been lying in a slit trench with Lyon during a Stuka raid in Tunisia. A bomb was coming right for them, and as they watched it twist to earth, George said, "This is for us, Gorgeous. Nothing we can do."

Said Gorgeous, expecting eternity but bucking up his officer in the last seconds, "Never mind, sir! Never mind!"

A good man—or woman—Gorgeous, to say that. The bomb landed fifteen yards away.

While there, a medical sergeant said to me, "Sir, would you move your platoon? This is a medical station now, and no combat troops within two hundred yards of it, according to international law."

"We're going back to Calvo immediately, sergeant." I have never seen or heard of Anglo-American troops violating the Red Hospital Cross. I was to see Germany break the rule time and again on the Western Front.

While we slogged to Calvo, British tanks followed by infantry attacked Mozzagrogna, Santa Maria, and Danciano. I was covered in mud, wearing a green ski jacket, my bootlaces broken, but Sergeant Cook had a brew, mail, and Watt waiting. The dog jumped all over me, whining, the farmer brought me two eggs and Tom arrived with four drinks of gin he had scrounged off a knocked-out German mail truck.

Gallagher, Cook, and I took a touring drive to Scerni the next day to visit our Italian friends and leave some laundry. Julie and the mother kissed all of us and asked for salt, almost nonexistent in Italy during the war. They invited us for Christmas, and if we would come they would kill a pig.

Julie's father said the Indians had replaced us in Scerni, and the first day a soldier had raped one of the young girls. The villagers thought it was to be the German story all over again. Immediately, Indian officers marched the man down the main street under guard while the Italians shouted at him. At the far end of the village, he was shot. No more rapes occurred, and the Italians were satisfied with the justice.

At another small village, we heard a roar—a noise like a fight crowd watching a knockout, or as I imagine the spectators' deep full cry was at the guillotine in the French Revolution. Investigating, we found the one main street jammed by muddy, tattered civilians armed with clubs, pitchforks, axes, and shovels. Like a slow, thick python they were moving from one end of the village to the other. At thirty-seven houses they stopped, and men were dragged out to the unified mob. Only one man resisted. He was immediately stuck and kicked to death in the street. We watched, fascinated. The Fascists were being gathered for trial. The Italians had waited for revenge until it was certain that we were across the Sangro and the Germans would not return.

In a field, we looked over four of our Shermans and two German Mark IV Specials destroyed a few weeks before. The tankers were burned in their vehicles. Beside the tanks were some of the graves—the size of a cigar box, a blackened helmet covering the earth, shell cases outlining the four corners. Inside the twisted, scorched iron of a Jerry tank was a leg, the boot covered foot still pressed against the accelerator. I reached for a German identity disc on the ground. I tugged on it before realizing it was on the neck of a loosely covered Nazi, just as the stench of disturbed earth and decay surrounded me. Nearby was a scattered pack of playing cards.

We watched the American Field Service ambulances and YMCA doughnut trucks moving toward the front, some driven by *conscientious* objectors, who perhaps realized that during war civil and human laws were more important than Divine. These drivers were not combat men, but they were up there with us, doing an important job for humanity. It was a more important job for humanity at the time than those objectors who elected to go to jail or remain at home passing out pamphlets. The red crosses on the ambulances reminded me of blood to be spilled, and I wondered how and why we kept going ahead when death and wounds waited.

Returning to Calvo, I found that the Battalion was pulling out for a long rest and to await further orders. The motor companies had caught a bad packet. The last casualties had been a C Company sergeant and driver sitting in a jeep after the battle had passed. They had gone to salvage the Browning in the Bren carrier where Basil Cochrane had lost his life. An Indian stepped off the road to relieve himself, exploding an S mine, and all three died immediately.

Hugh Hope took command of our Company, Hunt becoming battalion second-in-command. Tall, redheaded, overseas five years, Hugh had escaped from prison camp dressed as a shepherd, having been captured at the Sidi Rezegh coating in 1941. He elected to remain with us when he hit our lines on the Sangro, though he could have gone home immediately. We became close friends.

"With your build and red hair, I don't see how the Germans let you through as an Italian shepherd," I said to him.

"They are so stupid sometimes, those Germans."

"How stupid are they?"

"If you ever get captured, you must escape in the first forty-eight hours. After that it is almost impossible. They aren't really stupid."

"What kind of a time did you have getting here?"

"It took me six weeks. I walked all the way, staying with friendly Ities. One night I shared the only available bed with an eight-year-old hunch-backed grandmother. We took turns with the bed pot. Usually I stayed in barns where the cattle keep it warm.

"The Jerries are not fooling with the Italians. They search about the hay ricks and if they find any toilet paper there, they shoot the Ities. Jerry knows the Ities don't use toilet paper. It is proof the farmer has been hiding British or Americans.

"At a farm near me an Italian was shot after digging his own grave. Escaped prisoners were found there. When Italy surrendered and we all got loose up there, parachutists told us about destroyers which would pick us up along the coast. But it looked too risky to most of us. The plan flopped."

Christmas dinner, 1943, we had in a barn five miles behind the front, the officers and sergeants of the company waiting on the men. The barn was decorated as well as we could. For days beforehand we had purchased wine and meat from the farmers. Colonel Bill dropped in, and we listened to the King's speech. I had Watt decorated in red ribbons and silver bells. With all the food, he enjoyed his Christmas more than any of us. The men heard the rumor that day we were returning to England. Like all armies, the Eighth longed for home.

In the evening, Cook, Brown, Gallagher, Simmons, and I went off to see our family in Scerni for their Christmas dinner. All the men ate first, and I sat next to one of the in-laws who wore his hat the entire meal. Between each course we toasted each other. And there were ten courses, starting with spaghetti and bacon. Then the women had their meal.

Montgomery sent us a personal message in the field. ". . . my best wishes and hearty greetings to the great family of the Eighth Army. And I send greetings from us all to your loved ones and friends in your homelands; they are, indirectly, part of this Army in that their courage and fortitude is essential to the morale of the Army itself. And today we recall the Christmas message 'Glory to God in the highest, and on earth peace, goodwill toward men.' Surely this describes exactly what we are fighting for. Let us, therefore, take it as our battle cry and motto. When peace has come, the spirit of the Eighth Army will be a factor for good in the unsettled and difficult days. When the war is over and we all scatter to our various tasks, let us see to it that the spirit of the Eighth Army lives on. May it be a great and powerful influence in the rebuilding of the nations. . . ."

Guns were silent that Christmas. We were stalled in mud and snow. We sang our favorite song, the one good thing to have come out of Germany during the war, "Lili Marlene."

Boxing Day, Tom and I left in my jeep for a week's leave in Naples on the other side of Italy. We passed Vasto, Termoli, the Trigno, San Salvo, San Severo, Castelnuova, Montecorvino, places we almost felt we owned. Because we had been the first troops there. It was strange to see them again, with no noise, no fear, no death. I think we resented the new vehicles, faces, and signs that were not about when we had gone North. The shell holes were plowed under. Only some rusting, blackened husks of tanks and a few graves reminded us that we had been there before, reminded us of dead placid faces.

We pulled up at the Lucera prison, giving the guards cigarettes for a free run. Micucci was the warden, and he had a healthier, sanitary, wholesome, better-managed place than any of the six prisons I have visited in America and England. We talked to killers, Fascists, and juvenile delinquents. We had an excellent meal in their spotless kitchen. In the filth of Southern Italy, the prison was like a pearl. Near it is the castle built by Charles of Anjou in 1350, finished by Frederick II of Sicily who imported twenty thousand Arabs to work for him. They have left their traces of architecture and skin coloring in Apulia.

The castle is run down but was used as an army garrison before the armistice. We rummaged about the ruins, finding cartoons of Churchill and Roosevelt being led around the world by the hand of a Jew, Churchill with a mustache and great grin, surrounded by skulls and graves. I showed them to an Italian soldier picking in the scraps, asking him what he thought of them. He said it was true because the printing underneath the cartoon said it was, and anything in black and white was not a lie.

Germany and Japan are not the only countries with warped minds that need a thorough flushing followed by constant vigilance to prevent another stoppage.

As we entered Naples, we saw a large sign, "Beware of V.D.! Flies spread disease. Keep yours buttoned!" Stopping to ask directions, we were approached by a young Neapolitan selling his sister. "Spaghetti, ristorante, very good," he said as he pointed to her. We talked our way in to the "Albergo Sirena" on Garibaldi Square, a hotel reserved for colonels and above, the only place in Naples where brandy, sherry, champagne, whiskey, beer, and good food were available. Snapping on the electric light was a pleasure we had forgotten about, and we had our first bath in a tub for seven months.

During the first night, my jeep was stolen. The MPs found it, but some Italian had removed my camera and all films of Africa and Italy that were in the catchall. Tom and I had had enough, deciding the front was much better than Naples. Off we went to the Fifth Army sector to visit Fowler, Danielson, Thomson, and Alsop, just in time to catch Al and Turk on the way to Naples, preparatory to transferring to the American Army.

"I thought if you guys were going to transfer you were going to let us know," Tom said.

"Ted Roosevelt came to see us and this all happened in a rush. We were going to let you know."

"Yeah, I know. You'll spend months transferring anyway. The Yank Army has something or other about proper channels on all this. Anyway, let's have a do in Naples, the four of us."

We did. New Year's Eve was what New Year's Eve might be any

place among four old friends just out of the line in a foreign metropolis. The only bad part of the evening was Turk hiring Neapolitans to sing to us in high and low pitched yelling wherever we went. He did, however, engage a cantatrice who did "Lili Marlene." She used to sing for the Afrika Korps. She sang "Lili" better than anybody we had ever heard including Lala. Her leg was bandaged because of a Jerry officer shooting her with his pistol because she would not accept his advances the night before Naples fell. Or so she said.

New Year's Day, 1944, we drove to the ruins of Pompeii where we learned that Somma, not Vesuvius, destroyed the city with volcanic ash and that the Romans in the first century spent most of their time making love to music, thinking about making love, eating grapes, vomiting, watching gladiators, and spreading political propaganda.

Al said to me on the drive back, "It's certainly surprising that one doesn't become paralyzed with fright under fire. I'll miss this whole éclat of being an officer in a snobby British regiment. After the age of twenty-five, these English are really great guys. Do you think you and Slack Jaw will transfer soon?"

"Maybe. The rumor is that our battalion might go back to England for the second front bloodbath. That would be the time to transfer."

"When this war business is over, I'm going to spend my life in a hot bath, with a good cold whiskey in one hand and perhaps occasional side trips to a well-appointed toilet, white and glistening, with smoothly functioning flush."

"What about Tish? Are you going to marry her?"

"If I get to England, I am."

"How's Danielson making out?"

"We've got a new name for him, Bruto. He was marching smartly at the head of his platoon, thinking himself very much the handsome, colorful young officer. An old hag offered him some mangy grapes, and when he didn't turn to her, she exclaimed loudly to an aged crony, 'Bruto!' When he goes out to do battle he carries two pistols, one in a shoulder holster and one strapped to his leg. Then he has a large bowie knife, brass knuckles, a Tommy gun, and he bulges with grenades. His platoon bristles with scrounged Brownings and Vickers. He's having the time of his life."

"I hadn't realized how long I have been away from Americans, Al, until I talked to a captain in Naples the other day. A Military Government guy or something. I asked him what he did before the war. 'I was state sales manager for the Metropolitan Life Insurance Company in Indiana, with my main offices in Indianapolis. I'm from the Middle West, thank gawd.' The English would have said, 'Insurance, old boy,' and let it go. Then this fellow started to tell me the reason he was overseas is because he had a lot of old scores to settle from the last war. And he named the Gray twins and a lot of chaps killed from Indianapolis in 1918. He's never heard a shell this war, and he wasn't overseas last time. But he's got a lot of cock he's dreamed up being here! I doubt if between the wars he thought of the Gray twins more than once."

". . . the time has come for me to leave the Eighth Army. I have been ordered to take command of the British Armies in England that are to operate under General Eisenhower. I feel I have many friends among the soldiery of this great Army. I do not know if you will miss me; but I will miss you more than I can say, and especially will I miss the personal contacts and the cheerful greetings we exchanged together when we passed each other on the road.

". . . What can I say to you as I go away? When the heart is full, it is not easy to speak.

". . . And so I say good-bye to you all. May we meet again soon; and may we serve together again as comrades in arms in the final stages of this war."

It was Montgomery's farewell message that Tom and I first heard on our return from Naples. Monty was going home. He promised to take his desert troops wherever he went. Would he keep his word?

The air was full of rumors. I listened carefully to the other ranks who always had the gen before the officers. In late January, just after the landing at Anzio, Colonel Bill called a battalion meeting. "General Montgomery has kept his promise. We are going to England. In England, they have victory gardens and salvage campaigns, and we must play the game there, just as we have down here, and support those things. England will be interested in Eighth Army troops and we must be polished and smart. We must wear the proper uniforms, and not dress as we do here and as we did in Africa. We will turn in all our ammunition and most of our vehicles day after tomorrow. But you will receive instructions about this.

"Do not discuss this move with anyone. Just one more thing. We will have to dispose of all our pets. In the next day or two, try to find homes for them among new units or with Italians who will treat them kindly. We are not allowed to land the animals in England."

Hugh Hope saw the Colonel immediately about my dog. "Colonel, what about Watt? Don't you think we ought to take him back?"

"Ted's dog. Yes. Now what can we do? No pets, the order states. Still, Watt came out from England. He should return. The other pets we picked up here and in Africa. Yes, I'll see the Brigadier, and if it is all right with him, which I'm sure it will be under the circumstances, we'll keep Watt. Of course, there is the captain of the boat who might object."

And so we reached the Naples staging area. We had left behind our desert painted vehicles, our blackened brew cans, our Benghazi cookers which were petrol cans cut in half and filled with petrol-soaked sand or earth, our leaking tarpaulins, our animals, and all the tangibles which immediately distinguished the desert rats. In Naples, there was a new army, with fresh, healthy eager faces, new equipment, clean clothes, steel helmets, and all the gadgets that open and shut—the troops that would slug it out for fifteen heart-breaking months, whose necessities of life would be K rations, raincoats, grenades, bullets, rifles, and some mail.

While champing for the boat, Tom and I drove to the Fifth Army front again to see Fowler and Danielson. We took a ferry across the Garigliano River, locating Plow Boy in the wet sand on the seashore, the left hand platoon commander of the Fifth Army, one thousand yards from Jerry. Danny was in position near an ancient Roman viaduct. Tom and I didn't stay long. It was not our war there, and we were too close to home to take a chance on a stray shell. Fowler was jealous, and his good-bye to us, with a big grin was, "Hey, it wouldn't be half-funny if you guys got hit going back on that cross-roads up there. Two jeeps had it yesterday. They shell there."

We scooted past that cross-roads with our hearts pounding, glancing quickly at some fresh, red, formless bodies smelling like burned paint. In the distance we identified a place called Cassino.

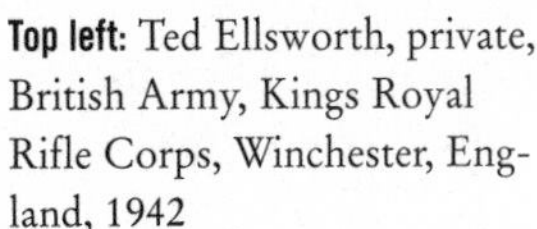

Top left: Ted Ellsworth, private, British Army, Kings Royal Rifle Corps, Winchester, England, 1942

Top right: Ted Ellsworth, Kings Royal Rifle Corps, London, 1943 *(portrait by Janet Jevons)*

Bottom left: Ted Ellsworth, mug shot, 1944

Bottom right: Ted Ellsworth with Watling Street, Dubuque, Iowa *(Hruska Photography)*

Top left: Barbara Lange Ellsworth, author's wife, circa 1943 *(Hruska Photography)*

Top right: Ted Ellsworth, American Army, 1945

Bottom left: Watling Street, the author's dog and wartime companion in England, Africa, Sicily, Italy, and the USA

Bottom right: British Lt. Ellsworth and his dog Watling Street look over ruins of Sabratha in Libya, 1943.

Ted Ellsworth (center) with British officers and pals in North Africa in 1943. Left to right: George Thompson, Stewart Alsop, Ted Ellsworth, Harry Fowler, and Tom Braden *(photo by an unknown soldier)*

KRRC Reunion, 1960. Left to right: Harry Fowler, Tom Braden, George Thompson, Ted Ellsworth, and Stewart Alsop

Top left: Church and graveyard in Sivry. Lorraine, France, 1955. Author in lower right of picture *(photo by Don Carl Steffen)*

Top right: Closeup of author in churchyard picture, 1955 *(Photo by Don Carl Steffen)*

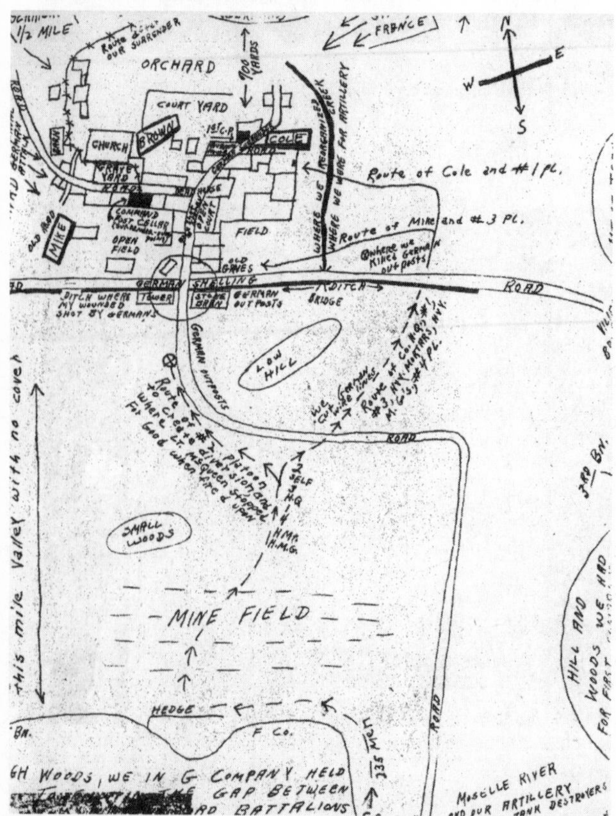

Bottom: Map of church and graveyard battle plan

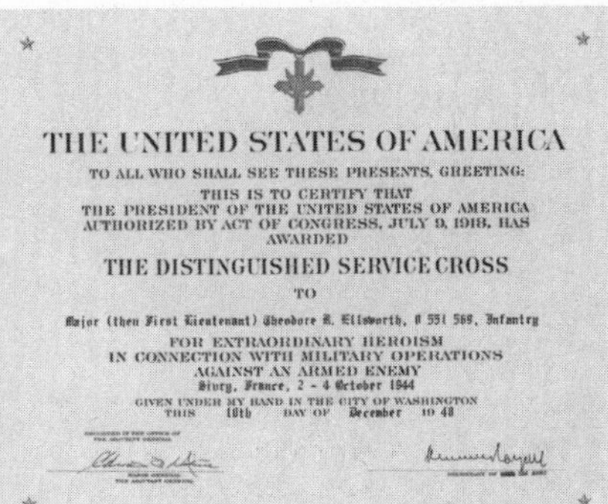

THE UNITED STATES OF AMERICA

TO ALL WHO SHALL SEE THESE PRESENTS, GREETING:

THIS IS TO CERTIFY THAT
THE PRESIDENT OF THE UNITED STATES OF AMERICA
AUTHORIZED BY ACT OF CONGRESS, JULY 9, 1918, HAS
AWARDED

THE DISTINGUISHED SERVICE CROSS

TO

Major (then First Lieutenant) Theodore R. Ellsworth, 0 551 569, Infantry

FOR EXTRAORDINARY HEROISM
IN CONNECTION WITH MILITARY OPERATIONS
AGAINST AN ARMED ENEMY
Sivry, France, 2 - 4 October 1944

GIVEN UNDER MY HAND IN THE CITY OF WASHINGTON
THIS 18th DAY OF December 19 48

Top left: Author in France, 1955 *(photo by Don Carl Steffen)*

Top right: Distinguished Service Cross Certificate awarded the author for bravery in battle in Sivry, France

Meeting the Queen of England, 1955

Left: Three war buddies 20 years later Oceanside, California, 1965. Left to right: Tom Braden, Stewart Alsop, and Ted Ellsworth.

Right: Ted Ellsworth and his four daughters, Dubuque, Iowa, 1952

Red Riding Hood and Wolf by Paul Hey

This picture I found on the nursery wall in the home of German Baron Von Rosen where his grand-children had slept until the family's flight to Germany in the face of the Russian winter drive through Poland. I was sleeping in Von Rosen's home, left just as the family lived in it while the Nazis were in power. I smashed the frame and glass which covered the picture, rolled it up, and carried it in my pocket while hitch-hiking by box-car through Poland and Russia, into Turkey and Egypt, thinking that if I ever got back and had children, it might be a nice picture for their room. I took it ten days after my escape from a German prisoner of war camp in Poland. Von Rosens lived in Exin, about 100 miles south of Danzig. I had it in my possession constantly in the ninety days from Von Rosens to Dubuque, Iowa.

Signed: Theodore R. Ellsworth, Captain, U.S. Army

DSC AWARD FOR TED ELLSWORTH

Second Dubuquer Honored For Service in France

Ted R. Ellsworth of Dubuque, who left the army with the rank of captain, has been awarded the distinguished service cross for leading his company into the outskirts of the Maginot line during some of the fiercest days in the invasion of Germany.

The coveted medal, which has been presented to only two other Dubuquers during the second world war, Maj. (the Rev.) Albert Hoffmann and Maj. Harold Hantelmann, will be presented to Ellsworth at a later date. It is the second highest award given army men for actual heroism in action.

Ellsworth

Ellsworth, who has lived at 879 W. Third street after receiving his release from the army late last year, had been recommended for the congressional medal of honor by the 317th infantry regiment. But since many of the eye-witnesses to his heroism were killed, the Pentagon building felt compelled to substitute the DSC for the nation's highest award.

Battle of Sivry

The engagement mentioned in the citation took place at Sivry, France, on Oct. 4, 1944. Ellsworth led his men in a grim onslaught upon the Germans holding that village, and killed or wounded all but two of them.

The Nazis counter-attacked, however, and wiped out many members of Ellsworth's company. He himself was captured and was taken to Oflag 64 near Danzig. Managing to escape, he hid in a barn with some Polish slave labor until the arrival of Marshal Zhokov's White Russian army, which sent him by horse-cart to Odessa.

At Odessa, he boarded a British boat for Egypt. From there he went to Italy, and then on to the States, where he arrived on VE-day—a day which he had helped achieve.

Fought Under Two Flags

Ex-Capt. Ellsworth has the unique distinction of having fought under both the British and American flags, since he served as a first lieutenant in General Montgomery's Eighth army during the Mediterranean campaign. He transferred to the American army prior to the invasion of Europe.

Ellsworth was a member of the late Gen. George S. Patton's Third army.

The spirited 28-year-old Dubuquer was in service for four years and was overseas for three years. He recently joined the insurance agency of his father-in-law, Harvey Lange.

Ellsworth is the son of Mr. and Mrs. Clyde Ellsworth. During World war I days, his father commanded local company A of the Iowa National guard when it was mobilized to safeguard the American border from the raids of Pancho Villa.

THE HILLS OF HOME

Letter from a Dubuque boy now with the British Central Mediterranean Forces:

Dec. 4, 1943.

"Dear Mr. Mulgrew:

"A few moments ago I finished reading your 1943 edition of 'And Life Goes On,' sent to me by my family for the third straight year.

"The 1941 edition I read in Montreal, the 1942 book in Yorkshire, England, and this year's book on the Italian front where our battalion had just crossed the Sangro river after ten fairly sticky days. And it was grand to get your book. I only hope that the 1944 one I may read in Dubuque.

"I don't think you are the greatest columnist in the world, but I know of few I like to read better than you. My love for Dubuque is great, and you seem a sort of symbol of my home town to me. My mother-in-law, Mrs. Harvey Lange, usually encloses a few of your poems in her letters to me. My favorite this year was 'The Hills Of Home,' and I was disappointed that you didn't include it in the 1943 edition. A fellow doesn't think of the hills of home when he's being machine-gunned, or shelled, but only why wasn't he born the size of Tom Thumb! But it's wonderful to think of home after things calm down.

"During my summer vacations from Dartmouth College I worked at Molo's Oil Station at Fifth and Locust and used to often see you passing on your way to the post-office. I thought perhaps one day I'd talk to you. But after the war I'll stop you on the street sometime. Please don't bother to answer this inadequate note. I just wanted you to know—well, how you've made me feel occasionally when I'd read something of yours. Thanks a lot, and all the best for 1944.

Sincerely,

Ted Ellsworth,

Lt. 2nd Bn., King's Royal Rifle Corps, 8th Army, British Central Mediterranean Forces."

(Editor's note: "Inadequate," he calls the above letter. Well, Ted, if that's an 'inadequate' letter, I don't know when I've received one that pleased me any better. Thanks a million.)

Top right: Feb. 24, 1946 *Telegraph Herald*, Dubuque, Iowa

Top left: Barbara Lange Ellsworth with Watling Street, Dubuque, Iowa *(Hruska Photography)*

Bottom right: Ted Ellsworth, Barbara Lange Ellsworth, and Watling Street, Dubuque, Iowa *(Hruska photography)*

Bottom left: Dec. 1943, *Telegraph Herald*, Dubuque, Iowa

Ted Ellsworth with his wife and family at his summer cottage on the bluffs of the Mississippi River "Shawondasee," 1969

U.S. Congressional candidate Ted Ellsworth and his wife, Barbara, campaign in Iowa, 1972

Queen Elizabeth II visits Washington D.C., 1975. Author is on the far right in black tie

Ted Ellsworth with his children and grandchildren at Shawondasee, Iowa, 1983

Chapter Thirteen

I poured out my story to the Chief Officer of the "Almanzora." He asked the Captain of the ship, who gave approval, and I waved to Tom to take the dog on board. There was no use for the duffle bag Tom had in his hand in case we couldn't legally bring Watt. I was ordered to leave Watt in the ship's potato hold, care of the butcher, and I tied him there with a German pull-through. We were to sail that night after taking on oil, but in the morning we could still see Capri. We hadn't budged.

After a leisurely breakfast, we descended to the bowels of the ship to walk Watt. We couldn't find the dog and assumed the butcher was exercising him. The butcher had assumed we were exercising him. I didn't worry, as the gangplanks were up and Watt couldn't have made shore. We whistled for a time and visited our platoons crowded below decks.

Sergeant Bateman met me, saying, "Too bad you couldn't get Watt aboard, sir, after all he's been through with us."

"What do you mean?" I almost shouted.

"He's out there on the quay. I thought you left him there."

"Show me!"

Three hundred yards from the ship was Watt, forlorn, sniffing at each soldier who passed.

I yelled to a soldier to grab that big black dog. Hearing my voice, Watt ran for the ship. We were five yards from the edge of the dock and I was afraid he would jump in the water. The Chief Officer and Captain were near-by, supervising final sailing preparations.

"The dog is out there, sir. We can't go yet."

"Your dog is with the butcher. That is another dog."

"I'd know my dog anywhere."

"No one is allowed to leave the ship. We are leaving straight away."

Tom took over. A rope ladder was being dropped to pick up the last seaman. Tom started down it as the seaman reached the top.

"Get the kit bag, Elmer."

As I ran for the cabin, I heard the Chief Officer say, "No one is allowed off the ship."

But I guess Tom didn't hear that too clearly, because when I came back, he was on the dock with Watt jumping all about and happily whining. The ship's motors were going and I visualized Tom and Watt vacationing in Naples and what I would have to say to Mrs. Braden about why her son didn't return.

Watt was too big for the kit bag, but Tom jammed him in, while a seaman tossed down a rope and hauled the dog aboard. A cheer went up from three hundred riflemen who were watching the proceedings. Tom came up the ladder, and twelve minutes later we sailed for Gibraltar and England. We learned that Watt had broken loose the night before, found his way to the gangplank in search of friendly smells, and waited on the quay all night. Hugh Hope kept Watt in his cabin for the voyage.

There was no aura of despair in leaving Italy. We thought we might miss the always-dependable sunsets and their splendor of streaks of gray lit with electric patches of brilliant orange over the pale purple outline of the ever-present Appennines. Otherwise, we had Italy.

On King George V pier, Glasgow, we argued and drank and spent pounds with customs men, pursers, fisheries officials, and adjutants. The answers were always the same. Watt could not remain on board, and Watt could not land in England. Cox and Kings came to our rescue, sent the dog to the Croydon kennels, making arrangements to ship him eventually to Barbara in America, by permission of the Bank of England.

On the rainy, windswept, cold beach at Worthing, Sir John Davidson welcomed us back to England, talking about the Battalion's great achievements in the Mediterranean, the new chapters we had added to the history of the Regiment. There were tears in his eyes as he shook each man's hand. Why, I wondered. Tears of gratitude? Because he was thinking of the Battalion in the days of the Boer War? Or in the Great War? Or in Calais? Or tears for the men who didn't come back? Or tears because he was thinking of why we had come back—for D-day in Normandy?

The 2nd 60th was given a month's leave, and Tom and I permission to spend it in America, if we could get there.

Noisy and happy, we visited our old haunts in London. Rosa and Edith kissed us, gave us the suite they called "the colonel's room," sent us gin and Pimms by the grinning Bennett. Bernham Porter, Fred Blakeman, and Colonel Spencer bought us a champagne dinner at the Ritz. Tom Joyce hired a Rolls Royce one night. Mrs. Dexter had food parcels for us at the Eagle Club. It was a thrill to buy a "today's newspaper" instead of leaping on something weeks old. War had become an efficient routine to London, and it was no longer the fun of the early days. Or perhaps we had changed.

Goring's "little blitz" was falling on the Old Lady, and the red glow of incendiaries outlined the Town in the night sky. It was three months before the rocket bombs and D-day. The American invasion of Britain had begun. The bottle clubs were filled with strange, new faces from the New World that had stepped forth with all its power and might to lift the curse of Hitler from the brows of mankind.

Some of the Americans thought the English did all their fighting in England. Some believed that the English accent was "put on." Some felt that we should have asked Britain for something before we instituted lend-lease, because when they were standing alone we could have had anything. Some pooh-poohed the invaluable, intangible reverse lend-lease of experience that was to save thousands of American lives. A few reminded others that England had not paid its World War I debts. Americans griped about London's high prices. Some wrote home, "The Limeys are Nigger-lovers."

But most tried to get along with their Ally in the unhealthy waiting period.

Looking out of the window of his office, his face tired, white, and worn from the war, Ambassador Winant asked Tom and me, "Was it tough down there?"

"Yes, sir. It was tough." But we felt embarrassed, because it was not as tough as Mr. Winant seemed to think. Deep feeling, pain, and sincerity were in his question. We knew his son was a prisoner of the Nazis, and it didn't seem right that he was doing all this for us.

"Well, gee, I'm glad to see you. I'm so glad you're back safe. I'll see a fellow about getting you home. But it isn't easy. Have a good time, and call me in three days."

Those three days Tom and I bought presents for our family and clothes for ourselves. We had only our battle dress to stand up in. We knew in the end all would come right, and it was so.

I sent a cable to Barbara to go to New York, and Tom and I flew to Prestwick. A C-54 of the Air Transport Command took us home. Our only stop was in the green, cultivated Azores. Eight of us were on the plane, including a friendly chemical warfare colonel named Chamberlain from Iowa who told us where we could get a "real swell beef steak" in Washington, and a British major who brought out a bottle of scotch which we drank flying over New York less than twenty-four hours after leaving Scotland.

The lights of Washington that early evening in the spring of 1944, were the first of such we had seen for more than two years. Circling the airport, I was tired, dirty, excited, wondering how I would find America and all that was there.

I remember a Coke machine, seeing my first WAAC, ice cold drinking water, a neon sign of "Drugs" and another of "Bowling," a man selling cheese sandwiches, and a shop in the Washington railroad station where souvenirs were sold and Tom got a great chuckle out of that. Then a train ride and a cab to Sixty-eighth Street.

Had Barbara received my cable?

The elevator took forever. She opened the apartment door, and I kissed her. We were both nervous, embarrassed, and never happier. She was wearing a house-robe I had never seen. After a while, everything was all right and we were no longer embarrassed. The next day I phoned my family.

We drove to my uncle's Mill Race farm near Washington's Crossing in Bucks County for a week, worrying about minor, unimportant things to forget about going back, but that time-clicking-on feeling was always there.

Every soldier thinks about his return to the hometown. I wasn't disappointed in Dubuque, only I was impressed with its smallness—

smallness in distance, streets, and buildings. Main Street, which I had thought of as the one and only Main Street before became just a main street. Men whose names I knew only as store-fronts before the war stopped me, shook hands, engaged in light conversation, said:

"We're all glad to see you back."

"How do you like the English?"

"That Italian war is a flop. I can't understand why we invaded there. If we bombed Italy, we could win easily. I've looked on the map. Italy is a narrow place. Just bomb hell out of it, and it'll all be over."

"When's the second front going to open?"

"Germany isn't our war. We're after Japan. That's what I figure."

"Are those Heinies as tough this time as they were last? I got over there just as the last war finished."

"I go duck-hunting every season, and I know I could shoot down a German plane."

"The Jews have all the scotch. That's why we haven't got any and have to put up with this bourbon."

"My personal opinion is, and you can take it for what it's worth, that England won't send any of their own boys in on D-day. We Americans, as usual, will be the suckers."

Generous America would do anything for the "boys." I thought that spring, if our post-war thinking and living are as active as the effort to entertain service men, the nations will not split wide open with hate, confusion, and fear.

At the Elks Club, the Country Club, the road-houses, family dinner tables, and the barber shops I found that during the war anti-Semitism had become fashionable, a sort of social habit. There was an increase in the social stigma attached to the colored race. We had enough complex troubles with the war, but America was bedeviling itself with a tension of closed mind prejudice on race and religion superiority without honest investigation.

The war also precipitated a new and defiant attitude on the part of the Negro.

The world was wicked, and America knew it. Many of my friends blamed it all on the Jews. They said it was the Jews who had the soft jobs in the war, who manipulated currencies, who brought on the war, who struck at the root and core and brain of society in an effort to gain their own ends.

"Did you ever see a Jew infantryman?" they asked me. I replied that I had seen plenty of them, but I knew they did not believe me, or that perhaps I had seen two or three.

I was a soldier, getting jittery about going back to action. I did not have the solution to the Negro and Jew question, or opinions on capital vs. labor. All I knew was that the talk bothered me, that we were not facing our problems squarely, that production and blood were not going to preserve the American idea. In the bumptious post-war world, Western civilization was going to end in failure and utter destruction if we refused to act in large terms and cease our thoughtless monkeyshines.

Post-war peace and prosperity must be earned by sweat and common sense. When death was swallowed up in victory, troubles would not evaporate if we washed our underclothes in Lux. America's social unrest, which was part of the worldwide chaos would not disappear like a bad dream. Peace would find the nations thrown closely together, on the verge of perishing within a few years if we did not find and make work, a rational form of global organization that our moral dignity demands.

The soft peace sob sisters would have to remember that racism would not die with the defeat of Germany and Japan. It was a racial disease, and millions of soldiers and war prisoners would be propagandists for Hitler. Perhaps unknowingly.

I knew America could not outlaw prejudice and maintain our way of life. The pressures that keep alive evil racial and religious doctrines must be liquidated in social engineering.

Now, long after that spring, our last enemy has been defeated. It was a sudden defeat brought on by the atomic bomb. We can dominate the sudden peace only if we quickly understand the nature of the war we played the major part in winning. The war was not for marbles.

"Elmer, I think we ought to transfer to the American Army."

"If we're ever going to do it, I suppose now is the time."

"The thing is this. I have very little money, as you know. This month in America has cost plenty. Financially, I remind myself of the story in *Alice in Wonderland*. Alice is running as fast as she can, and the Red Queen keeps yelling, 'Faster! Faster!' Finally, when Alice, quite breathless, stops and looks around, she finds herself in the same place she was when she started, and the Queen says, 'You'll have to run much faster than that if you want to get somewhere.' I plan, and contrive, and save and think I am getting ahead, then—boomstick! Something hits me and I'm just where I was before.

"The English don't pay us much, and I ought to have a bit of dough if peace ever comes."

"I'll tell you, Tom, if you line us up some place in the Yank Army, I'll transfer with you. We always intended to transfer some time. But it looks rather shady pulling out now, just when Europe is about to open up."

When I said that, Tom immediately made two long distance calls from Dubuque. One, to Major General Charles L. Bolte, commanding the 69th Infantry Division in Mississippi. The other, to the British Embassy in Washington. General Bolte said he would take us, and the British Embassy agreed to arrange it with London.

With a minimum of red tape, the British and American Governments worked together on our case and my father-in-law, a notary public, swore us into the American Army as first lieutenants, transferring in rank. The ceremony was not impressive. We had on sports clothes, my father-in-law was in shirtsleeves, the breakfast dishes were still on the dining-room table, and Barbara and her mother in their aprons watched from the kitchen door.

It was difficult to realize that we would never again see our Regiment and the people who had given us the most wholesale laughs, sheer kindness, sympathy, friendship, and bountiful breaks that we ever had had in our lives. I suppose we were rather maudlin about the 60th Rifles. I felt a bit jealous when I thought some new subaltern would take command of my old platoon of Sergeant Brown, and the cockneys, looking like ragamuffins, swearing, joking, dirty, bumming, singing, talking their own language, and disciplined.

On arrival at Camp Shelby, we had an hour's talk with General Bolte, cousin of Chuck Bolte who lost his leg at Alamein and who was one of our group of twelve Yanks in the 60th. We had known the General in the early days of the war in London, having used his room in the Dorchester and tagged along with him when he took us all out for Chinese food. Before Chuck left for Egypt, he asked the General to get him a plane ride to America for his two weeks' embarkation leave so that he could get married. A good soldier,

General Bolte refused, saying, "If you went on a plane it would mean that much less mail getting home in a hurry to the families of the soldiers over here."

"How do you think you'll make out in this army?" he asked us.

"Infantry is probably the same all over the world, sir. But we are having a bit of difficulty bringing that English salute down to a mild roar. We had our uniform insignias on all wrong at first, but some officers put us straight."

"We spend a lot of time in the field here, on bivouac. I can't promise you action for a time, but eventually the Division will go overseas. Get the feel of things here. You'll get along."

Then followed a barrage of interviews, filling out forms, answering questions, signing our names, and meeting our Battalion commander. We felt strange, looked strange to each other, and we asked strange questions. But soon it was the same old thing—the army. The men were healthy, hearty, intelligent, had little enthusiasm for going overseas, and they didn't like the infantry. There was more amenity and much less of a definite distinction between the commissioned and non-commissioned than in the British Army. At the same time there was more consciousness of rank among the American officers.

There were few combat veterans in America at that time, and our training lacked the final degree of realism which only those who have been up there can inject. The men believed the Germans were afraid of cold steel, that Jerry couldn't fight at night, and they held in contempt the enemy soldiers as soldiers. They later learned in action that Jerry was an owl in the dark, did not run at the rattle of a bayonet which was rarely used anyway, and that the Nazi was a well-drilled professional.

The 69th Division was continually sending men overseas as casual replacements, and it was almost impossible to build up a pride in the unit among the soldiers.

Our lunches in the field were steak, orangeade, mashed potatoes, cauliflower, salad, cake, and a paper napkin, a far cry from the haversack rations we had while training with the English, an old piece of cheese, a thick slice of bread, a fat sardine, and a mug of char.

Within a week we had been thoroughly attacked by mosquitoes, jiggers, ants, and our ears were sunburned. We had seen innumerable rattlers, cottonmouths, and coral snakes. My personal feeling is that I would rather lie in a hole all day like a human potato with a fat Hun on the next ridge with a Schmeisser than suffer the snakes and insects of the infantryman's life in Mississippi.

Eating my breakfast on the hood of a jeep near the Leaf River, I heard two pieces of news from the Battalion runner. One, the Allies under the supreme command of General Eisenhower had landed on the Normandy Coast. Two, eighteen officers were needed for a new overseas posting list. The date was June 6, 1944. I had been in the American Army just over three weeks.

I hurried to Tom.

"Have you heard the news?"

"About the second front? Yes."

"How do you feel?"

"I feel that life is a series of anti-climaxes, and we're in one right now. How do you suppose I feel, sitting here in Mississippi?"

"Let's go, Tom."

"How?"

"There's a new overseas posting list coming out. Maybe we can get on."

"Suits. Let's see some of the big gears—now."

The Battalion executive officer, "No, you can't go. You guys just came back."

The Battalion commanding officer, "You don't have a chance. No."

The Regiment commanding officer, "No. You've been here only three weeks and have a lot to learn."

"Sir, infantry tactics and so forth are the same the world over."

"You don't know enough about American logistics. Stay here and we'll give you a command."

"Colonel, sir, would you ask the General if we could go?"

"Certainly. I'll ask him. But he won't let you, probably. Are you two insane? You just got here."

About that time, I was thinking that perhaps we were insane, and how funny it is that people think you are insane when you volunteer for the job for which you are trained. Then I remembered the letter I had from Barbara the day before and how she said she was so happy getting used to the fact I was in the States, and what peace of mind the family had now, and how she planned to come to the crowded carnival of Hattiesburg, live in a single room, see me once in a while, and eat all her meals in a restaurant.

We thanked the Colonel, saluted, and left.

"Elmer, maybe we are a bit impetuous about all this. After all, there's a lot of Cokes and music and good food here. Maybe this is dumb on our part."

"Maybe, but we've shot our bolt now. Besides, I want to get home. We'll have a few days delay en route."

"That's true. Volunteer for overseas duty so we can get five days at home. About as sensible as Al taking us to Africa so he could get out of a battle course in Wales. But what the hell."

General Bolte gave his immediate permission and wished us the best of luck. A few days later he left to command the 34th Red Bull Division in its heartbreaking Italian campaign.

We checked in our rifles, binoculars, and compasses, endured hectic, hot hours of red tape, and managed to catch a plane from Jackson to Chicago. I got to Dubuque for four precious days, to find that Watt had arrived the night before, the end of the trail—for him.

Chapter Fourteen

There were no tears. My family had tapped that hidden reserve in themselves that we call upon in emergencies and strains. A mature calm had settled over Barbara, a sitting-back-to-wait attitude. But I knew this move of mine was harder on her than that first time I left. I thought of how it was better to be married when there was a war on; one has something tangible to think about and return to. But it is awfully wearing on the tangible.

"Are you sore about this, Barb?"

"No. I'm a bit dazed. Rather numb. It is sudden. My chin is up. I didn't think I could stand it if you went again. But I seem to be. It will be hell to read about a battle in the papers and wonder if you are in it. I'll be glad when these lonesome years are over."

"This time won't be fun. There won't be the glamour and the laughs like before. It is strictly business. I've no desire to close with the Hun, shake under his shells, get excited, and run all over the place with a carbine and map case. But when that overseas list happened, and the second front, I just somehow forgot about everything else."

"Don't worry about it."

"I'll go over, go in, come out, and I'll probably be one of the first sent home. Maybe by Christmas. Then I promise you we'll raise a family and have a house. As I say, it's strictly business this time. While I'm gone, pamper yourself in little ways and things. Queer how one does things he knows are right and best, and yet it usually means unhappiness for somebody."

I had spent the afternoon with my father's old friend, Joe Myers, who had served with Dad in Europe in 1918.

We were walking on the golf course. Mother was sitting in the car. Watt was playing with an indoor baseball on the green fairways that I had always promised him when he was in the scrub of Libya, plagued by flies. He was the only war souvenir I managed to get all the way home, a memento of the boredom, terror, homesickness, and fun which go to make up a soldier's life. I had instructed Barbara on how to praise, scold, and call him as well as the special little games such as each man has with his dog.

Tom and I left that night.

A final, quick army physical examination, and our package of replacement officers marches to the train at Camp Kilmer, New Jersey. A band is playing college songs, and it is rather embarrassing. A captain is in command of us. West Point '32, the kind of guy who keeps his eyes shut, with occasional blinks, when talking to you. A bird-dog, and privates say, "He'd better watch out or I won't give him his old job back after the war."

We have finished a week of buying as much ice cream as we can eat at one sitting, of countless formations, of long lectures and last minute warnings through which most of the officers slept, of long distance telephone calls. We have had our first taste of the replacement system whose horrors defy description.

On our most secret three-hour ride to Staten Island, the women of New Jersey who live near the tracks watch our every move, throwing us kisses, few of which we return because going overseas has lost all its glamour and we have been messed about too much since our initial burst of enthusiasm. We keep our self-respect by continual grousing and criticizing.

The cheery Red Cross is by the gangplank giving us doughnuts, coffee, lemonade, cigarettes, and chocolate. It is a seven-thousand-ton Victory ship and it will pitch and toss, and sleeping will be difficult. There are twelve officers to each narrow cabin with a single aisle and bunks three deep. Tom and I sleep across from each other. We hang our steel helmets on our bunks and use them for ashtrays.

A crap and poker game starts in the latrine and continues the entire voyage. Six destroyers protect our convoy of thirty-eight new and mass-produced ships carrying planes, men, guns, and gas. These men from America who have never sailed the ocean take the trip in their stride, and there is no cheering or waving when we leave, because this is just one more thing the army is doing to them.

The food is good, and the ship is crowded. We read and perspire in our bunks most of the time. The privates have been in the army just over three months, and they are to fight the professionals. As we land in the country of flat and slippery beer, we hear that an attempt has been made on Hitler's life, and we pray fervently that it is the end of the war. But many of those on the boat who pray will meet death in Germany.

England is silent. This is the pay-off summer for her "finest hour," and she is holding her breath. It isn't like the days of, "Hell, let 'em come. We'll take off the gloves."

The Red Cross gives us doughnuts and coffee as we wait near the

Liverpool Cathedral. The old familiar scene of Yanks examining an English bicycle and seventeen-year-old girls who have been denied so much and know so much, and were born five years too soon hang about us and are chased away by a bobby.

"Best of luck to you. Cheerio," the Americans mimic.

"Why do their policemen wear medals? They look like drum majors."

"So this is the country of the men of well-brushed bowler hats and tightly-rolled umbrellas. I'll be damned!"

"You ought to see the laborers, hey. They all wear coats, ties, and caps. No overalls."

"Ellsworth, you've been over here before. Aren't the girls any better looking than that?"

"There's some bomb damage over near that insurance building. First I've seen."

"What's the matter with this country? Their streets are narrow, their cars are small, and the newspapers are only four pages. They really drive on the wrong side. I'd have to see it to believe it. Give me America for my dough."

Our packet is issued rough English blankets and straw ticks under canvas on a majestic green estate with a lake and some swans in Wales. Tom and I ask for a two-day pass to London, and an impassive, dull lieutenant colonel of the type who commanded those early replacement centers tells us that we will be in Normandy any day and no passes allowed. There is a save-food campaign, and we must serve ourselves to only what we want, and we must eat all we take. We check the men as they leave the mess tents to wash their mess tins. They are throwing away no edibles. Because they have already tossed under the tables the food they do not eat. But the campaign is a big success because they throw no food in the garbage buckets.

The replacement center is riddled with ugly, false rumors. The English like the Negroes better than American whites. A Canadian soldier got V.D. during the nine hour Dieppe raid in 1942. The commanding officer is not giving us enough water because we are to learn what it's like at the front. We feed all of England except for tomatoes and lettuce. America is paying the owner of the estate fifteen cents a head daily for the fifteen hundred of us bivouacking on the land. The wounded from Normandy say there is no chance for us to be alive this time next week.

Most of the rumors are believed. Homesick, scared, and uninformed, the Yanks take it out on what they can. And the only thing around to take it out on is England. There is no mail for replacements, and there might be USO shows some place, but replacements don't see them. We censor the men's letters, and there is no trace of idealism, vehement eagerness, or pride in their role.

We move to Warminster on our way to France, and we have a game of baseball. Tom painfully twists his knee, and is classified for temporary limited service. Two days later we have a quick handshake on the cricket pitch where I had once drilled my English platoon.

"So long. I'll see you."

I've forgotten what he said. I was struggling with some special way we had been ordered to pack our tackle. In war, you always lose army friends one way or another.

We marched past the gate where the soldiers had left for Crecy and Agincourt on the fourteenth-century quay from which the Pilgrims had sailed to Plymouth.

The night before we had been issued final battle gear—some francs, V.D. preventatives, trench knives, entrenching shovels, hand stoves, gum, matches, water purifiers, anti-louse powder, gas ointment, and a warning not to marry French girls. The day was beautiful and sunny, the English Channel calm, and Dinah Shore was singing on the radio. We landed on sandy Omaha from a personnel beach landing craft in ankle deep water and we crawled to the top of the cliff, wondering how men under fire had ever made it. The climb was difficult enough for us, with the Germans fifteen miles away.

Resting that first night in France among the long, gray, stone farm houses and wicked, thick Normandy hedge-rows which had lately sputtered death, I watched the artillery blinking in the night sky. I thought about the wooden shoes I had seen the Normans wearing, and the girl near the dusty road, who had proudly patted her fat stomach and said, "Petite Boche," and about my invasion booklet which said Normandy is a grazing, cheese, egg, and butter country—but that it didn't much look like it at that moment. I wondered what Calvados was made of and about the man who had given me a rasping drink of it. He had told me the Germans had paid for what they had taken, married their girls, and treated the peasants well during the occupation, and I wondered if it would be like that farther inland.

If France is filled with well-mannered men, gay songs and talk, hard-boiled women, prostitutes, and good food, I didn't find them. We went too fast, and when we stopped, it was along the god-forsaken Moselle, out of gas.

After the German counter-attack at Avaranches, which failed to cut off the Brittany peninsula, the Germans were through. We knew it, but they would not quit. That made us hate them the more. But the soldiers thought it would be all over by the middle of October. We saw their wooden carts and horse-drawn artillery, an indication that Germany could not produce the machines of steel they needed.

The chase across France that August was a lark. Grandmothers who remembered the war of 1870 and children who did not remember 1940 cheered us. The gamins in the villages were dirty, friendly, and incessantly thanked us, shaking our hands. They had not yet learned to ask for "a cigarette for Pa-Pah." Pears, apples, and tomatoes were tossed to us as we went by in our trucks. Wine and cider were offered at halts if we could produce an empty bottle. We threw cigarettes in return. We talked about how soon we could go home after the surrender and if wives would be allowed to join the army of occupation. There was little thought given to post-war solutions by the liberating troops.

Homemade American flags fluttered from the windows, flags with six to a hundred stars, some of them six pointed, with the blue field in either the upper right or left hand corner. We bought eggs in any quantities for forty cents a dozen, and General Patton insisted his Third Army wear ties and steel helmets behind or at the front and looting was to be strictly punished. "Welcome to Our Friends" and "We Honor Our Liberators" banners were stretched across the highways lined with poplar trees.

As it always was and shall be, when an army packs us to move on, it leaves waste and litter and salvage. While dogs licked at our empty C and K ration tins the French appeared from nowhere with gunny sacks to pick over our discards before word had spread throughout the unit that we were going on. Sometimes we had good cognac that made us clear-headed and talkative. The moon was lovely that month, and casualties were light enough to add a small amount of exhilaration to the gallop. We no longer hoped for the Russians to finish the job. We could do it ourselves. Europe was not the expected minefield and our air of superiority was complete.

Only the bumblebees and yellow jackets plagued us, settling on our food in yellow bunches as thick as the black flies in Africa.

As we looked at comfortable chateaus tucked away in the hills, and grew bored with shouts of "*Vive L'Amerique*," we talked about Paris after the surrender and what we would do. The only city I had a junket was Le Mans where prices were low, shops loaded, and expertly rouged women in short dresses paid no heed to the French warnings plastered on walls that it was dangerous to walk alone. The Germans had left two days before, and I was able to buy perfume with no trouble and few francs—perfume that I intended to mail home and never did.

I walked in La Cathedrale du Mans as my father had in 1918, viewed the thirteenth-century tomb of Berengere, queen of Richard the Lion Hearted, and saw the relics of saints protected by sand bags. Twenty-four loads of German prisoners, standing sixty to an open truck, passed through the town, the French hooting at them, and the Nazis jeering back. I experimented. I smiled at a few of them. They smiled back. I had tried this dissimulation in Italy and Africa, receiving only stony glances in return. Perhaps the treacherous creatures were cracking and quitting after all, I thought. I wanted to think that.

Southeast of Paris, on the way to Troyes, I joined the "Blue Ridge" 80th Division and was the first replacement officer assigned to the 2nd Battalion, 317th Infantry, acting as Lieutenant Colonel

Murray's S2, intelligence. I then informed Barbara I was in France as I needed mail and didn't want her unduly anxious prior to the Moselle.

We drew up behind Pont-a-Mousson, a half-mile west of the Moselle River, between Metz and Nancy. We dug foxholes in half-filled World War I trenches which contained the original, twisted, rusty wire entanglements with huge four-pointed barbs. Scattered about where shell cases of 1918. Along the river we heard the probing 88s and the spasmodic tear of the German "paper-cutters" which sound like the ripping of bleached canvas. We questioned wandering civilians, because across from us was Alsace-Lorraine, a mixture of French and German sympathizers. But we trusting Americans probably didn't treat them as discriminately as we might have, and Jerry undoubtedly learned much from civilians who claimed they were moving back to their homes, just as we gained intelligence about Jerry from the French who roamed almost at will between the lines.

As S2, I handled the battalion patrols along the Moselle, reporting information to Major Jim Hayes at Regiment in preparation for the crossing. It was "poor bloody infantry" work, and we smoked at least five cigarettes before breakfast.

The plan was for the 80th to secure a bridgehead across the canal and river, while the engineers placed the vehicle bridges. The great 4th Armoured Division was to roll through us and dash for Germany followed by the 35th Infantry Division on trucks. To our left, the "Red Diamond" 5th Division would widen the breach. We were to keep Jerry on the run as soon as supplies came up.

At 9 P.M. the night of September 11, 1944, we marched four hours through the dark and mud to our assembly area. I had spread my six-man S2 section among G, E, and F Companies with orders to get all possible information back to me. Harold Kinder, private first class from Mishawauka, Indiana, who had an uncanny knack for scrounging, stayed with me. He and I wore raincoats and carried rifles, four grenades, a map case, extra clips, six K rations, sixteen packs of cigarettes, and eight candy bars. A river crossing is never much fun, we thought, but after the first night it would be all right. The war's end was a matter of weeks, and the hills we could see on the other side were "the last ones between us and Germany." After that it was all flat, and tank crews could handle things and have the headlines, once we got the river.

At 03:00 hours, we left our assembly area, with the actual crossing scheduled for 05:00. Colonel Murray and I watched the terrific half-hour barrage from the hill overlooking the river, while our infantry companies lurked below by the small canal. As we left the hill, Colonel Murray's runners and wireless men disappeared in the dark, not because of fright, but because it was difficult to keep contact. We stumbled on G Company, which was lost, having failed to locate the engineer guide. Kinder and I found the starting place for them—only by luck, but it was our job. It meant that we would cross the river in light, instead of the dark, and that bothered me. The clumsy ten-man combat boats were ready for us, and like school boys on an outing, we paddled across the swift river. I had a feeling I was on the Mississippi River, and thought it strange I should feel that way, because the Mississippi was quiet, I worried about Colonel Murray being out of touch with his companies, but remembered the plan was well known to all the battalion, and if everything went according to plan, Murray would not need communications for another half-hour. By that time the sun would be up, we would be on our objective, and we could locate the runners and wireless to report success to Regiment.

The far banks were steep, behind which was an eight hundred-yard field, stretching to the base of the hill. Over this flat were slow, arching tracer machine-gun bullets. It was grazing fire, not much chance to avoid it, but it was coming from only three guns. The Germans were not in strength. Huddled along the bank were thirty men, windy about getting up for the dash. It was almost full daylight, and the Germans would begin to mortar the river. Better to take a chance on the bullets than lie there. I went over the bank, ran twenty yards, fell on my belly, Kinder five yards behind. "Come on!" I shouted to the bank.

Lieutenant Moye appeared, and five men followed him. We moved on another twenty yards and hit the dirt. We all yelled back to the others. In groups they followed us. "Run and flop! Run and flop!" we all screamed. The secret was to keep moving. In six minutes we caught the rest of the battalion approaching the hill on their feet, German machine guns occasionally chattering. I was tired. So was Kinder. We stopped in a ditch for a smoke. To the back of us I watched the German mortars start to slap about the river, but we were all across. Ahead I saw two unarmed Germans rise and run forward with their hands in the air. An F Company sergeant stopped and fired eight rounds in to the chests of the Germans, fifteen yards away from him, ran to the fallen bodies and let go two more shots, and hurried on to join his company going up the hill.

I talked to him later and he said, "No sons-of-bitches are going to fire at me until the last thirty yards and then try to surrender. They could have given up before that."

Kinder and I finished our quick drags, and were about to move when some more of F Company searching ditches fired at us. “Hey, we’re 2nd battalion. Hold it!”

“Sorry, we thought you were Krauts.”

The hill was ours by 07:00. Captain Talcott, our battalion artillery liaison officer, hurried the German retreat with 105s and we watched them speed away in trucks to the East. We had few casualties, were confident and cocky. This was going to be like the rest of France since St. Lo. But I didn’t like it. There were no mines. Jerry had given up this valuable high ground without the proper fight. I knew how he scrapped for high ground in Italy.

On the perfect target of the hill, slowly digging in, we received some 88 and mortar fire, and a few of our men were wounded. One blast blew off my helmet. Kinder and I had a sleep in one of the last war trenches that ran all over the hill like messy telephone wires down in a storm. Two of my S2 section with the companies had been killed before they had given us any information. We wouldn’t have felt so badly about it if they had been killed doing some good. But they had just been following along and died before they could help us.

“Kinder, I don’t like this,” I said. “Jerry should be tossing more stuff at us than these occasional shells. He doesn’t give in this easily. Things are too quiet.”

“Oh, well. You can see the bridges going up down there. The tanks will be through tomorrow morning. Then we can rest. Jerry is licked.”

At last light, I joined the battalion staff in a low crowded German dug out, all of us sitting on the ground with our knees forced against our chins, the damp seeping through our seats, and the wireless open to the companies.

Chapter Fifteen

"Enemy tanks followed by infantry are coming in to St. Genevieve, and we can't hold them." We could hear bullets over the radio as a background to the radio operator's voice.

"You've got to hold them. Fight the bastards!" Colonel Murray replied.

From that message on, there was complete radio silence from G Co. in the little village of St. Genevieve on the left flank of the thousand-yard hill. We crawled out of our cramped dugout to the battalion command post in the yard of a ruined stone house, the only building on the hill outside of St. Genevieve. A steady stream of mortar fire was plastering the hill, but the companies were dug in and the shells were falling far over our location. Fifteen minutes later all battalion radio communication was out.

"Ellsworth, get those tanks to G Company."

We had a platoon of tanks with the battalion, but they had arrived in the night and were going to wait until first light to move in to position. I took Dunaway, my jeep driver, with me and on foot we started in the direction the tanks were harboring. Dunaway stopped me at the edge of a hedgerow, crawled around the end of it, rose up and lunged his bayonet —into the dead body of a horse.

"Don't frighten me like that, Dunaway."

"I thought it was a Jerry," he whispered. "Look at there."

Two hundred yards from us two red flares were shot toward our C. P., directing light machine gun fire which started immediately.

"Those are Jerries. If they have come this far, they've overrun our tanks." In the vicinity of F Company in the old quarry we heard German burp guns. "This must be serious. We'd better tell the Colonel."

Murray would not believe me when I said the Nazis were closing in, but he told me to get his blankets. I walked to the dugout and thought perhaps the Colonel was right. Maybe I was frightened down there and didn't want to look for those tanks of ours. The Germans couldn't have advanced this quickly since the message from G Company. Coming out of the dugout, I heard idling motors of tanks and loud voices about sixty yards distant. I walked over to them, thinking they were our tanks that had moved when the attack started and were reporting to the battalion Command Post. I wanted to tell the tankers to quiet down or they would give us all away. I wanted to tell them that Jerry was tough and just because they had armor around them was no reason Jerry wouldn't knock them out. I wanted to tell them I would show them battalion headquarters for which they were searching. Ten yards from the tanks, I stopped. What were our men shouting? The voices were high-pitched and unintelligible. The outline of the tanks were not those of Shermans. But I might be wrong. It was dark.

I woke up. I was surrounded by three Mark IVs and some Jerry foot soldiers. I had walked right among them. Well, I'd better not say anything, I thought. I'd better just get out of here. But I'd better do it in a casual, matter of fact way. Walk slowly. Don't run.

They might not see you in the dark. They seem drunk. I guess they are. They sound it.

And when I was twenty yards away, I raced, my heart pounding. Raced for the Colonel and the battalion command post behind a wall near the house, forty yards down from the dugout. When I arrived I was alone with the stone wall. All battalion headquarters had taken off. They had heard the Jerries, too, and battalion H.Q. has no weapons for tank fighting. Burp guns opened, and tank guns fired at the house.

Then I ran. I ran in the first direction any frightened boy does—toward home. Down the hill, west to the Moselle and America. At the bottom, I stopped by a knocked out ambulance. Across the eight-hundred-yard piece of farmland before the river I heard other men running and American voices. German tanks and machine guns had infiltrated on the flat, and I saw their tracer bullets cutting through the retreat to the river. I could hear two men screaming. Maybe more were beyond screaming, but I guess the Colonel went that way, and I'm supposed to stay with him, I thought. It's better to get to that river and take a chance on getting hit than staying around here with Jerry. He's got the hill now. Besides, all our communications are out, and Regiment is on the other side of the Moselle. I'd better get over there and report the chaos to Major Hayes. With not much hope of making the river, I jogged along. More men were yelling, and German tracers were making a celebration out of the entire river flat. I ripped my hands and clothes on the barbed wire fences. My raincoat was in shreds. Was I running away? Was I making the report to Regiment that was my duty an excuse to put the river between Jerry and me? Had the Colonel really come down the hill, or did I want to believe that? Was I yellow?

I didn't know then, and I still don't, and I've thought about it many, many times.

At the river's edge there was much confusion. It seemed every man for himself. I knew I had committed myself, that I could not go back up the hill, that I must cross the Moselle. In the dark we heard cries of "Help! Help!" Men who couldn't swim were trying to get across the river. We'll never know if two or twenty drowned. Ten yards from me Lieutenant Rideout of the Ammunition and Pioneer platoon received a direct hit and slumped dead with a loud sigh. I tore at my wet, muddy leggings, but my fingers fumbled. With leggings on, I could not remove my boots. Forgetting my training I had already tossed away my carbine and helmet for the swim. There was no longer any time to struggle with the leggings. I should have had paratroop boots, I thought. Then I slipped in to the ice water, feeling it soak through my clothes, meet the sweat, and chill my body. When it reached my stomach, my breath came in gasps. I thought about cramps and what they were like and if there was any way to overcome them in the water. I gathered courage, gave a shove from the bank, and started to swim, slowly. My boots were heavy and I did most of the work with my hands. Twice bullets sprayed the water, but it was all like a dream and didn't bother me. I didn't fight the current, and after what seemed like hours, my two hands dug in to the thick slime of the home bank. Like a lungfish climbing out of the Nile to live on land, I crawled to the grass. Grazing fire was covering the route, and I ran a few yards, and dropped, ran a few yards and dropped, until a voice directly in front of me said, "What in hell is going on up there? I almost shot you as you came toward me."

It was an ack-ack private in a hole, on guard near his gun.

"Jerry counter-attacked." I looked back on the hill, which seemed in another world. Tanks were on fire, lighting the night sky. They were our tanks, the ones I had tried to locate. I thought of my bedroll, pictures, one hundred dollars cash, and shaving kit up there with the Germans. I suddenly felt tired, but I had to keep going, or it would be just a plain case of running away in the face of the enemy.

At the Military Police station in Dieulourd, I made a direct telephone call to Division, which was flapping. "Hurry up. Hurry up. Tell us what is happening so we can take counter measures. There is no time to waste."

I grew calm. I gave Division the hour of the attack, that St. Genevieve was in German hands, that they had tanks and infantry, that the 2nd Battalion had been overrun, that the Germans had reached the flat and must have caused casualties among the 318th Infantry Regiment, that communications were in a bad way, that we had lost several tanks, and that Jerry seemed to be making his way toward the bridges.

The MPs gave me cigarettes and coffee. I walked a few yards, and Major Hayes came by in a jeep. I worried that he would think I had run away. I gave him the information about the attack, he gave me a breakfast C ration, told me I had done good work in getting word to him so fast under the conditions, and dashed away, I felt better. It had made sense to make a report. In Dieulourd, the engineers manned machine guns, and prepared charges to blow the spans if the Jerries reached them. On the other side of the bridges, the 313th Field Artillery was winning a distinguished unit citation by acting as infantry and fighting the Germans at close quarters in an effort to save their guns. Artillery General Sirby was killed at this time when he attempted to make a Mark IV button up, firing at it with an M1 rifle. To misquote, "*c'etait magnifique, mais ce n'etait pas la guerre.*"

In Dieulourd, I looked at a sign put up by the French, "Americans! You must kill all Germans! Take no prisoners. For eight days they have shelled us wildly. Take no prisoners! Kill all!"

The 4th Armoured attacked as planned, and their strength was overwhelming, driving the Jerries back, pushing on to the East and taking seven hundred prisoners. I watched some of these Nazis marched through Dieulourd, and they moved not a muscle while the French threw stones at them and ran along their column spitting in their faces. I met several soldiers of our battalion in Dieulourd, and from questioning them, I realized that they had run away in blind terror. My guilty feeling returned. I walked back across the bridge under mortar fire, stopping to take a helmet and an M1 from a dead American. The rifle had a girl's picture pasted on the butt.

On top of the hill, battalion headquarters was slowly gathering. I was ready to be accused of turning yellow, had my answers ready. Colonel Murray was gloomy because his battalion in their first big action had taken a beating. No one was quite certain of just what had gone on during the night, and all had dispersed shortly before I had started for the river. My jeep was covered in blood, but intact. How the blood got there, I never learned. We took up the same positions we had the night before.

And at midnight, it started again. Steady artillery and mortar fire and small arms. G Company was immediately overrun in St. Genevieve by tanks followed by infantry. Bullets were singing all around the C. P. and Jerry was on the hill again. Our 4th Armoured had pushed miles to the west, bypassing the groups of Germans that we now had on our hands. We had learned something. Instead of taking off, we set up a perimeter defense around the stone house. In the morning, Germans were within one hundred yards of us, but the tanks had remained in St. Genevieve. When they came out, we brought down artillery fire on our own F Company but also on the Jerry tanks. We had casualties, but the battalion held the ground, except for the village. Ten of the eighteen tank destroyers that had joined us were knocked out in a half hour. The fog was thick all morning, and we had no idea where the German infantry was except for their occasional bursts.

At noon the fog suddenly lifted. Murray gave me a direct order to guide a platoon of tanks that had arrived at the C. P. to F Company in the quarry. I almost dropped dead. It was an order. What could I do? I had to take them. The Company was seven hundred yards away, through ground covered by snipers, possibly German squads, mortar fire, in direct view from St. Genevieve and 88 antitank fire. I talked to the tank platoon commander and was consoled. He was more scared than I, if possible. He knew the tanks would draw all the fire Jerry could command. My mouth was dry and I was mad. Mad that I had come back to Europe instead of holing up in the States.

We waited after one hundred yards while three tank destroyer men who had lost their guns killed a sniper in some brush. I walked on, motioning to the tanks to continue, my hands in my pockets, rifle hanging on my shoulder, the sweat pouring off my face and soaking in to my collar—sweat from fear only, not physical exertion. I was glad the tanks were making so much noise, because then I couldn't hear the shots directed at us. I dropped behind a fold, the tanks stopping. In my sights, one hundred yards distant, was a black-shirted S.S. light machine gunner prone behind his gun. I fired three shots in to his body. I thought it strange he did not jerk when I hit him and that he was alone. Then I almost dropped dead from surprise that we all reached F Company alive.

Around the quarry were many bodies of Americans and Germans, swelling and smelling. In front of one of the platoons was the body of its commander, blown in half. And the men had to look at it. Jess Barton, the company commander, had removed the wedding ring from the mangled left hand to mail to its wife. There was no time for burial, no evacuation facilities, very little blood plasma. Many wounded bled to death or died from shock who would have been saved if they had reached medical aid.

Through the network of old trenches, I made my way back to the C. P., coming to the body of the S.S. man I had shot. I kicked at it, found it stiff. It had been dead at least twenty-four hours before I had ever seen it. In and around the trenches where their fathers and uncles had fought were dead Nazis in their thick, weird, camouflaged, hooded suits. Scattered among them were the Schutzstaffel boys, injected throughout the ranks to prevent desertion and increase the army's fighting qualities. The death's-heads on the collars of these janissaries looked vicious even in this extinction of life. Small arms fire increased as I slithered along the rocky, muddy trenches, and I took my time. I waited for a bit by the body of a dead Jap soldier in German uniform. Our intelligence stated that a few Japs were with the Germans, but this was the only one I saw. I thought he was a Mongolian, as many of them were fighting with Jerry, but his papers said he was Japanese.

At the C. P. vehicles were coming and going. A yard from the muddy road was a German who must have been very fat, and now he was puffed out to three times his size, like the dead French cattle which stay for days on their backs in the fields before disposal, their stiff legs pointing to the sky, legs like matchsticks in comparison to their bloated bodies, always reminding me of baby giants' discarded toy animals. Whenever vehicles passed the body of the German I watched with fascination, like being charmed by a snake's eyes. I wondered what would happen to the balloon body if a wheel ran over it, at the same time hoping that the wheels would continue to miss it.

That night, Major Warmbroad, battalion executive officer, and I sat up with Captain Jim Mullen and E Company. Under the faint moon, I shared a blanket with the wireless operator who had a strong body odor but was warm. It was a nervous strain while we waited for word that the third counter-attack had started. At 4 A.M. the barrage began, with the Germans in St. Genevieve. The shells wounded some of the men in their holes and lives were lost because we did not evacuate them in time. But the Nazi infantry did not come out of the village. With the dawn arrived the fog, which lasted until noon. Visibility was about thirty yards and the Germans could easily surprise us, and it would be hand to hand in the trenches. We had our grenades placed in front of us, rifles resting on the edge of the trenches. I took up a position with an American private from the Bronx, who had no idea why he was in Europe except that he was drafted, trained, and shipped over. We had both been without sleep for ninety hours, making us more nervous than the situation authorized. A few bullets were coming at us, but we knew Jerry could not see his target.

I said, "There's no use in asking for rubber bayonets, or chocolate bullets, or stick grenades that blow up and shower into beautiful dancing girls. But it isn't out of order to ask that it be warm, that my clothes were dry, that my socks were not small lakes, that the rain would stop for a bit, and we could get about five hours' sleep."

The shivering private grunted, rubbing his bare hands together and blowing on them, rain slowly dripping off the edge of his helmet, a maudlin character.

"Where would you rather be, here in this rain or back home in New York with your mother bringing you bacon and eggs?" I asked him.

He gave me a fierce look. "Are you nutz, man? You know where they can shove this war. Christ!"

"But New York's sidewalks are hard. See how nice and soft this mud is."

Then we both gave big grins, for some reason. Maybe because the situation was so ludicrous. And we both felt better. Especially when word came on my radio that we should keep our eyes open, that the 4th Armoured was returning from its fling to the East and would clear out St. Genevieve on the way back. With the village in Jerry hands, we could not supply the column and it had to return. In addition, it had received severe casualties. It was dawning on us, and the generals, that the Germans were going to fight, that this war was not over, that we would have to punch our way at a high cost all the way to the border, that the quick dash to Saarbrucken was off.

The private and I watched St. Genevieve cleared by our armor. He was killed ten days later.

That night I slept. Just dropped in the mud by Sergeant Charley Price and my S2 field telephone. There were a few shells over, but we could not be bothered. It didn't matter anymore.

We got off that hill the next morning, even if it was for another attack. But we got off the hill. That was something. I made a reconnaissance with Kinder for the Colonel of our objective, the bald pimple past Vil-au-Val which Jerry was using for artillery observation. We jumped off an hour late, without the tanks that were supposed to help us. Most of the men were not in the picture, many of them not even knowing the direction of the attack, the sort of thing which creates unnecessary widows and gold star mothers in the States. Murray sent me after the tanks with Major Warmbroad. Leading the tanks toward the objective, we were heavily shelled in a field, and machine guns and snipers opened on us. There was no protection. We hit the dirt, and the tanks moved on. Kinder, a soldier who had become lost from his platoon, and I rolled under a barbed wire fence, psychological protection only, while the machine guns zeroed in on us from a flank. I waited, hoping the bullets would give me just a Blighty wound. When the firing let up I pushed the feet of the man in front of me, telling him we were going to make a dash for it. He was dead. I yelled to Kinder to follow me and off we went. I couldn't find Major Warmbroad. Afterward I learned that he was in the field for an hour, while Germans pecked at him. He was returned to the States because of wounds.

Behind the battalion, Kinder and I saw many shell-shocked Americans, some being led by two men to the rear. One man I remember was foaming at the mouth and screaming, walking like a drunk. We knew this was an old trick—the two men getting a chance to get out of it while taking back a battle fatigue case. One soldier would have been sufficient to handle several crack-ups. When they reached rear headquarters, they helped the supply sergeant until we had time to go back and round them up for another skirmish. Some soldiers made a regular business of returning battle-fatigued men to a quiet location. It was often the same when we sent prisoners of war to the rear. The soldiers who delivered them to Regiment stayed there as long as possible. They had a fairly good excuse, and I can't say I blamed them. The amazing thing is that it didn't happen more often. At the front there was little we could do with the shell-shocked. We kept them a day or so to make certain they were not feigning and sent back the genuine cases. We worried about them no more. After they left us it was a problem for the hospitals and Government for the next generation.

Before I got to the foggy, bald top of the pimple, Kinder was hit in the leg, and I never saw him again. I had two men of my eight-man S2 section left. The artillery observation team of eight Germans, commanded by a sergeant with the Iron Cross won in Russia, stayed on our objective and purposely surrendered, an act I have never seen or heard of in the Allied Armies. They were the pus of the pimple. Murray told me to return to Regiment, three miles away, ask for tanks at dawn, take back the walking wounded and the prisoners. Two guards who could speak German accompanied me. The German sergeant suggested we carry Lieutenant Raymond of the mortars, badly wounded in the stomach and bleeding at the mouth. There was only one medical aid man with the battalion on the pimple and Raymond was bound to die if we didn't get him to a doctor. The Germans made a litter out of two of their raincoats, and our party started back. Halfway to Regiment, I sent the walking wounded on alone. It was getting dark, we were receiving some time-fire shells overhead, and making slow progress with Raymond. Two of the Germans wanted to drop Raymond, whining he was too heavy. I threatened to shoot them if they did not carry him, as they had offered.

In the last light, I thought we had passed no-man's-land, the pimple being inside the Germans jagged line. We wheeled right toward the road bordered by a deep ditch. We all struggled to get the moaning but still conscious Raymond across the ditch without lowering his head and prevent a gush of blood. As we reached the side of the road, one of the raincoats ripped, and Raymond dropped in the dark with a low, long sob. As this happened up walked a fifteen-man German combat patrol. I had turned too soon, missing our lines. I could make out the soft, peaked caps of the Nazis. The two guards and I remained silent. All was quiet. I could have heard my heart beat, but I believe it had stopped. I had my rifle pointed at the back of the Iron Cross sergeant, planned to fire twice if he gave us away, jump in the ditch and run.

The patrol leader asked what the party was all about. The sergeant answered, "We have a wounded American prisoner we are taking to our lines."

Satisfied, the patrol passed on, the guards telling me of the short conversation in German. It was too hot a spot for us, and I told the Germans to march on, as I didn't want the three of us, and our prisoners to bump another patrol.

Raymond must have heard me. In almost unintelligible words, he said, "Don't leave me. Don't leave me."

It tore my heart out, and besides we had worked this hard to get him almost to help, why not just a bit more? I ordered the Germans to lift Raymond. The sergeant ripped off his blouse, tied it to the raincoat, and we went straight down the road for two hundred yards until an American voice said, "Halt. Pass word."

"Hell, am I glad to hear you! Orange." I was jubilant. Never had I heard that nasal twang with more joy. I warned the American a

Jerry patrol was near. Relieved, we found a jeep going to Regiment, put Raymond on the hood, telling the occupants to keep his head up, get him to a station and he might live. I gave the Jerry sergeant a cigarette, which he shared with the seven prisoners, and the three of us smoked one in cupped hands. Through the two guards, the Jerries told me they were tired of war, wanted to be prisoners, that they could have escaped from us in the dark and when the combat patrol questioned them, that they would willingly go along with us to the stockade.

Chapter Sixteen

In the center of the small pimple was a basket and Jerry lobbed shells at us, and sooner or later he would land in the basket. That's where we had Battalion headquarters, and in it I dug one of the few fox holes of my life. At noon, I walked out of the basket to get my K rations. I was gone five minutes but during that time a shell scored, demolished my foxhole, killed four men of the battalion headquarters and wounded seven. Two of Hitler's own soldiers were killed, also. I had finished questioning them, but there was no opportunity to send them to a POW cage. They were young Luftwaffe boys, fighting on their feet, arrogant, sneering, and they had been Hitler Youths for nine years according to their papers. Our patrols had picked them up that morning. They had none of the thumbs-along-the-pants-seams discipline such as some of the German Army displayed while being interrogated. I looked at their bodies, limp like dead snakes, and my back crawled. I thought it small of myself to hate boys of seventeen, but it was the way they had acted during questioning.

At last light that day, we moved off the pimple in to the woods, digging in two hundred yards from the chinking of the working spades of Jerry. I slept in a last war trench with Sergeant Price under a blanket I had taken from a dead man. First thing in the morning, Jerry attacked the battalion in the woods, throwing mortars at us. We loathed being stonked in a woods, the tree bursts spreading accurately the deadly fragments. Shells that hit the ground were limited in killing area, and the soft mud was friendly in its absorption—the only good thing about the mud of France. Three mortar bursts alone killed thirty-two huddled and frightened replacements of G Company, bunched up due to inexperience. Those in action for the first time were scared by the Germans' yelling, "Hall-ow-ow-ow! Hall-ow-ow-ow, Ameri-kan! Hall-ow-ow-ow!"

It was eerie when Jerry called to us, and he always did. When he attacked, he gave queer screams and calls, a form of the Old South's "rebel yell." I don't know if it was to build his morale, but I do know it was successful in lowering ours.

Murray sent me back with a squad in the afternoon to the bald hill to recover lost radio equipment, weapons, and identify the dead. It was a horrible scene of crusty, black blood, smashed weapons, shell holes, foxholes, K rations, bodies, and equipment. Occasional snipers' bullets snapped at us from the wood, and when a machine gun opened, with a forced calm I suggested we leave, having accomplished our mission. Small mortars, embellished with crackling Schmeissers followed our route to battalion.

At twilight, back in the woods I was able to read six copies of the *Stars and Stripes* I had been carrying for a week. I couldn't smoke after dark, but during the intervals of sending and receiving battalion radio messages I thought of some of the dead boys I had seen on the pimple during the day. "Killed in action" the telegram will read, and he might have just been sitting there looking at the words on K ration food. But the telegram sounds like a gallant bayonet charge. It might have been his first day with us. The dead body means nothing to us, except maybe to take the wristwatch and wallet to send to the next of kin. You can't call on him anymore for a patrol or to draw rations. The person is not easily recognized by the dirt, whiskers, and drained face. You wonder if he means anything to people in America, and you suppose he does but that place is awfully far away. His family will probably think he was winning the war single-handed until he was killed.

I had forgotten just why we were fighting that first week after crossing the Moselle. I was conscious of abstract reasons somewhere in the back of my mind. There were reasons, I knew, why sitting up in the woods with the radio was necessary, but I hadn't even thought of Barbara more than twice that week. But I dimly realized it would all come back to me when I was clean and dry and had some hot food and a couple of blankets. The Presidential election, Anglo-American relations, my teeth, or any of the things one talks about just weren't in our world. The main thought was to fight to stay alive, but it wasn't as important to stay alive as you thought when you first joined the army. I thought about home, then, and that I hadn't had any mail since kissing Barbara goodbye, and I consoled myself by thinking I wouldn't have time to steal away and appreciate the delicious words from the land of make-believe anyway.

I thought about the twenty-three officers lost of the thirty-five who crossed the river with the battalion.

I wondered why America was sending us cooks, bakers, ack-ack, tank destroyer, quartermaster clerks, ASTP, and ordnance personnel for replacements—men who had three to six weeks infantry training and shoved up front. It seemed a shame, because they didn't last long with their brief training, and I wondered why we had miscalculated and not raised enough dogfaces in the first three years of war instead of frantically trying to make combat men in a hurry. A few of the replacements had never fired a BAR or rifle and here they were. It's surprising so few desert in the face of the Germans.

As usual when I started to think, orders came to move. "Advance through the woods clearing out the enemy." There is no place worse to fight than in a woods. Places as bad, but no worse.

Three days we fought in those woods, seventy-two hours of death, Kraut calls, one K ration a day, and hoping the Germans had no more idea of our location than we had of their whereabouts. We could literally smell where the enemy had slept and where he might be crouching. Those who have been around the Nazi know what I mean. It is a musty stench of sweat, rancid sausage, old damp leaves, sour bread, synthetic rubber, and stomach gas.

I was taking two sections of G Company which was without a company commander to consolidate near a surrounded German strong-point. Isolated Jerries were harassing us, and they were almost impossible to find in their green and brown camouflage suits. We had to expose ourselves to cross a narrow, dirt road. Feeling guilty, I went first with no hesitation. I remembered Hosington's advice to me in recruit days about his fighting in Calais. Going first looks brave, is safest, and an officer can't very well ask an NCO or private to give a trial run. Master-Sergeant Downes followed me, and he was across before a "paper-cutter" ripped at him. He made a dive for the large tree I was behind, a spot the Germans had used for a latrine. We thought it was neither disgusting nor funny, just taking it for granted. A buck-sergeant was third, receiving two holes through his field jacket. The Nazi gunner was getting the range. He was five yards away in a slit trench, and the bullets were going C-R-A-C-K, which means very close to old-timers.

Before we could hold the fourth man, he dashed and his leg nearly spun off in the air, but his momentum carried him across the road and we pulled him to comparative safety, applying a tourniquet. Downes, the buck-sergeant, and I set up our little defense near the latrine and fired at every bush. At twenty yards, Downes and I together hit a flushed Jerry who was probably as surprised, confused, and frightened as we. Bullets were cracking off twigs above our heads, and the main force sent a storm of lead at intervals in our direction. It was an extremely warm spot. A vehicle passed down the road and I fired on it three times before I recognized it as a German medical car. I doubt if I hit anyone.

A few hours after this the First Battalion entered the woods and we had virtual control.

Continuing along the axis of advance to the East, we started out of the woods with one night's sleep. I had reorganized my S2 section with five new men and two veterans. I was beginning to think that I might get through the war alive, having survived thus far. As the point-company emerged in to the open, I received a radio call from Murray, ordering me to take command of G Company immediately, at the Regimental combat team commander's suggestion. I realized a rifle company commander did not last long, so promptly changed my ideas about getting through the war alive. It was raining and foggy. G Company, with no original officers remaining, was scattered and in a high state of disorganization. Walking to its general location, I asked a bewhiskered GI where the men were and how many of them. In the meantime, machine guns and mortars were falling about the first part of the battalion leaving the woods.

"There's about fifty of us. Most of the men are new. Is this an attack we are in, sir?"

"What's your name? I'm the company commander now."

"Feig. Call me 'Charley.' That's good enough. I've been with this company a long time. Since Camp Forrest."

"Okay. You're my runner. Stick with me. Line up a couple more runners. Is there a first-sergeant?"

"No first-sergeant. Jimmy Frank has been acting as much. We've two lieutenants with us, but they have no platoons."

I talked to the lieutenants, Byddle and Cahill, gave them each twenty men, told them to move immediately and follow me, while Charley, a Mexican named Roy, a Jew called Sol, Frank, and a few others formed company headquarters.

"What's our weapon strength?" as we filed along the edge of the wood.

"They all have rifles and a few grenades. We've lost all our BARs and mortars. We have one light machine gun and one bazooka. About half the men have entrenching shovels. No medical aid men are with us."

At this time, General Horace McBride, Division commander, directing the advance from personal observation, startled me, saying, "What kind of a company is this? Get moving faster. You should be just leaving the wood. Hurry up."

"Yes, sir!" there was no time to explain that I had assumed command eight minutes before, that the company had been wiped out three times in twelve days, that the men had not received attack orders until eight minutes ago, that we were doing our best and would do better.

It was the sort of chaos I had heard about in war and which isn't generally explained in the newspapers where neat little maps with arrows satisfy the readers that all is well. The men could see the humor in the situation, and that helped no end.

By noon we had secured our objective, some more high ground that was once again "The last high ground before Germany." Digging in, the men uncovered the skeleton of a soldier of the last war. The trenches we were in formed the line as of November 11, 1918. The company took a few prisoners that day, and I had a paratrooper's Iron Cross for a souvenir. Several of the men picked up Lugars, P38s, and long jack-knives. One Nazi I interrogated was wearing a massive, ugly, silver death's-head ring. I asked him about it, through an interpreter.

"My mother gave it to me," he said.

"Tell him it's a hell of a looking thing for his mother to be giving him."

I knew it as an SS ring, removed it and gave it to a sergeant who had no booty and wanted it to post it to his little brother in Virginia.

Sending the prisoners back in those days meant giving direct orders to the guards not to shoot the Nazis after a walk of about six hundred yards. I said it was not a gentlemen's war in France. Who started it, I don't know. It might have been cold, wet, homesick Americans, confident the war was nearly won. Or it might have been Jerry who started it. Both sides were guilty. In our battalion I have seen the bodies of sixteen Germans who had surrendered and were shot in cold murder. I heard of other cases. It was foolish, and we received a direct oral order from Division, via General Sommers that the shooting of POWs must cease. Naturally the Germans would retaliate by slaughtering our men after we surrendered. It was not the best soldiers who shot German prisoners who had given up according to international agreements. Again, it was not the best soldiers who shot themselves, usually at dawn or shortly after dark when there was rumor of an impending attack. It was an old gag and happened in all the Divisions. A single shot would ring out, and the wounded man was invariably hit in the foot or hand. His excuse was that he was cleaning an enemy pistol and was unfamiliar with it, or he was cleaning his own weapon and didn't know a round was up the spout. Sometimes he claimed a sniper shot him, but afterwards the empty M1 cartridge was found near by. There was no way to prove the man had done it purposely, and we sent him back to the medical station and never heard from him again. The surprising thing is that it didn't happen more often. Most of the GIs were brave, disciplined, willing.

A popular fallacy that blew-up on the front was that the worst soldiers in garrison were the best in action. In a few outstanding cases this was true, but generally speaking, the "eight balls" in training were the same in the line, and those good in Stateside duty were dependable overseas.

The first week I had the company we slugged about in the mud with few casualties. I recommended the old-timers for the combat infantry badge and the ten dollars extra a month. Sergeant Frank and Sergeant Eichorn were put in for commissions-in-the-field. We had privates first class and corporals doing sergeants' jobs, because replacements were scarce, and we quickly promoted these men. Company strength was brought to one hundred and three, well below normal but a fighting force. We moved slowly and always bumped the droppings of Jerry. Empty champagne and cognac cases and bottles, the best liquor of France, helmets, blankets, mess tins, pocket stoves, their heavy and coarse bread, camouflage shelter halves, copper, shiny, black, snakelike machine-gun bullet belts which they carried around their necks like scarves providing the extra fire power of the Nazi infantry, neat weapon pits dug deeper and more elaborately than ours. They fought in their shirts, sleeves rolled up like a half-back's, and in flight they usually lost their coats which they had taken off when it looked like a scrap.

The big difference between us up there was in all the liquor they consumed.

Our army was well equipped in the beginning, but when we lost things, we had a difficult time replacing them. There were not enough small mortars, Browning automatic rifles, shovels, and bazookas reaching us. America was cutting down production and the First Army in the North was receiving priority, while people back home read that we had everything we wanted at the front.

Fresh second lieutenants joined the company. Mike Dankowitch was one of them. Mike was worried and willing about being at the front. Having recently left the harrowing replacement system, Mike was confused but eager.

"Mike, our first attack you will police up in the rear until you get the swing of things. Then you take over a platoon. When one of your men is hit, don't be gloomy and assume individual responsibility for it. MEN HAVE TO BE HIT. You'll never get used to all this, but you will overcome it very shortly. The War Department says that replacements don't go into action until they are with their unit for at least three days. That's not so. The men are sent up to us, and a couple of hours later they might be in a hot mix. Some are bound to panic. You stop this, so it won't spread.

"Don't go first on patrols until you know what you are doing. Don't lead the leading squad in an attack to prove to the men you are brave. They will find this out later, when you are sure of yourself you can take all the risks you want. The replacements coming up now are hastily trained. Pick old-timers for the hot jobs. We're all terrified up here. You never get over that, but when things start, you feel better and gain confidence. Pretend to yourself you are calm, and you will grow calm. Keep thinking about the men, not yourself. You'll be all right."

One never knew if he said the right thing to replacement officers. But Mike was the only officer at that time to stay with the company until VE Day.

Major Hayes left Regiment, replaced Colonel Murray as our battalion commanding officer. The first day with us he got us our first hot meal since crossing the Moselle—and it was steak. From then on we had hot chow at least once a day. He supplied V-Mail forms, and many of the men sent word home for the first time in three weeks. As they wrote, rain dripped from their hands and helmet rims on to the paper, smearing the ink in light blue splotches. At the front, they underplayed the danger in letters. It was impossible to exaggerate. I remembered how I had unconsciously overstated the hazards of 1942 nuisance air raids in England in writing to Barbara. But I had learned war that September in the rain. Hayes also immediately secured dry blankets, more ammunition, new field jackets and boots, raincoats, socks, and barbers. Life was almost pleasant, until "Moivron, bloody Moivron," as we called it.

A rainy, bleak, solemn, dawn, austerely lightened the broken rim of hills and the battalion trudged slowly through the villages, being given sour as well as cheerful looks from the mixed populace of Loraine. The shapes of trees were black and strongly drawn, and the birds were beginning their cries and tiny trills. Another morning, and I wondered why is it that the calls of birds sound sad. Moivron looked too quiet. Our artillery opened for twenty minutes, plastering the town. Supporting tanks had not appeared. We were not close enough following the barrage, and Jerry had fifteen minutes to recover before we attacked. As we neared the railroad tracks one hundred yards from a disemboweled grave-yard on the edge of the village, all hell broke loose. Machine guns, rifles, machine pistols, 88', and mortars. Cahill's Number Two platoon killed five, captured two first thing in a beet patch, but from then on it was all Jerry, Moivron was supposedly lightly held, and we were to clear it in a half-hour and push on toward Mt. Toulon from the rear. Pinned down by the fire, we were perfect targets for the accurate snipers' fire. Never had I seen the Germans snipe like that. We were up against crack paratroopers, which we hadn't learned in our pre-battle intelligence reports. Medics were few and overworked. All we could do was let the wounded howl for the time being. Steaming bullets slapped in to steaming bellies, and as each man was hit, blue smoke poured from his clothes as though he were on fire, and he would drop his rifle, hold his wound with both hands, and scream like a child stung by a bee. From the graveyard, the Germans waved a white flag, and we yelled at them to come out with their hands up, revealing more of our positions which were promptly sniped. The pitiful, shrill cry of "Medic," the worst sound in war, was blending with the snap of bullets. We would tell the wounded everything was okay, that a medic would be along soon, gently patting him, at the same time comforting ourselves. We called them "Doc," and one good calm aidman did more for our morale than two Shermans. They carried no sidearms and that touch alone was enough to remind us of a life we had known and wanted again. Few of us liked going around like little arsenals of democracy.

Through all this the rain continued steadily, but we didn't notice it. Twice more German white flags appeared and we held our fire, giving the enemy a free chance to change his positions and open from newer and deadlier angles.

About noon I grew careless about sniper and mortar fire. The men took my casual wandering about for bravery. It was only because I was so tired I could not expend the energy safety requires. Nine times I ran over the railroad tracks, flinging myself in a ditch filled with mud and water, trying to organize the platoons, calmly wondering if I would shriek like the others if I were hit. I crawled two hundred yards up the ditch, water covering two-thirds of my body to contact Captain Miller and F Company. As I reached him, his radio operator was handing him the walkie-talkie. As Miller grasped it, his radio operator slumped when a bullet caught him squarely in the head.

Miller merely said, "Jesus! Somebody must be close to us." The dead operator was almost restful to look at, lying there in another world. The bayonets on our rifles mocked us. We didn't have a chance of getting in close.

Charley Feig, always with me, said, "This Moivron is one spot where the goldbrickers are out of luck. There just isn't any safe place anywhere for them to take it easy."

Hayes gave me two tank destroyers that had arrived, and with Jimmy Frank I was able to direct fire on two houses holding up Cahill's platoon. Three tanks arrived, and Hayes committed them with Lieutenant Moye's E Company, held in reserve. Over the tracks they went, the men foolishly bunched up behind the tanks while the Germans dropped mortars with rifle-like accuracy on the foot soldiers. One squad under mortar fire and surprised by a concealed machine-gun froze on the ground instead of moving to cover despite casualties. Jerry methodically eliminated each man.

I reorganized the company, gathering twenty-eight men. Moye with tears in his eyes had run back for more help from Hayes.

Hayes clapped me on the back, saying, "Ellsworth, go take that town!"

"Okay, G Company. Let's go. All twenty-eight of us." I went over the railroad track first, remembering Hosington. Through mortar and machine-gun fire right straight in to the middle of the village where three of our tanks had set up shop. My carbine was almost useless from the wet. I asked Cahill where his rifle was and he said he had to throw it away, that he could hold nothing in his arms, that a shell had done something to him, though he hadn't been hit. "You mean you came up here with us when you knew you couldn't fight?"

"Yes."

He could have gone back to the aid station, but he preferred to come unarmed just to be around.

The presence of tanks kept the machine guns silent, but snipers were pecking at us. A message arrived to hold tight, a battalion of armored infantry was going to help us, to remain in Moivron. E Company was down by the graveyard, and F still pinned along the tracks. I walked around the fifty yards square park we were in, a silly thing to do, but it bucked up the men, and I didn't get hit. Finally I got under one of the tanks with Lieutenant Walker of E Company and his runner. It wasn't much better. The runner was hit in the scrotum, the only time in the war I saw that happen. He was stoical about it. Then, without warning, the tank backed away, twisted on its tracks just as it passed us, and the armor left the village. It was so sudden; we were not frightened, though we could have been smashed. As the brutes ambled away, machine guns from all sides crackled in to the park. I ran for a slit trench with Frank. We stayed there five minutes.

"This armored infantry should be along soon."

"I guess so. But do you know, sir, we are the only ones left here? Just us of G Company. See past the tracks there."

I looked up from the low slit trench. The remnants of E and F were making haste out.

"Well, twenty of us aren't much good here." I called out that groups of four men should make for the hedgerows and get through the culvert under the tracks. Frank and I were the last two to leave. We didn't run much. We were too worn out. A tracer flicked through my flapping raincoat and I laughed.

We picked up one of our wounded and helped him through a small creek under a culvert.

"Am I bleeding much?" he asked.

"No. Just a little bit. Nothing at all." I could see the muddy water turning bright red as we eased him across. As we came out of the culvert, a streak of machine-gun bullets went through it, ricocheting off the sides. The battalion was in full flight a half mile from us. Major Hayes was waiting for me near the tracks."

"Ellsworth, I don't know why the tanks left. Tell the men they were not whipped today, but that they just had too much for us in Moivron. Let me know about your casualties. Go back to the assembly area and dig in." I gathered thirty-one of the one hundred and six who had jumped off with the company. The rest were killed and wounded, including five of my officers.

That night I thought of the bravery, the countless dead lying about, the soldiers killed I knew, the sound of mortars, the mistakes, the few chicken-hearted men, the smoke, the excitement, and the whole messy thing. The next day information reached us that eight hundred well-placed Jerries had fought our force of four hundred, most of whom we lost in the first ten minutes.

Chapter Seventeen

"Charley, you and Jim just write bravery stories today. Go around and interview the men. See what they've done. A lot of them have been very good in action, and it seems Patton wants more medals handed out in his army, according to headquarters. You know, bronze and silver stars and so on."

A very fine soldier, Jim Krohn, from Saginau, Michigan, said, "What are they doing? Chucking those things out and about now?"

"The General probably thinks it's good for morale, and it probably is."

I had heard a lot about Patton in the rear echelons. He was popular, no doubt about it. But at the front, I rarely heard his name mentioned. We had never had much chance to see the headlines the Third Army was making and didn't realize America's admiration for the General. Therefore, there was no beating of the chests about being in Patton's Gang by the men who were doing the actual fighting. And in any case, up to full colonel was about as high as the combat officers' minds worked, while the men were conscious of officers up to the rank of captain.

He achieved results and that's what we wanted. He pushed us

until we were so tired we didn't much care what happened. Not as cautious as Monty, Patton did not husband man-power and was willing to make sacrifices to hasten victory. All soldier, Patton thought of us as machines and not as men with families. That is war. Patton was very flashy in his dress, such as the pearl-handled pistols, while Monty had a studied sloppiness and carelessness in his clothing. Both showmen, both successful in their own way, both colorful, Monty was deeply religious and very friendly, while Patton was profane and a martinet. Monty's words to his soldiers were usually understatements while Patton's were overstatements.

The Englishman might say, "One or two Boche were bothering us a bit." And the American would say of the same situation, "Thousands and thousands of the enemy were flung in to the battle."

After Moivron, the battalion was taken out for a rest. That is, all except G Company. We filled in a gap between the 1st and 3rd Battalions, were under very light shell fire, a temporary minefield and booby traps which I had placed with the engineers was to our front, and we were concealed by trees. Looking across the big valley, we could see the Nazi-held village of Sivry at the base of the German strongpoint, Mt. Toulon. At night we heard Germans talking and singing in Sivry, while their heavily loaded horse-drawn vehicles moved in and out. In that position, I received my only mail in France, three *Newsweek* "Battle Babies," though I knew Barbara was writing four times a week. One hundred forty-six replacements joined our company there, including Lieutenant Douglas Cole, Syracuse, New York, and first-sergeant Humphrey. The men were not completely trained, having been converted to infantry from other branches of the service six weeks prior to arriving at the front. This did not bother me as we had been promised baths the next day and a week's training program ten miles behind the lines.

The day following the arrival of the replacements, Sunday, October 1, 1944, Sergeant Humphrey called me to the phone. It was Jim Hayes.

"You are to take Sivry by eight o'clock tomorrow morning. I'm not sending in one of the companies which have been resting because you know the terrain. We'll relieve you twenty-four hours after taking your objective. I leave the entire plan to you. Come back to Regiment and arrange for artillery support. I will meet you there. Miller is on his way up to replace your company in the gap. There's about one German company down there. I've tried to get white phosphorous shells for you to burn the village, but it seems the Germans claim these are illegal and the General has ordered us not to use them for awhile. Machine-guns and the 81mm mortars from H Company will be under your command. Any questions?"

"No, Jim. The men will probably question me if Sivry is where those promised baths are, however. I'll see you back at Regiment. I'll make a reconnaissance first. We're short on 60 mm mortars and BARs. Could we borrow some from F?"

"I'll fix that. I'll also send the chaplain up right away to give the men a service. Incidentally, six of your men are wanted by the Inspector General for testifying in the shooting of German prisoners back there along the Moselle. The Jerries lodged a complaint. I've put the I. G. off for a while until this attack is over. You'll need all your men."

"Right, Jim. In regard to the particular shooting they are talking about, the two men responsible in the company are no longer with us. One wounded, the other killed."

At Regiment, I arranged with Lieutenant Colonel Ellery for artillery. The American Army had shot eight million artillery and mortar shells in September. The AEF in the entire World War I had used only ten million shells. We had to conserve because ammunition was running low in France, but Ellery promised me a fair quote.

I pulled the company back two hundred yards to an assembly area and called together the platoon commanders and sergeants. With the only map available in the company due to a shortage, I went over the plan, first in a field order, then in detail, followed by questions and synchronizing watches.

"The Jerries hold this Sivry in strength. I imagine their C. P. is near the church you can see from our position. The center of town. On the edge of the town is the crossroads. There will be a lot of automatic stuff there, and it should be quite a hair-pulling contest at that spot. Our company is to take the town by early tomorrow morning through the embarrassments of street fighting. We attack from the right, the East, at 5 A.M. following a ten-minute barrage and intermittent fire during the night. We must be close, and go in as soon as the barrage lifts. Remember Moivron when we weren't near the village when the artillery stopped. Surprise is essential. It will be getting light as we hit the village, but we can get there undetected if you will keep the men quiet. No talking and rattling of equipment.

"Lieutenant Cole's Number One platoon and Lieutenant Mike's Number Three will go in on a two platoon front, Cole on the far right. Number Three will go in from the South, creating a diversion. Number Three platoon, don't attack until you see our red flare. Number Four is in reserve. Heavy machine guns and mortars stop with Number Four and set up fast in the village for a counterattack from the North. I'll be with Mike's platoon. Sergeant

Anderson is clearing a path for us through the mines in front and will guide us through. If we bump outposts, kill them so they don't warn Jerry and try to do it with as little noise as possible. Remember, surprise is important.

"Make sure every man in your platoon is in the picture. None of this stuff of not knowing what our mission and plan is. We've got plenty of time. Each man must have four grenades. They will be handy in this street fighting.

"Don't let the men get the idea that they have to hold their fire until they see a Jerry. In an infantry company there are about twelve dependable killers. The rest will fire only when they have to. Once we attack, make as much hullabaloo as possible. Have them toss lead all over hell whether they spot anything or not. Keep an old-timer at the back of your platoons. These men are new and will have to be pushed, maybe. Though they seem like a good lot.

"Remember, we leave here at 03:50 hours. That will give us plenty of time to cover the mile. The moon will be down then. We'll be well in front of our own lines, right under Jerry's. So consolidate in a hurry. Don't think it's all over and breathe a sigh of relief once we get the place. Jerry's best weapon is his well-executed counter-attack. This will be a hole in his line, and he is first-class at puttying-up holes.

"Tell the men we'll get those baths when this is over. Have everybody get sleep as soon as you pass out the ammo and information. Don't forget K rations. We'll be cut off there for awhile and will want to eat. Our total force will be two hundred thirty-five men.

Another half-hour of thinking over every last detail, and then I forgot about things, lying in Captain Talcott's pup-tent, telling him about the trip to Alaska I made in 1939. I realized he was tired and wanted sleep, but he knew I wanted to talk, and he listened. He was to support our assault with his always-dependable artillery.

Sergeant Humphrey got the company on its feet at 03:40 and we moved off, silently, almost too sleepy at first, which was a good thing. By the end of the minefield each man was wide awake. Few were really frightened, because they all felt it was the other man who would die, not he. A house in Sivry was burning, and we used it as a guide in the still black night, the only noise being sergeants continually whispering one word, "Silence." Near the first road we had to cross, I cut three wires which might have been Jerry listening posts. It was there I sent Number Two platoon off to the left. They were to attack at our flare. I walked one hundred yards with the platoon commander to make sure he was all right and knew the plan.

Over the radio, I asked for an eight-minute delay in the barrage as it had taken us too long to get through the mines. I was between the two assaulting platoons with Krohn, Humphrey, artillery observer Bobby Gorenson of Illinois, and Shorty Blodgett, an older man whose brother had recently been killed. I saw a dark form disappear in to the ground like a mole one hundred-fifty yards from the edge of Sivry.

"Are you American?" I whispered at twelve yards.

"Nein! Nein!"

I fired my carbine three times at the hole. Humphrey tossed a grenade that rolled short, and we all got flat waiting for it to explode. The German fired his machine pistol. Blodgett rushed the hole, and the German was dead. And the barrage opened, ten minutes of death, light, thunder. I watched the minutes go by on my luminous dial. On ten, I gave Mike and Cole the go-ahead on the walkie-talkie, and in they went, yelling and firing. I sent the flare for Number Two platoon. Our initial momentum carried us nearly to the church, where I placed company C. P. in a garden by a wall next to the street. Mike's platoon was advancing thirty yards ahead of the C. P. with Sergeant Atkin of Arkansas doing most of the fighting—going wild his first day in action. We had bayonets fixed to bolster our morale.

Krohn reported two Germans in the street near the wall. I ordered a replacement who had attached himself to us in the confusion to guard the garden gate.

"I can't. I have a bad heart. I'm not even supposed to be overseas. It's my heart, the doctors said."

"If you don't guard that gate goddamn right away you won't have to worry about your heart much longer. None of us will have any worries." He watched the gate and was killed later in the day.

I peeked over the garden, saw the two Germans, and threw a grenade. Humphrey peeked over, gave me directions on two more Jerries behind a wall across the narrow street, pulled the pin for me, and I lobbed it. Humphrey said it was short.

Shorty looked over the wall, said in a whisper to me, "There's one just on the other side of the wall, only a couple of yards from us."

"Shoot him, Shorty."

Shorty took another look. "He's got a grenade in his hand and he's looking for you."

"Shoot him!"

Shorty bobbed up again. "I've got him right in my sights. He's about five yards away now."

"Shorty, pull that trigger!" I was almost hysterical with Shorty anticipating the kill.

Shorty fired once. There was no yell or moan, and we couldn't hear the body flop in the mud.

"Did you get him, Shorty?"

"Right through the neck. He sure wanted to find some place to throw that stick grenade."

The firing increased in front of us, and streaking back down the road came Mike and his platoon. "They've got too much for us up there. They are organized now. If I'd had some mortars we could have taken this place," Mike yelled to me. The mortars were with Cole as that is where we expected the heaviest resistance.

There was nothing between the German company and us. I took off after Mike. "Mike! Stop your men! We aren't licked. Get them by the creek down there and reorganize."

At the creek, Sergeant Atkin said, "We saw nothing of Number Two platoon. They were supposed to come in just where the Jerries are now. If they'd have gotten there, it would have been a cinch."

Mike had lost one-third of his platoon, which might not have happened if Number Two had assaulted on time. I learned later from Major Hayes that the commander had taken off, left his new men in a ditch where they remained for nine hours, their first time in action. The platoon commander was killed that day by a mortar shell in the valley where he was hiding. This is the only case I know of in the war where an officer left his men in the face of the enemy.

Charley Feig came out of the North end of the village to the creek. "Lieutenant Cole has a good toe-hold in there. No opposition. We've taken a few prisoners. He wants orders."

"Let's go, Mike. Let's get this village so we can get those baths."

We entered on Cole's position, and Mike led his platoon from house to house up the main street. I put Number Four under his command. The impetus of the advance was Sergeant Atkin. He climbed on roofs, fired bazookas through windows, caught three prisoners, sniped, directed mortar fire, tossed hand grenades in cellars, while the Germans around the church graveyard shouted at us and each other.

I got hold of Atkin and said, "Sergeant, you'd better slow down a bit. You're doing fine, but I'm afraid you'll get hit one of these times."

"Lieutenant, I'm either coming in or going out," he said in his Arkansas drawl with a big smile.

When Jerry reinforcements trickled in from Mt. Toulon, we called for artillery on their route, the 313th F. A. and our own Cannon Company giving immediate and accurate support. We pumped 81mm mortars in to the church and graveyard. As we advanced, we alternated leading squads so that no one had too much of the fight, except Atkin, who was always up there.

At 16:00 hours came my great moment of the war. A German medic came down the street with a white flag shouting in a tinny voice, "Kamerad! Kamerad!" The remaining force wanted to surrender. Krohn, a medic named Murphy, an H Company machine-gun sergeant who could speak German, and I went to the church. Besides the medic, there was only one other German who was not already in our hands, or wounded, or killed. The German officer in command of the town had head wounds. I had a short talk with him.

"How many men were holding this village?"

"Ninety-eight."

"How many reinforcements did you get?"

"About eighteen."

"Did our attack surprise you?"

"Yes. We expected you to attack in three more days. We didn't know you were here until the barrage started and you fired small arms on the edge of the village."

"Did you know we were up in the woods the last week?"

"We could see movement up there. May I have a cigarette?"

"No. Not yet."

"Is this village important to you?"

"Our orders were to hold it at all costs, to the last man. But only two were able to fight when we gave up. Reinforcements were coming down tonight."

"Why is this village so important to you?"

"It is obvious. From it you can attack Toulon and gain the high ground. With you Americans in Sivry, it is a break in to our lines. May I smoke now?"

"No. Not yet. How do you feel about being a prisoner?"

"I am glad the war is over for me now that I am prisoner. But if I had been captured one day later I would have received my promotion. Will we go to America?"

"What do you think of the American Army?"

"Your infantry is not good. We have better weapons. You Americans do not know war. You are very brave, but we kill too many of you. We do not like your air force and artillery. If we had half of your air force and artillery you would not be in France."

"Who is going to win the war?"

"Germany will win by Christmas. We have a secret weapon."

"How many Germans are on Toulon?"

"I don't know. May I smoke now?"

"No."

At this point, Jim and Atkin came to me. "The wounded in

Number Three platoon we left when we were booted out this morning are all dead. Neat round bullet holes in the backs of their heads. Their helmets are lying by their sides. They were shot. Murdered after they were wounded. Let's shoot all these bastards!"

I took the German officer wearing the Iron Cross earned in Russia, to the bodies of our four men. He admitted they had shot them, but that it was drunken Mt. Toulon replacements who had done it. He said members of his original company did not do it, and he did not know their names. I made a full report on the wireless to Major Hayes after I sent the walking-wounded prisoners to battalion.

Somebody found Number Two platoon at the spot they were supposed to create the diversion, and I spread them among the other three platoons to replace casualties. We collected all our wounded and the German wounded and put them in a barn to await evacuation in litter jeeps. I asked for ammunition from battalion, and we sat up our defense of the village. Two French boys were fighting in my company, and we supplied them with everything but pay. They had been a great help to us. One was killed instantly in the fight, and I gave the other a drink of sparkling burgundy just before he died of wounds on a bed in a battered house an hour after the surrender. Krohn had found the burgundy in the German C. P. and when the Frenchman died, he and I drank it.

We destroyed the German machine-guns and burp pistols. The town was a mess. Dead and wounded chickens, dogs, cows, horses, and suckling pigs were in the streets. We had no chance to move the dead Americans and Germans because of mortar fire from Toulon, the hill that had figured in the world's battles for fifteen hundred years. The graveyard was torn up, revealing twisted, shattered, wooden coffins. In the church were dead Nazis and French civilians piled around the altar in a sickening, sweet stench. We connected four German telephones among the three platoons and my C. P. There was no relaxing in victory because Jerry was looking down our throat. Gorenson and Lieutenant Haverland, the artillery forward observers, plotted artillery concentrations for the night. Only three French had remained in the town, and they were very happy that Americans had arrived—until I put them in custody.

For his action in Sivry, higher headquarters recommended Sergeant Atkin for the Congressional Medal of Honor.

Our Command Post was a reinforced cellar under a blown-out three-story house, the same one used by the Nazi commander as a German C. P. during World War I. Twelve yards long and five yards wide, it contained mattresses, tables, chairs, one bed, an oil lamp, an alarm clock, two dozen loaves of black bread, and broken bottles. At the back was a door leading to steps in to the house, and the front door was seven steps below street level. One barred window was near the ceiling and looked on the sidewalk. Near the front door was a shallow cesspool covered by a barrel.

At 02:00 hours, the second day in Sivry, our patrols detected enemy activity. I thought it might be the counter-attack. I asked Gorenson for artillery. He gave the concentration over the radio and we listened to our shells whistle over. We hoped we were breaking up their attack before it started."

"Do you want any more?" he asked me.

"Yes."

"Send over some more ice. Same thing."

"On the way," the radio sputtered.

There was no more trouble that long night. At first light, Shorty came in, looked at me with serious, tired, woeful eyes, said, "Counter-attack."

"Where from, Shorty?"

"North. Seventy yards from Lieutenant Cole."

"Take another look, and let me know. We'll shift some help down there if you need it." Fifteen minutes before dawn we had received a concentrated shelling, and that usually preceded a good Jerry thrust.

We waited ten minutes. I met Shorty in the street. He said, "Wrong dope. No counter-attack. They were cabbage heads and the light was bad and they looked like Germans. There was a patrol, though. We got one prisoner."

"I hope all the counter-attacks are like that, Shorty. Send the prisoner up here."

We were out of food, and K rations reached us from carrying parties to give each man only one meal. Though it was against the policy of the American Army to live off the land, I gave orders to kill any live stock such as pigs and chickens that might be around and supplement the K ration. Under the intermittent German mortar fire, the company lost no time on those orders and had more fun than at a Tennessee barbecue. A wire team laid a direct telephone line from Major Hayes to my C. P., and we fed them roast pork.

Hayes phoned me, "How are you doing down there?"

"Okay. We've sent the 81mm mortar platoon back to you as per orders. That leaves us with one hundred twenty-five men of the two hundred thirty-five who came in. The rest are wounded and killed. We'd like to get the wounded out of here. At least the Americans. The Jerries, too, if possible."

"Nine jeeps are coming down to you with food, blankets, grenades, and that BAR firing pin you asked for. Send the wounded back on the jeeps. I can't relieve you as I said. We're afraid of an off-tackle play up here. Can you hold them?"

"We're spread pretty thin, Jim, for the size of the village and the number of men. We can hold off a platoon but more than that and the Jerries will get in the village, which will neutralize it. But we'll fight. The men will be disappointed on no relief, but what the hell."

"You fought hard enough to take Sivry. Don't lose it."

"I'll tell the men that."

At dark the jeeps arrived, we sent back the wounded, a few of whom had died in the garage. On my inspection of positions before dark I found two men shaking like puppets. They were not scared but had let their imagination work too much. I sent them with the jeeps. When Murphy left with the wounded it meant we had only one medic in the village, Richards. We should have had at least five.

Jim Monaghan replaced Gorenson as cannon company observer, and his radioman went out with Krohn and me to repair a telephone wire that mortar fire had smashed. When I returned to the C. P., Kennedy and Rittenhouse were there with two big, smelly, sobbing prisoners crying, "Don't shoot. Don't shoot."

"Tell these guys they won't be shot. Tell them Americans treat their prisoners well," adding "most of the time" under my breath.

Rittenhouse said, "They were told Americans shoot their prisoners. We got them infiltrating in the East end. There seems to be more Jerries out there, and I think they are setting up machine-gun positions about two hundred yards from the edge of town. We can't see much by the moon."

"Can I have this guy's watch, sir? I caught him," Kennedy added.

"No watch-taking in Sivry, tonight, Kennedy."

"Yes, sir."

"Sergeant Humphrey, you, Charley, and Jim get word to each man in the company that Jerries are setting up machine guns around us. Tell them we expect an attack, and no man, no matter how tired he is, sleeps in those blankets tonight. Tell them I will try to get another company down here to help us, but not to count on it. That we probably will have to fight it out alone. Tell them to hold their fire until they are sure what they are shooting at. No trigger-happy business or revealing their positions. Jerry knows enough about us in this town as it is."

Chapter Eighteen

"I have given myself up because I am tired of it all. I have been fighting for five years. That is why I came to Sivry."

"And you were at the battalion staff meeting when the plan was made to attack this village?"

"Yes."

"What is the plan?"

"I do not know it all. You will receive a very severe shelling early in the morning. The troops are young and fanatical. They are going to officers school near Metz and have been brought especially to recapture this village."

"How many will attack us?"

"About two hundred. They will have thirty machine guns and other automatic weapons. They are now on Mt. Toulon resting. Your defenses cannot hold out. Now will you take me to your lines? I must get out of here or I will be shot when our troops take the village."

"They aren't going to take this village," Jim Monaghan said.

"You have no chance, I am afraid. They are determined to get this village."

"The hell with that. Charley, get me Major Hayes on the phone."

"Jim, we're going to have a fight tonight. It might be smart to get another company down here. I've got a Jerry prisoner in the C. P. who has given me all the information. He was at the German command meeting tonight and then came down here to surrender as he has had the war. They will outnumber us in men and firepower. We've got one light machine gun, two heavies, and one BAR. The Jerries will have thirty machine guns and a lot of these burp affairs."

"Send the prisoner back here. Let me talk to him, and I'll get Regiment to see if I can send you help."

Lieutenant George Herr, 313th F. A. forward observer from Lancaster, Pennsylvania, arrived in the C. P., having laid a direct wire from his guns, and replace Haverland. I plot concentrations with him, explaining where we expect the Jerry attack, and tell him to get some rest until the fight opens. I see that he doubts me, thinks I am exaggerating our predicament, but is willing to play along. Clean clothes, shaven, fresh, he looks out of place in the grime of the C. P.

The phone rings. It is Hayes. "There will be no help coming down. Colonel Ellery has given you all his guns. That means you have fifty-two of them with Cannon Company."

"Okay, Jim. We won't get the company together in a central strongpoint, or it would be a cinch for Jerry to get in the town. I'm leaving the South end wide open with a few guards only. He probably won't attack from there. That will give us more men for defense on the other three sides. If they aren't too strong, we'll hold them. The men will fight though they've had no sleep for three nights. I'll keep in touch with you."

"Good luck."

At 02:30 hours I double the guard around the C. P. and we get the grenades out of the boxes. We have sent back the English-speaking

German to Regiment. Two other prisoners are huddled in a corner eating a K ration we have given them. They are relieved they will not be murdered. One wants to go to the toilet, and we let him, even furnishing the K ration toilet paper.

Feig and I have giggles for a minute, because the situation is ridiculous and fantastic, and we are very tired. We are from the mid-West and never thought we would be in a cellar in Lorraine looking like tramps waiting for two hundred men to arrive to try to kill us. I make a quick tour to Mike's and Cole's platoons, and the men are alert, but they don't like the waiting.

Mike phones me in the C. P. "We think we see some movement out in front of us. Is it the attack?"

"It might be, Mike. Keep your eyes open. They might be sneaking up. They sure as hell won't come in playing the 'Stars and Stripes Forever.' I think they'll come in your side of the village first. Do you want some artillery in your concentration?"

"Yes."

I ask Monaghan for some shells, and he gets the ice on the way.

"How was that, Mike?"

"Just right."

We hang up.

At 03:00 hours, the heaviest concentrated barrage any of us have experienced begins and the dugout and ground shakes.

I say immediately to Monaghan and Herr to open all the guns. But Herr's radio and telephone wire are knocked out. Monaghan has contact with Cannon Company and four of our guns fire. Cannon Company relays the message to the 313th, but this takes time. I ring and ring for Hayes on battalion line, but that is gone, too.

The barrage lasts twenty minutes, and stops. Mike phones.

"They are all around us. They are coming right through us. What shall I do?"

"Stay there and fight, and if you have to retreat, come down by the church across from the C. P. and set up there."

"Okay. We'll stay here as long as we can. There's a hell of a lot of them." He hangs up.

Private First Class Brown, commanding twenty men on the North edge phones. "We got two in a tower in the courtyard here. But there don't seem to be any more about. We lost a few in that shelling. It was a son-of-a-bitch, that shelling."

"Keep watching, Brown. They are coming through Mike now."

"Yes, sir."

Outside our C. P. our men are throwing grenades from the cellar steps. Machine pistols are firing in to the top three stories and raking the empty streets. We hear Jerry shouting. One soldier who was waiting to be evacuated with hemorrhoids has forgotten all his ailments and is doing great work with the grenades. "I just cut one in half with a grenade. Give me some more," he says.

Sixteen of us are in and around the C. P., four of them neurosis cases that we were unable to evacuate. The two Germans are cringing in the corner, but we don't notice them. I give messages to Monaghan to pass on to Cannon Company who will contact Major Hayes.

It goes on for two more hours, and at 05:30, Germans are well spread in the village. The phone to Cole is out. I pull all our Command Post in to the cellar and say, "We don't control the village. That English-speaking Jerry gave us the right information. There's about two hundred of them, and they are well armed. We have four grenades left in the C. P. here. I will keep trying to get help down here through Cannon Company. One grenade or Jerry bazooka round in this rattrap will finish us all. But we might get help, and if we do, this will be a strongpoint where we can fight. They haven't kicked us out of the village, but this is not a nice spot to be in, and with no ammunition, we can't do much fighting until help gets here.

"I myself am not going to surrender. We can't pull out. Our orders were to stay in the village.

"But if any of you men want to surrender, you have my permission. But you must do it right away, before it gets light."

I walk to the cellar steps and look out. It is dark and the burp guns are sporadically firing from houses where the Germans have located themselves. I hear Jerry talking and he doesn't sound drunk. Behind me are whispers of my C. P., and Sergeant Humphrey comes up. "The boys have decided to stay here with you and no surrendering. We'll sweat it out."

I go to George Herr. "What about you? How do you feel? Got any ideas?"

"Whatever you say goes."

Hayes sends a message through Monaghan's radio. No help will be coming to us. They can't spare a company from the main line of resistance. I tell Humphrey to barricade the front door so no German will walk in and surprise us. He quietly moves mattresses, tables, chairs, a barrel, and blankets. We have put out the oil lamp. It is dark. His job finished, Humphrey stumbles in to the cesspool where the barrel was and lets out a stream of swearing.

"Quiet, Sergeant!" I whisper, and Humphrey climbs out in the dark, and I can hear Charley laughing next to me. I distribute our last K rations, cautioning the men to open them quietly as Jerry is in the two houses next to us, and we can hear his hobnails stomping on the sidewalk. From Cole's position in the east end are the sounds of fighting. Jerry has control of three-quarters of the village, and our C. P. is in the center of Jerry's portion.

Brown phones, and the ring sounds like a free-for-all on a tin roof. "They know where we are in this house. Ten of us. They are trying to knock us out with grenades and everything. I think we can hold them."

"Is there any talk of surrender?"

"No."

"Don't surrender. Mike's platoon is washed up."

"Any news of help from battalion?"

"Not yet."

"Yes, sir," and Brown quietly hangs up. Brown, who asked to be a cook on his arrival to the company and was refused, is now acting magnificently with the chips down. A private, he is doing an officer's work. He will get no medal for it, because he is not in the right place at the right time.

It is light outside now, but dark in the cellar. I take off my shoes to rub my feet. The alarm clock clangs unexpectedly at 10:00 hours, and no one can find it in the dark. It is located, and the man doesn't know how to shut it off. He finally muffles it, and we wonder if Jerry heard it. In fact, we wonder if it can be heard in Paris. Dead tired, the men fall asleep and snore, and we have to kick them quietly, because Jerry can hear the snoring and he is methodically and brutally searching all the houses for Americans.

I have guards posted on all three stories of the house. Gathering momentum in the street rumbles what we think is a Goliath mobile mine, a well-drilled machine-gun team, a headless horseman, or a mortar on a wooden cart. We wait silently for the thing to shoot through our door and blow us to bits, but it passes on. "That was very eerie," whispers Charley to me.

Humphrey comes from upstairs and says it is a runaway team of horses dragging Jerry ammunition on a wooden wagon.

We keep the radio open to Cannon Company, but sometimes we can't answer their calls if Jerry is right outside the cellar steps. We smoke incessantly and the tension grows as we hear Jerry and his burp guns. We think how cushy it is to die up in the sunlight, or in a cool field at dusk, but what a hell of a place to end in is an old stinking, dark cellar.

I take a guard with Williams on the top floor, and a mortar team is stopped right below the house. I tiptoe slowly to the window, two grenades in my hands, the pins pulled. I can't miss, and our position will remain undetected. I wonder why I should presume to say who shall die by these grenades, or why I can limit life's duration. But I am going to kill a foe, someone I do not know, and it will give me grim satisfaction. As I near the window I can hear them excitedly talking. And then I see I am too late. The mortar team moves on as I reach the window and they are outside my throwing range. I am disappointed. But Jim Krohn later kills one full in the head with his M1.

Down below, a message comes to us. E Company is on its way to enter Sivry and help us. From which direction should they enter the village? I tell them to enter from Cole's end, but this message is never received by E Company though acknowledged by Cannon Company. Major Hayes, with the company, has to take a chance, and comes in from the Southwest and the men are cut to bits, and they don't get within three hundred yards of the village. But it gives us some hope. We know we have not been abandoned. Some of our guards do a bit of careful sniping from the windows.

I try to get the battle-fatigue cases to do some guarding, because we are very tired, and we can feel ourselves slowly snapping. "They have lost all pride in themselves and plead to remain in the cellar," I say to one.

"I can't go up there," he says. But he slowly walks up the steps.

Five minutes later he comes quickly down and I meet him at the bottom. "What the hell is this?" I ask him.

"I can't stay up there. I can hear them talking."

"What are you going to do when we go out of here tonight?"

"I don't know."

You don't know whether to comfort him or smash him. A brave, worn-out man goes up the steps to replace him.

I arrange the men in pairs for leaving the cellar in the dark and return to battalion. It is 16:00, thirteen hours after the opening of the barrage. I have sent a message to Regiment on Monaghan's weakening radio that we are across from the church and that we know E Company has not been able to break in. It is the low point of the 317th Regiment that later goes on to win great victories in the final smash-up of Germany. Brown phones that some of his men made a break for it and were cut down before they had gone five yards. What is my last message in combat comes at 16:15 hours from Regiment, "Tell Ellsworth not to worry."

Passing this on, I can see the men are amused, for none of us ever has been in a tighter spot. But I know that Hayes will not let us down, and he has sent this message through Regiment to inform us further attempts are to be made to get us out of Sivry. It is no longer a question of controlling the village after E Company has been slaughtered. It is a matter of salvaging what manpower is possible.

B-r-r-r-r-i-t! B-r-r-r-r-i-t! B-r-r-r-r-i-t! Red flashes dazzle us. Schmeisser bursts through the barricade. The world stands still.

Then two more insistent, efficient, automatic bursts. Two of our men cry out, wounded. My heart sinks and quickens with disappointment and fright.

It is all over. It is *der tag*. "Surrender!" I yell.

B-r-r-r-i-t! B-r-r-r-i-t!

They had found us. They were going to kill us. No chance for surrender. No chance to fight.

"We surrender," I try again, and am answered by the red bullet flashes in the stodgy dark.

"Try 'Kamerad'," Charley says.

I motion to one of the German prisoners near the light by the rear door. He understands immediately. He is not immune to Nazi bullets and he does not want to die. The night before he had cried because he thought he was going to die. Like a rat he scampers to the back door, up the stairs in to the house, out in to the street, shouting in German to stop shooting. I put a grenade on the back of the neck of the second German. If Jerry is going to commit murder, one German will go with us. The prisoner returns, indicates to us from the top of the back steps to come up with our hands behind our heads, helmets removed.

"Son-of-a-bitch, Charley! What a damned thing this is."

Monaghan destroys vital parts of his radio. Herr does the same with his .45 pistol. I tear up my maps and written messages, put our four grenades in the cesspool, and still find time to shake hands with each man as he goes up the steps. I am the last to emerge and I help one of the wounded across the street into the graveyard where we are quickly searched, being permitted to keep our wallets, snapshots, personal letters, money, fountain pens, and cigarettes. I see the Germans are excellent, well trained, experienced fighters handling their weapons as though they had come out of the womb with them. Occasional bullets snap through the graveyard during the search. They line us up against the gray church, put a machine-gun in front of us, tell us to raise our hands. A blue-eyed Nazi gets down behind the gun. We think we are going to be shot, but we are so humiliated, tired, disgusted, surprised, disgraced, and shocked that we don't care.

They don't shoot us, but march us in to a barn near Mike's old position which is their C. P. The German officers are there, directing the attack, not personally leading it, thus saving the officer class for future battles. The Nazi soldiers are well disciplined and it doesn't seem to bother them that the junior officers do not take the risks of the British and American line officers. There are many wounded from my company on the floor of the barn. I ask permission to talk to them. Some of them have belly wounds and are crying for water, but we don't give them any. One Mexican dies while we are there. The Nazi commander looks on me with contempt. He is well pressed, and I am shabby. He is the winner and I am the loser. Otherwise, he ignores me. We begin to laugh and joke among ourselves and this surprises Jerry. It is because the terrific fourteen-hour tension has suddenly been lifted, and we feel giddy.

Krohn is forced down the street under guns to ask Cole to surrender and Cole refuses to give in. His men are well set at strategic windows and have limited ammo. We are then lined up in the barn, and once again the blue eyes get down behind the machine gun. But again they don't shoot us. We think it is to break our morale for later interrogation. A year later we learn from a German who is captured on VE Day that they were to take very few prisoners in

Sivry. But the two Germans who were with us in our C. P. plead that we gave them good treatment, and the Nazi captain does not give the fire order.

We are marched over Mt. Toulon, bristling with soldiers and several heavy self-propelled guns. Our own P 47s strafe us. A cub plane circles us, directing 105 shells on our group, scattering the guard. It is the time to escape. I remember Hugh Hope had told me to get away in the first forty-eight hours. Our men wave handkerchiefs and hands at the artillery O. P., and he understands, halting the shelling. But our own shells hit three of our men. One of them is Monaghan. We pick up our wounded and it takes all our strength for the four-mile march. Monaghan says to leave him and try to get away. But we think the Germans might find it easier to shoot him than carry him themselves, so there is no escape attempt. We have stopped his bleeding with a tourniquet. His blood is on our raincoats and khaki pants. I tell him he will get a Purple Heart, and he says, "Hell, I've got one of those already."

A lantern-jawed German of the pre-historic man type keeps counting us and muttering, "*Marche.*" We swear at him in English and he doesn't understand. At dark, we arrive at a large farm with many buildings, an important German combat headquarters, protected with huge red hospital signs. We are not surprised because we know this is a German habit and that one day there will be retribution.

There are eighteen of us now, and we are herded in to a small room with straw on the floor, and we go to sleep, exhausted. Krohn wakes me because I am saying in my sleep, "Get machine guns. Get machine guns. Our only chance is more machine guns!" But I don't remember this and in the morning I think I have had a nice ten-hour sleep. Herr is called out for questioning, but gives only his name, rank, serial number and asks the Jerry lieutenant how long he thinks the war is going to last. The Jerry answers one more year—with Germany and Japan the winners because of a secret weapon. The German guards tell us the same, and we can see they believe this.

Monaghan is evacuated in an ambulance. We are permitted to wash in a horse trough but receive no food. At noon, Herr and I are called upstairs to a clean, comfortable room. There are four English-speaking Germans in it. George and I salute smartly. We have no hats, and we are dirty and unshaven. We do not look like American officers, and we try to make up for it by our best military courtesy. A Colonel returns a Hitler salute, politely tells us to sit down, calls me Lieutenant Ellsworth. He opens a new bottle of cognac, pours three drinks, gives George and me one each and takes the other for himself. The other three Germans are standing against the wall silently staring at us. "To victory," I say, raising my glass. The Colonel smiles, says in Oxford English, "To victory," and the three of us drink in one gulp.

He pours another, and George and I refuse.

"Lieutenant Ellsworth, if you think we are going to ask you questions about your unit or division, we are not. We know all that. You Americans are so careful and yet so careless. We get all the information we wish about your units from divisional patches on your sleeves, from your A. P. O. numbers, and from the signs on the front of your vehicles. By the way, Major Hayes, your battalion commander is in good health."

"Are you asking me or telling me?"

"I'm telling you."

"Why did you fight so fiercely in Sivry? You must have known it was useless. Why could you accept responsibility for such waste of men's lives? It was an empty gesture, yours."

George and I remain silent.

"Lieutenant Herr, you are artillery. What are you doing with the infantry?"

George gives me a grin, says, "You Germans should know that."

" 'Herr' is a German name. When did your family go to America?"

"1719."

This causes the Germans to wonder why anyone left Germany in 1719.

"The French boys you had with you in your company, where are they?"

"I don't know," I answer. But it shakes me to know the Germans had learned about our Allies, and I wonder silently how they got this information.

"You will go to a camp in Germany, go on parole hikes, ski, and be treated with dignity."

"I hope so," says George, refusing a cigarette the Colonel offers.

"You had a lot of new men in G Company, Lieutenant Ellsworth."

"Are you asking me or telling me?"

"I'm telling you," nodding his head slowly.

"How long will the war last?" a German lieutenant interrupts.

"A few months. We will win."

"Look how long you have been stopped in the Moselle valley."

"Look how suddenly the war ended last time."

"That is because Germany was betrayed within. It will not

happen again. When you get to Germany you will see how hard our people are working for victory."

"Why are you allied with such a country as Russia? We have no quarrel with Americans. Why are you in Europe? If you must be in Europe, you should help us fight the Russians."

George and I say nothing because we know how Germans twist prisoners' statements for their newspapers and propaganda broadcasts.

"Your Army is not to be compared with the German Army. Your soldiers are not trained. Your non-commissioned officers are new and have been in the army a short time. It takes a long time and much fighting to get a rank in the German Army."

"We beat you in Africa."

"That is because the despicable Italians let us down. They are to blame for the defeat in Africa. They would not fight," he snaps.

A sergeant with only half his nose, the other half being on the Russian front, asks, "Why did you want Sivry?"

George and I do not reply. They are writing down the questions and answers and our every word.

"What was your occupation before you joined the army, Lieutenant Herr?"

Lieutenant Herr just looks at me, raising his eyebrows.

A sergeant comes in the room, salutes, says, "The prisoners are spoiled. We have fed them, and they threw away most of the bread, potatoes, and gravy we gave them."

A line officer of World War I, stiff-shouldered, straight-backed, frozen-jawed, narrow-eyed, the Colonel looks at me, says with a trace of smile, "Your men, Lieutenant Ellsworth, will have to learn the Prussian way."

"Yes," I say.

For the action in Sivry, the Regiment recommended me for the Congressional Medal of Honor. But I was not a hero. I was not made for it.

The Battle of Sivry made the German High Command Communiqué and furnished material for propaganda pamphlets to be shot at American troops the following month.

Chapter Nineteen

George and I were given our first food following interrogation—potatoes, a thick, brown gravy, and a piece of coarse, heavy, dark, sour, wholesome bread. A Nazi corporal watched us eat. "You Americans," he said, "do not know about your country. You do not know. Do you know that your President Roosevelt is a Jew? Or that his wife is part Negro? Do you know that one hundred Jewish families rule your land? Of course, you don't know it. You are not told these things."

Herr and I looked at each other, our eyes popping. We couldn't believe that Hitler had actually taught these things and the people actually believed them. It was like meeting a man who was firmly convinced witches ride the sky every Halloween.

He continued, "Not one American soldier now in Europe will come out of it alive."

"How about prisoners?"

"Oh, you will be all right. For you the war is over. You will be sent to America in about five years, and you can rejoin your families.

"When we destroy your Army, we shall then wipe out Finland. They have betrayed us. They have made peace with Russia. We don't know what this secret weapon is. We know it is coming. One of your airborne armies has been destroyed recently in Holland. We don't know how, but it was probably our secret weapon."

He talked to us for another twenty minutes, and we listened, saying nothing. Two German privates also added choice tidbits. Their minds, fairly typical, were depraved, wicked, and cynical. Freedom and democracy were empty rubbish. They held in contempt humankind and personal happiness. In addition, their ideas, Nazi ideas, were impractical, phony as the Aski mark, and were not the answers to the world's sickness.

We marched ten miles that day, spent the night in a farmhouse, and I peeled potatoes the next morning for our noon meal. But a German guard stopped me after a while, saying, "In Germany, the officers do not work. They just think."

Jolly German guards took us in a truck to Forbach outside Saarbrucken. On the route, we gave the V sign to the population who stared at us, afraid or unwilling to show friendliness. After the Maginot came the Seigfried Line. A big guard tapped me on the shoulder with his rifle barrel, pointed, snapped, "*Da Vest Vall*," and his eyes gleamed. The series of pill boxes, trenches, gun emplacements, dragons' teeth, all combined with the natural folds in the ground, looked formidable.

Charley glanced at a medal one of the guards was wearing on his left breast pocket, asked what it was about. The guard gave a stainless-steel grin, said, "Olympics. Three sports. Berlin. 1936." He indicated boxing, jumping, and shot-put movements. It was actually a medal for participation in three major battles on the Russian front.

The garrison guards at Forbach lined us up, searched us, and took from us our watches, pens, money, matches, cigarettes, and cigarette lighters. It wouldn't have been so bad to be looted on the front by the men who had captured us, but to have these show-off, loud, cruel rear echelon troops get our pickings made us livid. But we did not protest, after an initial outburst of mine. Because four Russians walked slowly by carrying a dead soldier to the outside for disposal. One of the Russians made a pistol sign to his forehead, pointed to his dead comrade, then to the Germans. I had hidden my watch in my crotch and got it through the search. But they found the Iron Cross I had in my watch pocket—the souvenir I had forgotten about and had been carrying ever since taking it from a paratrooper. The Germans colored, and I felt our men stiffen. I could be shot for this. I talked fast, saying that I had traded one of my officer's bars to a German prisoner—that the prisoner had wanted the insignia for a souvenir. Whether or not they believed me, I don't know. Probably not, because Americans are the only soldiers who madly collect war mementoes. Other nations are constantly reminded of war without souvenirs.

French, Poles, Indo-Chinese, and Russians were in Forbach, and we joined thirty American privates from the 5th, 78th, and 35th Divisions. We had a piece of bread spread with lard for supper, and the next four days we each had a cup of ersatz, two ounces of bologna, and a sixth of a loaf of bread daily. Nothing else. No tobacco. Of course, we had lice and bed bugs shortly, but that didn't help our hunger. The Americans came to me, as their senior officer, and asked me to get them toothbrushes, razors, soap, and more food. Before, they had always been able to get these things through their officers. They did not comprehend that we were in the hands of the Nazis, and what that meant. For the record, I asked for these things.

After three days, we were marched to a railroad, crowded into boxcars, and locked in, after being issued a half loaf of bread per man. Herr sat on one side of me, Charley on the other. We opened a small window, but the guards came in and nailed this shut. Krohn protested about the window. A guard told one of our men who could speak German to instruct Krohn to keep quiet or he would have his throat cut. Krohn heard this. The guard looked again at Jim, asked the interpreter a question.

"He wants to know if you're Jewish, Jim."

"Tell him you're damned right I am."

The guard gave a slow smile and left, taking my raincoat with him.

We were in the dark for four days and four nights, spreading, twitching, itching, listening to arguments. Some of the men had used the bucket for stomach sickness and dysentery. At first the smell was unbearable, but later we did not notice it. It was our water bucket, the Germans said, and we could have no water unless we wanted to drink it out of the latrine bucket. Through the boxcar cracks we shouted "*Essen*" and "*Wasser*," but the Germans mimicked our pronunciation and laughed. I had the men stop this, because it did no good, made matters worse. On a siding we parked across from a train loaded with pink-cheeked Hitler Youths. They were eating. Silently we watched them through the cracks, occasionally muttering, "Bastards," or "Just look at the little sons-of-bitches."

I literally didn't care whether I lived or died—until American Thunderbolts strafed and bombed and missed our parked train. Then I knew I wanted to live and never lost the desire again. Our heads ached, and we talked about food, though we made agreements not to discuss the subject. Each man had one particular simple food in mind, something he probably had not paid much attention to in the States. A sergeant from Alabama talked about buns, another about malted milks, George about Milky Ways, Charley about a cherry sundae, Krohn about pancakes, and I thought about glazed doughnuts. I wondered who would get my bottle of White Horse back in my bedroll with Supply-sergeant Mario Donato of Abington, Pennsylvania. I had been saving it for Christmas or VE Day, whichever came first.

Charley said, "I don't mind losing my cigarettes, lighter, money, and all that. Or even being a prisoner and being here with no water. We couldn't help being captured. But that damned Kraut at Forbach took my list of phonograph records that I had made up during my spare time. They are all the names of the records I have at home. If I had that list of records, I might be able to stand this."

"Charley, that Jerry Colonel said we would be treated with dignity. I wonder if raw hips from lying on the wooden floor of a dirty, dark boxcar without food and water is what Germany means by dignity. I suppose it adds to our dignity, too, to listen to the guys argue about where the latrine bucket is going to rest, at whose feet, and for how long."

"Yeah. Do you think I ought to throw away my dog tags?"

"Why?"

"They show me as being Semitic."

"You've got to keep those. You have to be a soldier. They won't treat you any worse because of that."

"Why do I have to keep them? Where are yours?"

I smiled sheepishly. Charley knew I didn't wear dog tags because they were uncomfortable, and I, for some strange reason, considered them bad luck. "I wish you had not brought that up. If I am missing-in-action for a long time, Barbara will think I received a direct hit and they couldn't identify me because I had no dog tags.

She knows I didn't wear my identification. I can picture the effect at home of that two-star telegram signed by Ulio. Anyway, you keep your dog tags."

We crossed the Rhine, and peered through the boxcar cracks. There were hills. We had passed many hills on the way, and a private said, "I guess they are some more of those last-hill-before-Germany places we were always hearing about."

During the interminable waits and as we swayed along, I wondered why we were prisoners, where it might have been my fault, what we might have done to escape, whether or not it would have been better for us to make a futile stand and die in that cellar. I have never stopped wondering.

The last day we were dizzy if we stood up, so we remained on the floor, the men feebly arguing. There were no fights in the close confinement because the men were too weak. We swore revenge when the war was over, that we would get out of prison and comb Germany for the guards who were taking us on this trip and giving us no food and water and laughing at us. With much shouting and pig grunts, the Germans threw open the doors, making us blink with the light, and slowly we emerged, each step an effort, stepping carefully over the railroad tracks which seemed like eight-foot walls. Seven of our forty-eight fell to the ground, and we pulled them to their feet. Through Limburg, people jeered at us, spit on us, and one woman hit a sergeant with an umbrella. The civilians hated us. The guards did control this, shoving our hecklers out of the way. The guards in the peacetime concentration camp pushed and cursed us through a barbed wire gate and we were searched in a stockade, followed by delousing. George and I registered with the International Red Cross and were put in a building forty yards long and twenty yards wide, with one hundred British and American officers, all of whom crowded us for news from the outside. A Lieutenant Starkowitz gave us his precious bread ration. Major Cuff of the British Army produced a cup of coffee and three cigarettes, and that night we had our first hot meal since interrogation—four boiled potatoes and some ersatz jam, which we wolfed with our fingers.

We stayed there four weeks, and learned the tricks of the trade. How to cook on a "Smoky Joe," how to cut the bread paper thin and make five cigarettes out of one, shave every three days with a jagged blade, and how to make a frying pan out of a tin can. We never learned how to keep from getting up four times a night, to relieve our almost total liquid diet. That is what every "Kriegie" will remember about prison—the uncontrollable gush of water that might come as he staggers fully clothed past snoring, smelling soldiers to the latrine. He has awakened suddenly in the cold, damp dark, and climbed painfully and quickly from the triple-deck wooden bunk with a thin straw tick to the stone floor, groping for his boots.

In the mornings we had ersatz coffee that one gets used to, one sixth loaf of black bread, jam, and a dash of "Prima" oleo. At noon we had a cup of soup, either grass, barley, pea, beet, turnip, or cabbage, with a few small potatoes in the bottom. At night, another cup of soup. Seven of the eleven soups each week were the nauseating beet, and we lost weight rapidly. Lining up for soup was the only time I saw men rush for the rear of a queue. As the big soup container reached the bottom, more potatoes were in each helping. We took the potatoes out of the soup and fried them in the "Prima." I raised a mustache for something to do, and it drooped. But I got a mustache out of my system and will never have to have another.

The sick bay was in the middle of our room, and the wounded officers lay there, and we became accustomed to the stench they could not help. For forty-eight hours we were locked collectively in our building because one of our officers had talked with a new arrival in the next enclosure. It was a treat for us to get out and walk ten yards to the outside latrine, where we could look through barbed wire and see a microcosm of the United Nations—Russian, French, British, Yank, South African, Polish, Indian, Canadian POWs living in tents in inches of mud. In our building, we were fortunate.

Lieutenant Cole and Lieutenant Ackerman arrived, having held out a day after we were captured in Sivry.

Our only entertainment was singing, and reading the books such as well-meaning citizens might contribute to a POW book drive—old Victorian novels, religious discussions, directions on how to make puppets, or crocheting. I visualized the attics in which they had been for years. A biography of General Sherman was the only decent reading we had and the waiting list was prohibitive to ever getting at it.

After four weeks, I got a toothbrush from the Red Cross and removed the thick matting from my teeth, sent my first postcard to Barbara, became accustomed to the long, dragging hours after the pace at the front, made plans for reading, walking, living, and forgetting following the war. I had lost all my identity among the officers and was known only as "the bread man," having taken the morning job to divide the black stuff into sixths after the Germans issued us the leadlike loaves. Prison camp is no place to build up one's vanity.

Herr had been taken off for solitary confinement in the Dietz thirteenth century castle to prepare him for the German attempt to pick clean his knowledge. Near the Limburg marshalling yards, we heard the wail of the air-raid sirens several times a day, and someone always said, "There goes Hitler crying again." We were warned that we would be shot on sight if we went to our windows during an air raid as this would be interpreted as signaling to the planes.

We lived from soup to soup, and when worms were found floating we made the stock remarks, "Well, it won't eat much. Don't remove it," or "Fresh meat in our soup today. Good!" If we had beet soup, we would say that the Germans must be winning the war. If we had barley or pea, we would remark that the Americans must have taken a town and the Germans were trying to make amends to us.

Sex and drinking rarely entered our conversations. If we thought about women, it was with a desire to have a meeting of minds with them. Our calories were low. Often I have heard the question, "What would you rather have, a nice beautiful girl, whiskey, soft music, a wallet of money, a comfortable hotel room where you won't be bothered, or a big, juicy fifteen-cent hamburger with mustard?"

Sex lost every time.

Occasionally we were able to get raw turnips that satisfied our desire for something fresh. Indians risked their lives by sneaking them to us through the fence, or we got them by trading some of our precious cigarettes with the German guards.

I told everyone the story of the rise and fall of Sivry and listened to everyone's story on how he was captured. It was always the same. Captured on a patrol, a company, platoon, or squad outpost, a German counter-attack, and a few non-combat men who had been put in the bag while "out taking a look at the front" and bumped into ubiquitous Jerry. For this last group we had no sympathy.

It rained often that autumn, and though our roof leaked, we had one comforting thought besides being alive—we weren't out in the rain at the front.

On five minutes warning, we were marched out of our stockade, deloused, thoroughly searched, given French army hats and greatcoats, taken to boxcars headed for an unknown destination. Herr came out of solitary to join us, and twenty officers crouched behind chicken wire in one third of the small European boxcar while five guards lolled in the other two thirds. They gave us fresh straw to put on the floor and one latrine bucket. Nine of us sat on each side, and it was necessary for two to take turns standing up in order to make room for the others to sit.

One engineer officer did not join us. He remained behind because he had criticized the German harbor and mines defense in Marseilles, saying that Jerry had done it all wrong, and the Southern France landing was easy. Jerry had the officer draw a plan on how it should have been done. It pays to give only name, rank, and serial number. George was given a Red Cross parcel when he got out of solitary, and he shared it with Doug Cole and me in a corner of the car. The guards cooked meat and potatoes in the car, while we silently watched their every preparation and eating of the food. We ate cheese and bread. Several times the guards cooked us a gruel from their own rations making a great effort and display about it. When we asked for more water, they might shout and fuss at us in their guttural talk. Friendly one minute, antagonistic the next. We couldn't understand them, and neither can the world.

By threes we were let out for the latrine, while the boxcar became grubbier, smellier, more confining. In Posen, we all crouched at an imaginary latrine near the tracks in full view of the main boulevard. Nazi officers left the street and shouted at our guards about the exhibit. They took the reprimands at stiff attention.

Down Adolphe Hitler Strasse, Szubin, Poland, south of Danzig and west of Warsaw near the Vistula River bend in the old Polish Corridor, we marched into the well-guarded American officers' prison camp, Oflag 64. It was commanded by German Colonel Fritz Schneider and Colonel Paul R. Goode was the Senior American Officer. There languished the guinea pigs of Kasserine, paratroopers from Sicily, Rangers of Anzio, and the Normandy tank and infantrymen.

We were searched, questioned, given pails of G. I. coffee, and listened to a fantastic, guttural, shouting speech from Schneider, relayed to us in English after each sentence. The tone was that of welcoming new boys to prep school and how fortunate we were to be in such a fine institution with such a great record. The American prisoners gave us spam, potatoes, salad, and coffee, a meal that tasted better than any food I have had on Christmas Day in America. But it was to be a long time before we saw the like again. That night we got on standard Oflag fare, a large chunk of red beet, four boiled potatoes, ersatz coffee.

Nine hundred American officers were in the camp in a highly organized state. We were conducted to our quarters after a shower and haircut. I was given the only Red Cross parcel I was to receive in my first twelve weeks as a Kriegsgefangenen. The allowance was one a week when there was a supply on hand. We lived in one of the twelve long, low, narrow brick buildings with three German brick stoves, forty double-deck wooden slat beds with straw ticks covered by a blue-and-white-checked cheap cloth, a few tables, plenty of stools, electric lights, and lockers which we placed to form rooms or cubicles for six to eight officers. Herr and I shared a double-decker, while Lieutenant Paul Wiley, Portland, Maine, Dr. Julius Parker, Chattanooga, Tennessee, and Lieutenant Robert Breazele, Baton Rouge, Laouisiana slept next to us. Lieutenant Colonel Max Gooler, a very fine soldier captured as an observer at Tobruk, was in command of the building, under command of the Germans.

Americans who might have known us in the States, in our Divisions, at college, or some time in the past came in to identify each one of us as a precaution against the old Jerry trick of running in his own kind disguised as an American officer in an effort to learn our secrets of escape plans, morale, thoughts, army information, etc.

In Oflag 64, the average Kriegie was twenty-seven years old, from New York, college trained, food conscious, efficient, and making the best of it. He had chilblains and called the Germans "Goons."

Chapter Twenty

Books worth twenty-thousand dollars from the YMCA Prisoner of War Fund formed our library. I read Gibbon's *The Decline and Fall of the Roman Empire*, which I probably would never have done in my life if not taken prisoner. *The Robe* was the most popular book among the captives, and there was an eight months' waiting list on the limited supply of *Lee's Lieutenants*. The Germans had sliced the covers of all our books looking for escape tools or written messages.

Doc Parker, George, Wiley, Breazele and I each evening presented three words we had picked up in our reading during the day. If we knew the meaning of the other man's words, he gave us a cigarette. If we failed on the definitions of words from previous evenings, we forfeited a cigarette. We took turns reading aloud five chapters of the Bible following the word contest. In this way, we helped pass the time and kept our minds active.

Twice a day the Goons had us out for *appel* or roll call, in the three-hundred by four-hundred yards square area which was overlooked by seven guard towers bristling with machine guns and surrounded by three high barbed wire fences. Searchlights swept this square at night. Sometimes appel was only ten minutes; sometimes we shivered for two hours in the frigid clime. It was common for men to faint at appel from the cold and lack of sufficient food. It was not unusual to see a soldier wet himself because of cold kidneys while standing at attention as the Germans counted us out loud in their guttural grunts. Once an officer hissed "horse face" at the Jerry in command of the appel, and we all stood there for an hour.

German news was placed on the camp bulletin board each day, and it was amazingly accurate. I remember one item they had wrong, however. They said that Elliot Roosevelt had married movie actress Alice Faye instead of Faye Emerson.

Twice the Goons posted special atrocity stories for our benefit—that American soldiers were murdering German prisoners on the Western Front. A strict check was kept by American officers on the cigarette supply of each man and rations were made accordingly. The new arrivals who would have to wait a year for a tobacco parcel from home, therefore, did not have to wait twelve months for a smoke if Red Cross parcels were not coming through.

Sunday was a big day because we had gravy to put on our potatoes. The Germans fed us a slow starvation diet and did not give us the same amount of rations as the Nazi garrison troops, a violation of the Hague Convention. At that time there was plenty of food for the German Army, the people, and the war prisoners. It was a deliberate attempt to starve prisoners and Colonel Goode stated this to the Swiss protecting power. I lost thirty-two pounds I could not afford, and this was about average. The entire camp was fed twice a day, each sitting lasting twenty minutes. Ten of those minutes involved dividing the bowl of food among the eight men at each table. The Kriegies captured early in the war took their ration from the mess hall to their bunks where they added their own food sent in parcels from home. Our potatoes were always boiled with the skins on, and we were advised to eat the skins for their nutritious values. Once a week we received sugar and each day we had one-sixth of a loaf of bread. The sugar and bread we kept in our lockers, and twice rats ate mine when I left my locker door open. This does not sound serious now, but it was then. Very serious. We received eight hundred calories less per day than we should have to keep even on our weight.

Wiley and I heard about some rotten carrots, potatoes, and beets thrown out on the ground near the cookhouse, and for two hours we were on our hands and knees with ten other officers grubbing in the garbage to get enough parts of the vegetables which were not rotten to fill a frying pan. Again, I found a few stray cabbage leaves on the dirt near the cellar window where cabbages had been dumped from a truck. I gathered them and distributed the leaves among Doc, George, Breazele, Wiley, and myself. Our skin grew scaly. Doc Parker said it was due to lack of vitamin A. In the middle of each afternoon we received a cup of plain, hot drinking water. I have often seen groups of prisoners sitting about a table slowly drinking hot water and chattering as contentedly as at a high tea. One gets accustomed to things. Sometimes officers were reduced to cheating and lining up twice for hot water when there was only enough rations for one cup per man.

One had a chance of coming out of prison a much better man who had learned and thought about life's intangibles, or he might go downhill, like the officer who stole leeks out of the little prison garden and diluted coffee in Red Cross parcel trades.

Hunger was our dominant thought and talk, not the war. By and large, however, we, as American officers fared better than the other nationalities that were under Jerry control. But we did not live as well as Nazi prisoners in United States because our country followed the Hague Convention behind the front. In retrospect, few Americans taken prisoner would have had our country do otherwise, though there was bitter feeling about it in the Oflag during the last year of the war.

On Thanksgiving we brought out a secret supply of bully beef and mixed it with potatoes. I know of turkey dinners I enjoyed less. We attended church conducted by one of the five chaplains taken prisoner on the Western Front. He told us that we had things to be thankful for—our friends in prison, being a member of a victorious nation, for the bully beef we had that day, and that our families in America were safe. I added silently at the end of the service that I was grateful for my life.

In December, the first Red Cross parcels in several months trickled in from Sweden, and grown men who had held important jobs in civilian life and the army overseas, huddled in groups and haggled over food trades or told gleefully about bartering a can of meat and beans for half a tin of powdered milk. Our values had changed, and the unimportant in our normal lives had automatically assumed the important. Whether strawberry jam was better than pineapple jam was as momentous to us as our beliefs in happier days on which make of automobile was the better. Wealth might be two bullion cubes. Values on food such as bread changed according to supply and demand. When there were Red Cross parcels, bread went down. When there were no parcels, it was our main subsistence of life.

Each Red Cross parcel contained fourteen-thousand calories of jam, sugar, powdered coffee, powdered milk, crackers, chocolate, cheese, meat spread, salmon, oleo, prunes, bully beef, and spam. In addition, the package contained cigarettes, soap, vitamin tablets, and sometimes soup powder. Bob Breazele and I made puddings and cakes together. The pudding was twelve prunes, black bread, a spoon of milk, some sugar and heated over a Smoky Joe, a contraption made out of milk cans with cardboard from the Red Cross parcel for fuel. For our piecrust we used crackers. The longer a man was a prisoner, the better a cook he became. He had the knack of using headache pills and toothpowder for baking soda.

My Red Cross chocolate bars I would nibble on and put away to save. As I sucked the chocolate from my teeth I would think of the rest of the bar in my locker. I tried to discipline myself and remember that I had to make it last. But it was no use. The image of the bar was there, and I would go quickly to my locker, eat the bar, feeling the sugar seep into my system as far down as my heels. For a time, then, I would be as contented as a python harboring a doe. But I had to admire the men who could nonchalantly walk by their lockers and chocolate, go about their trumped-up business, and occasionally return for a nibble only.

Several lotteries were run. The prizes were fifty-dollar wristwatches with the entrance fee of one chocolate bar. The men putting up their watches garnered twenty-five bars each. In retail value, a Red Cross parcel was worth five dollars but in prison could not be purchased for one hundred dollars payable after release.

Our poker games were limited to a two hundred and fifty dollar total loss at which point the Kriegie was barred from further play. Each Saturday morning we had an inspection by senior American officers of our personal appearance and locker and cubicle condition. It was an effort to maintain our dignity as much as possible in the eyes of the Germans who would judge the American Army by our discipline. We tried to look and act like soldiers despite our makeshift uniforms of Polish, French, British, and American clothing. We recognized all German officers and they replied with the Heil Hitler salute. We saluted only our five full colonels among the American officers. The Nazis had a canteen for us. It contained hardened tubes of French toothpaste captured in 1940. That's all I ever saw in it. We mailed home thirty lines of writing a week, and the letters took anywhere from sixty days to a year to reach America. They were cheery, cramped, printed, and asked for dehydrated foods and family snapshots.

The YMCA furnished ample sports equipment but we did not have the calories to go with it. Bob Rankin organized a twenty-piece orchestra which YMCA instruments made possible, and we attended plays staged by the prisoners. Parlor games and Victrolas also reached the Oflag. Occasionally we had five-reel German films of 1930 vintage. We would go to see how many reels we could sit through, and once I managed to watch four. The movies were bad if even Kriegies could not stand them. I played several games of chess each day with Herr and Lieutenant Marcellus Hughes, Washington, D.C., who was bagged in Africa. After lights were out in the evening, we maintained strict silence as Germans might be listening inside the building. When Goons walked in our barracks during the day we yelled "at ease" and no one talked until the Nazis had finished their clumping about and snooping. It was an effective silent treatment that irritated Jerry. Near the camp was a V-2 location and two nights we saw rockets launched through the winter air toward the Vistula. We managed to get information on the site to Allied Headquarters.

I took short walks around the camp with Lieutenant Harry Schultz, Cleveland Heights, Ohio, a college friend of mine captured in the early days of the war and whose escape from Szubin was ended by the Gestapo near the Czechoslovakian border after six months of comparative freedom.

There were no individual escape plans. There was an escape committee, and any man or group with ideas on how to get away presented the scheme to the security committee for approval, refusal, or a priority number. Only three escapes took place while Americans were in the camp, all three unsuccessful. The feeling was that the war was about to end and we were to take no unnecessary risks, which may or may not have been a good attitude. We had a set of tools for necessary repairs in the prison and we were honor-bound not to use them for escapes. A group had dug a tunnel, but it was not used, nor was it discovered or clogged by the Guard Company that drilled holes and blasted the earth just outside the wire.

Old Kriegies advised the new arrivals to read as much as possible in the beginning, because the place had a wearing effect and the average man eventually became lethargic. A prisoner passed through four stages. One, the dull, dazed state of trying to realize he is captured. Two, the I'm-going-to-study-and-get-something-out-of-this, or I'll-read-now-what-I've-never-had-time-to-before outlook. Three, the itchy, unsettled, detective-story phase. Four, the patient, settling-down and waiting for the end attitude enlivened with petty arguments and the accepting of the abnormal life as normal.

No matter what a prisoner did in civilian life, or what his rank was, or his intellectual capacity, or his financial status, or how long he had been in the army, he had several things in common with all the rest of the officers. We all talked deals in food. We loathed the Germans. We practiced self-flagellation by thinking of what we would eat our first week in America. We all said, "I thought about being killed or wounded but the thought of being a prisoner never entered my head." We bored each other continually with feats we had performed before capture and the full details of how we were captured in a subconscious effort to justify our humiliating status. We all suffered from the cold of Poland and had fat, red, ugly fingers swollen to sausage shape and size. And we all disliked the few sharp traders who made two Red Cross parcels out of one by spending their entire time bartering.

I gave a talk to the field officers in the prison on the British Army as part of our sub rosa conducted training program arranged by Lieutenant Colonel John K. Waters. Our lectures were always well stooged and if Germans were in the vicinity or listening we had canned lectures on such subjects as "How to Raise a Vegetable Garden."

Every few weeks we had sudden Gestapo searches for which we were always prepared. The Gestapo found nothing out of line. Once we had a supply of coal that we had been saving for Christmas, and they stopped our meager rations for eleven days and cut future deliveries in half. After that most of us spent the time in bed fully clothed.

At the near-by hospital of Wollstein, one of our American officers of the Jewish faith died of stomach ulcers. The Germans were going to throw his body in to the lime pit used for dead Russians. But the sick of our camp in Wollstein strongly protested and got him a military funeral of a sort.

In December Lieutenant Colonel William Schaefer and Lieutenant James Schmidtz were sentenced to death. Jerry said he was going to place on the bulletin board a warning that to escape from prison camp was no longer a sport, that Britain had initiated a non-military form of gangster war, that Germany would shoot immediately any escaped prisoners as they would be considered enemy agents or sabotage groups, that we should stay in camp where we would be safe as "breaking out of it is now a damned dangerous act."

Colonel Schaefer interpreted this as propaganda and contrary to the Hague Convention. He ordered Schmidtz to stand in front of the bulletin board when the Goons came to place the notice for our consumption, as a token resistance. We had the right, under international law, to attempt escape with nothing but minor disciplinary punishment if recaptured. A German pushed Schmidtz aside, tacked up the warning, and the incident supposedly was closed.

Hauptmann Zimmerman, the type of man who pollutes the earth, and I hope he is now expiating his cruelties in hell with a lively devil to poke the fire, pressed charges and the two American officers were sentenced to die.

It sobered our senior American officers and we were told to tread as on eggs, by saluting without fail Goon officers in the vicinity, to have no extra clothes, soap, food, or cigarettes, to talk to no Germans except on strict business, to do nothing that might be interpreted as propaganda such as offering a Jerry a cigarette. The above could be considered, if so desired, as crimes against the Reich, punishable by death, with no appeal except to Hitler himself. We were warned to keep no diaries that criticized the Germans, and it was impossible to keep a prison record without writing a few nasty things about Jerry.

Tension mounted as rumors circulated that the Gestapo was going to run the camp instead of the German Army.

About the same time we were ordered to produce ninety American uniforms. Colonel Goode refused. We were called out for appel, kept standing for three hours while Gestapo squads ransacked our barracks and took the uniforms. We did not hear what happened to them until word came of Von Runstedt's great counter-attack two weeks later in which Germans in American clothing were infiltrating the lines of the Bulge. Nearly all American prison camps had undergone the same order and search.

As Von Runstedt stepped off with everything at stake, Christmas Red Cross packages arrived in Oflag 64. The entire camp paused to look at a display of a parcel that was put on in front of the main barracks. We filed past to look at the canned foods and spent the next week discussing when and how we would eat the contents. I would have traded my entire parcel for one scratch of news from home. It had been six months since I had had any contact with my family.

Lieutenant Ackerman was in charge of our barracks' Christmas decorations. The Germans allowed us to have a tree, and red and green paper streamers sent from the YMCA lined the low ceiling. We made ornaments out of tin cans and Ackerman had drawn Santa Claus cartoons to tack on our lockers. Christmas Eve supper we had cabbage and two boiled potatoes and afterwards listened to the Christmas carols sung by the glee club while our thoughts were far removed from the snow and barbed wire of Poland.

Christmas Day we had a big meal made out of our parcels, paid calls to other barracks, avoiding talk about the thought uppermost in our minds—the German offensive in the West and how soon the Russians would start. That night I ate all my Christmas candy in one sitting, receiving the greatest physical thrill since I left America while Doc, Bob, Wiley, and Herr watched me with vicarious pleasure.

New Year's Eve there was no singing. A few half-hearted "Happy New Years" were said, and George and I gloomily shook hands over a chess game at midnight, the Germans having allowed us to keep the lights on for two extra hours. We went to our bunks muttering four letter words about a happy new year. New Year's Day the entire camp was run through the delousing chamber as we had been scratching for two weeks.

That day we received word from new arrivals that more than sixty American officers had been killed outright by a British bomb that had landed on our Limburg transit quarters just before Christmas. They were waiting for transportation to Oflag 64 and it was just one more fact in a long series of facts that made us realize that life in war time is largely a matter of luck. The *Overseas Kid*, a German propaganda newspaper for American POWs, carried an editorial that the British had purposely bombed the American officers' building. It was a weak stroke on the wedge the Nazis were trying to pound between the Allies, a more dangerous wedge than Von Runstedt's in the West.

A captain who slept near me asked me each morning for the next two weeks as we crawled out of bed for appel, "Ellsworth, any signs of the Russians yet?"

I would look out the window. "No. No Russians yet."

The captain was to go on trial January 24—for his life. He had maltreated Jerry prisoners on the front. The Nazis had counter-attacked, captured the captain, released the roughly handled German prisoners who gave evidence of their alleged beatings.

"If that ground would only freeze, the Russians might get here in time," he would reply.

Then one day the ground did freeze. And twenty-four hours later we heard that the Russians had started their winter offensive one hundred miles due east of us and were running high, wide, and handsome for the final furious squeeze.

When Warsaw fell, a wave of optimism hit the camp. From our windows near the road we watched the civilians in the stiff wind and cold hurrying from the country to Szubin, carrying satchels, rifles, and sacks for the long awaited "emergency." Loads of Polish hay went by on peasant wagons, and on each one I made a wish.

Saturday, January 20, immediately following inspection, we were ordered to prepare to move on foot from Poland to Germany. Madly we packed our belongings, said good-bye to our friends in other barracks as we did not know what was in store, broke up the library, distributed three thousand Red Cross parcels which arrived that morning, made formal request to Colonel Schneider to permit us to remain in the Oflag, and he replied that he must follow orders and try to get us to Germany. Marcellus Hughes gave me seven cartons of cigarettes and these I distributed about my pockets. There was not water that day, and we melted snow to drink. Eight men were given permission to hide in the tunnel. Otherwise, Colonel Goode ordered us not to try to ghost out or attempt escape.

The German doctors granted permission for about seventy sick and wounded prisoners to remain at Szubin and be overrun by the Russians. Among those remaining behind was Breazele and he promised to contact our families in America. Two doctors cut cards for the Szubin job, and bearded Catholic Chaplain Brook, captured in Africa, stayed in the Oflag. The entire hospital party was under command of American Colonel Fred W. Drury.

Doc, George, Wiley, and I made an agreement to try to get away together after Major Jerry Sage, commanding our platoon, refused us permission to try that night, as per Colonel Goode's orders.

My last meal from the Germans was four boiled potatoes.

Chapter Twenty-One

The next day we looked out our windows to see the white roads jammed with wooden wagons drawn by old thin, sorrel horses. On the wagons were German families with their possessions covered with burlap. It was the evacuation of the East after five hilarious years of occupation. The transplanted farmers were trekking to Germany realizing the Russians would probably kill them if they stayed on their looted Polish land.

At nine o'clock in the morning we were called out for our last appel. Two hours we stood there while the Germans unsuccessfully searched for the missing prisoners hiding in the tunnel, and all that time we hoped and listened for the first shots of the rampaging Russian Army. I was wearing a French hat and overcoat, "Colonel Waters" British battle blouse, a pair of American trousers, a red football jersey, orange and black hockey stockings sent by the YMCA, a pair of socks on my chapped hands, and carrying my mattress cover as a rucksack.

German Colonel Schneider gave us a shrill speech on the appel grounds and Jerry Sage interpreted it for us. "We are going to Germany. We will walk, but later we may get a train. My orders are to get you there. You treat me well on this trip, and I will treat you well when we get to Germany. This first day we will march twenty-three kilometers. I don't know what our final destination is. I will stick with you to the end and give you protection. There will be no food or water today. I am in as much danger as any of you.

"Anyone who attempts escape will pay the maximum penalty."

Sage noticed one of us had nothing to cover the ears in the crisp wind, and he tossed the Kriegie an extra wool knit cap saying, "If we get out of this, give me back that cap. I was captured in it two years ago and would like to keep it to take home."

Sage then gave us each a cigar from a box he could not handle, and we walked through the wooden gate of the Oflag for the first time since entering, each man in our platoon puffing on a big cigar while Schneider counted us as we hit the road. We were happy, jovial, garrulous, not thinking about the future, but only how glad we were to look on the Oflag from the outside. In our fantastic column of humanity were the peasants stretched along to the horizon, the Szubin Gestapo and our World War I veteran guards loaded down with personals and weapons. To our right and left was the flat, frozen, snowy plain of Poland.

Our column of threes did not last long. We straggled, and put our belongings on the backs of the long, narrow wagons until a German guard ordered us to remove them or a peasant raised a fuss about it. The word was passed that Colonel Goode said it was all right to try an escape but was not advised because the Russians would soon overtake us.

The Kriegies carried their kit on hastily made sleds, wooden boxes with no runners, flat pieces of tin, and cardboard boxes. Field jackets, mattress covers, shirts, and extra pockets sewed on coats and trousers were used for our few precious belongings. One Kriegie had a wheelbarrow; another carried a violin, one a cornet. A woman threw away some onions from a wagon, and Wiley and I picked them up. A cold day, our faces were red and glistening with perspiration because of our loads and sudden exercise. Letters, extra shoes, pictures, books, and clothes littered the first mile. We threw away most everything but food. Wiley and I carried our mattress covers on a long stick slung between us, he walking in front and I in back. There were no organized halts. When we were tired, we sat down until a guard told us to "rouse."

In Exin, the Poles gave no indication of their feelings toward us. They had had five years of subjugation and were wary. I smiled and winked at the people crowding the doorways and curbs, but only a small boy winked back. Wiley and I got ready to duck down a side street, but we could not do it without Poles seeing us, and they might shout. The Gestapo was still in Exin.

As the afternoon went on, we made plans to get away by toddling in to one of the freshly dug slit trenches which lined the roads and were marked by sticks. Just at dark we were wheeled left down a road and in to a great snow-covered dairy yard enclosed by a brick wall and surrounded by a white Polish castle, a granary, a large building for pigs, two cattle barns, a stable, and several small houses. We were tired, hungry, and at a low mental ebb. It looked as though we would have to sleep in the snow. I ate a can of salmon sitting on the bumper of Colonel Schneider's car and felt I could not face another day on the road.

In an hour permission was given to sleep in the buildings, and Wiley and I made for the large, warm, crowded cow barn. The Holsteins chained in their stalls urinated over us and we were too tired to care or laugh. Wiley and I ate a can of his jam and looked for ways to clear out. Most of the Kriegies went to sleep. On pretense of getting some water and going to the toilet, Wiley got outside in the yard to look around, while I searched for an entrance to the loft from the inside.

"What did you find out there, Wiley? There's no entrance in here, and you can't get out the windows. A lot of these guys are ready to kill me. I've been stepping all over them looking around."

"There's no way to get out of the dairy yard. There're only three gates, and they are well guarded. You can see pretty well by the moon. Take a look. There's a door on the far end of this building on the outside. It might lead to the loft."

On the same pretense for getting out that Wiley used, I got past the Nazi. It was a cold, clear night, and ten yards from the door Wiley mentioned was a Nazi guard, his coat collar done up, his rifle slung on his shoulder while he smacked his gloved hands together and stamped his feet. I knew these veterans of the Kaiser's were more interested in saving their own lives than in preventing our escape.

"Let's risk it and see what the door is all about, Wiley."

"Okay. We've got food, and I've filled the canteen."

"We better wake up Doc and George and ask them if they want to try it."

Wiley found them asleep near the head of a Holstein munching on hay, and they were willing. Wiley went first, George second, Doc third, and I entered the door last. If the Nazi saw us he was not interested. There was no way to get out of the yard or the buildings. Inside the door the others had waited for me and had found some steps in the dark. We went up these, crashed and pitched around in the hay and made our way through three rooms until we were almost above the spot where we had eaten the jam. Below we could hear Kriegies snoring and coughing and cows stamping the stone floor. We crawled over the hay and back near the rafters and started to dig, the hay cutting our hands. We went down about ten feet, put our long pole across the hole for a bit of support and pulled bales of hay over us. We were wrapped up in each other's arms and hay was in every crevasse of our bodies. We knew the Germans might set the barn on fire, that they might shoot at random into the hay, or toss grenades into likely hiding places.

"If these Jerries come up in the morning and say 'rouse or we shoot,' what do we do?" I asked.

"The hell with them. We'll stay here. We've a fifty-fifty chance," George said.

"I can't face another day on that road. Let's risk it," said Doc.

"If they do find us and start talking maximum penalty stuff, we'll tell them we overslept up here and that we'd come up because it was too crowded below. These Jerries are too scared themselves to do much searching. I doubt if they will do any of the things they did when the Chieti camp in Italy was broken up. At least not until they get the column across the canal near here," Wiley answered.

I think we might have been able to sleep, but Wiley and Herr chose that particular time to be violently sick. Then the hay began to press down on us, and for the only time in my life, I had claustrophobia. I stood it as long as I could and then I could not breathe. I sent the hay every which way and George and Wiley had their turn to swear at me.

"I'll pull the hay down toward morning. It's dark now anyway. But I was about to go crazy."

"This is not the time and place to go crazy, Elmer," George said.

"This was not the time and place for you to be sick," I barked.

Toward dawn, Major John Dobson, Richmond, Virginia, and some Rangers came in to the loft and quietly argued whether or not they should try to hide out. At 5 A.M. we heard the Jerries getting the prisoners on their feet, and this was the moment. Would they make a search? The Rangers had dug in, and Major Dobson had decided to leave the hay and take the chance of ducking off farther down the road, saying, "They're bound to come up here and shoot tracers into the hay and that will be that for us." But it was too late. We heard the Germans counting the prisoners as they filed out of the gate in the dawn. Another fifteen minutes passed, and all was quiet. I had a terrific hunger and had to get at my Red Cross parcel at the top of our hole. I crawled up to it, opened a can of meat, and heard a high-pitched German voice coming through the rooms to ours. The hay was dry and I could not pull it over us without making noise. I sunk slowly back on Wiley's head, and he could not protest or move. The voice came nearer and I heard its owner climbing back to our rafters and hole. I kept looking up and waiting for a black Schmeisser to appear in the hole followed by its red flashes of death.

The face appeared. It was a boy's. I was about to reach up and pull him into the hole to keep with us for the next two or three days, when Doc from down under answered him in German. They carried on a short conversation.

"What does he say, Doc?"

"He says that the column of prisoners has left under guard and that he will keep us informed on things and his father will bring us coffee in an hour or so. He also says that about eighty of our sick were left behind in the castle too weak to make the march and that it is a declared hospital. He says we are to keep under cover because the German Army has yet to retreat past here."

"What does he say about the Poles here? Are they friendly?"

"He says they are friendly."

George says, "Let's take a chance he's telling the truth and won't turn us in. We can't make a getaway now that it's light anyway."

We had not been alone in the loft. Besides five Rangers, there were four of us and two other doctors. We held a meeting and decided to stay in the loft for the day and get out after dark. The Poles brought us bread, lard, and coffee. A medical sergeant was sent down by two colonels in the castle giving us direct orders to leave immediately as we were endangering the lives of the sick, creating an international incident by being escaped prisoners near a hospital, and jeopardizing the safety of others. This astounded us. All we were trying to do was evade the Germans. Dobson negotiated with the two colonels and received permission to hide in the loft until dark, at which time we would have to leave. He said that most of the men in the castle were only feigning sickness and that the colonels finally realized it would be impossible to make our way across the white plain during the day without being picked up.

We moved downstairs with the cattle where it was warm and found three more escapees. We kept an organized watch from the windows for German Army units among the long column of peasants slowly creaking past the dairy farm on the frozen snow of the road. It looked bad as the farm was a perfect place for the Germans to set up a headquarters in their retreat, and the others except Wiley, Doc, George, and I, left the barn about noon for a cross-country hike. Late in the afternoon a Pole came in with a pail of hot milk for us and said he could hear Russian artillery and that the Red Army would be at the barn before midnight. We listened and heard the guns—for once the sweetest sound imaginable. At last light we watched a small unit of German motorcyclists race to the West. We decided to leave about midnight after receiving directions from a Pole to a farmhouse that would hide us until the Russians arrived.

The four of us went downstairs into the barn that twenty-four hours before had been filled with prisoners, and milked a cow, immediately drinking the warm milk. The others went outside in the moonlight and I lit a cigarette. The huge door opened, and Doc said excitedly, "Get upstairs quick! There's a heavy column coming down the road! It might be Jerry, and if he stops here we're through!"

The others made for our old hiding place and I stayed by an upstairs window that looked toward Exin. I heard the clank and squeak of fast armor and watched lights draw closer. German or Russian? The column passed the castle in sixty seconds, and over the cold night air I heard singing—sweet, sad singing that I later learned was the Polish National Anthem. And then a song I recognized, "The Star Spangled Banner!"

"Christ!" said George from the hay.

'They must have been Russians!" said Doc.

We rushed up to the porch of the castle and there were thirty Polish slave laborers and our group of Americans all shaking hands and laughing. My captain friend who was to go on trial for his life was among the sick. The column had been Russian medium armored artillery, and we prisoners were free—and the Poles were free after more than five years of the evil things the United Nations had been fighting against.

Tears were in my eyes and for the first time I thought about getting home. Up to that moment it had been necessary to escape to avoid the grueling road-march to Germany where there was no security if we did make the entire trip.

Terribly tired, excited, cold, happy, dirty, the four of us returned to our hole in the hay and slept for ten hours. The next morning we had a close-up of Georgi Zhukov's First White Russian Army driving on Posen. They were riding about ten to a tank with American-made sub-machine guns in their laps, their worn, flat, red,

Mongolian faces bright from the sun off the snow. Fur hats with red stars on the front, high boots, worn, quilted clothes, gray overcoats, they were dirty and disheveled like all crack combat troops in action. A hard-looking lot, they had only cold looks for us —no stopping or waving—tanks on a definite mission. We later learned that the Russians use these Mongolians as front-line troops much as the French employ their Senegalese—never as rear area administration units. Like Senegalese, they had little curiosity about us. Elated at our freedom, we could see this was a fine modern army, but it was queer to be on the cheering end as soldiers raced after Jerry. I felt like the French or Italians I had watched in earlier days.

The two striking differences from the pictures and posters of Russia's army were that the tanks were not camouflaged white and the personnel did not wear steel helmets.

Like the crack Jerry outfits, the Russian weapons seemed to be a part of them, fitting like their clothes. It seemed to be a serious army and the vehicles weren't plastered with nicknames as in the British and American forces. It had all the earmarks of a rough, tough, formidable army that had fought hard for many months and many hundred miles.

Some of the trucks and motorcycles stopped and we explained about our bizarre group, and we all laughed and the big, friendly White Russians fingered our light clothing and we offered them cigarettes, but they had plenty of their own tobacco. Never were any of us as proud of our country as when watching the armored spearheads of Stalin. The manpower was Russian, and the mobility was American, with some British lend-lease. Shermans, Studebakers, and Fords gave the punch for Zhukov, and I never fully realized until then how we had been delivering the goods. The Russian soldiers had fixed the big American trucks with sheds and stoves. The light Russian trucks that came through were old models but recently built. They seemed to be living very well off the land, and half a cow might be tied to a tank hull, its frozen, dark, blood streaking the side. Trucks carried sheep or hog carcasses roped on the bumpers. No planes were paving the way for the armor that passed us.

In mopping up, they were thorough—too thorough. That first day we watched several armored cars and tank-riding Mongolians repeatedly search the same house or piece of ground for isolated Germans. Apparently the Russians did not have the Western Powers' systematic investigation ending in a radio report to all following units such as, "This road clear for tanks."

After the first well-drilled armored prongs, in which there was some order and battalions and regiments would be recognized, there followed a packed, shambling mass of peoples moving out of Asia into Europe. They jogged along in the dark, red wagons, placid and comfortable with their weapons on the bottom of their carts, their bundled women sitting stolidly on the straw. Lone Russian horsemen galloped along the road shoulders. For four days that army moved, as irresistible as a glacier. There was no waving, and they did not return our V sign. There was a great outdoor look to those Russians. Our men look as though they were tanned from a summer of hunting and fishing in Montana, but these faces from the East had the appearance of being beaten by sun and rain for generations. Except for the automatic weapons, the migration might have been the army that fought Napoleon.

The mass of man-woman-child power that ambled after the fast, motorized waves had none of the march discipline of the Western Armies. No one seemed to be in command. A cart would shuffle into our dairy yard, and if the occupants saw a horse better than theirs, they would take it and leave the old one. Or perhaps they would fire a burst of lead in to the head of a hog or hammer to death a fine dairy cow, throw the body on the cart and crowd their way back in to that moving lump. We then understood why we saw no supply trucks with food—only ammunitions and gasoline vehicles for the armored units.

Soldiers without women dropped in to our dairy—often a little drunk. They hung about with us for hours or ate and drank in the houses of the local Poles. There was no asking of an officer's permission to fall out. It was every-man-for-himself-but-keep-going-West. High-spirited youngsters of fifteen in fur hats and gray boots banged away with their guns at anything they might see—a bird, a fence post, a thin wobbling dog. These stray shots did not result in written reports and investigations as did ours miles behind the lines in France.

There were no ambulances, medical jeeps, or the standard provisions we make on a swift advance. The first day, in front of our castle, a tank-gun muzzle swung wild and knocked off two men. One of them couldn't walk, and the other had a mangled hand. The tough, cocky tank lieutenant brought them to our American doctors in the castle and had dressings applied. Both soldiers were in pain, but neither so much as groaned. In the American or British armies, the men would have been good for a month in the hospital. After the bandaging, the officer boosted them on the tank and away they went for the front and Posen. We later learned the Red Army had good hospital trains, but only for stretcher cases. The walking wounded were given battlefield dressings and told to come back when they had recovered. We met them in groups weeks later making their own way back through Poland, driving a cart they had taken from a peasant, sitting patiently in their bandages on the floor of a railroad station, or riding boxcars toward the Vistula.

The ranking colonel in the castle called us together during that first day of freedom, said, "I am the commanding officer here, and not the senior American officer. This is now a United States Army unit. Anyone leaving this dairy farm will be charged with desertion. If we stay here, we will not irritate the Poles nor hinder the Russian war effort. You are going to see more and more of the Russians. When you see some of the methods they are using, don't criticize them. Forget all about it. The Germans were in Russia and maybe the Russians want to even the score. Don't discuss politics with the Russians. Americans are very badly informed on world politics. When Russians wander in here, drunk or sober, officer or private, treat them with respect. The Poles have promised to feed us until we get out of here.

"I repeat no one is allowed to leave here. The men who hid in the barn may use the castle during the day, but at night they must sleep in the granary or one of the outbuildings. There is not enough room in the castle for everybody to sleep here. We will now go on the front porch and Chaplain Scott will conduct a service. We owe much to God and the Russians."

After the service, Doc said, "A hell of a thing. First the Colonel orders us to leave, and now he orders us to stay."

The four of us crowded some pigs together, put fresh straw in the empty pen, and lived there twelve days. The Poles gave us bread, jam, sugar, lamb broth, lard, sausage, milk, goat cheese, and pork.

Chapter Twenty-Two

We did not see the retreat of the German Army because it was being carried out on two parallel roads to the one in front of the castle. Jerry had also learned a lesson in the 1940 Battle of France—when the French and British could not conduct an orderly withdrawal because the roads were jammed with civilians. Falling back across Poland, the Nazis designated certain routes for the Army and other roads for refugees.

The third day after the Russians arrived, a Lieutenant Max drove into our yard in an American jeep, jumped out, was taken to our ranking Colonel, delivered a smooth salute, and said, "I have come to take you to Moscow. Your Embassy knows about you. Your families will be notified within forty-eight hours that you are free. Within two days you will be on your way home."

Max had spent four years at the College of the City of New York and returned to Russia to become a staff officer of Zhukov. Slender, dark-complexioned, sporting a natty little mustache and pompadour, he would be a smooth operator in any country. When he relaxed a bit, he said, "I'm not a Communist, but what do you think of our army? Wonderful, isn't it?" We told him it was.

He left a Lieutenant Micholovitch of Russian Army H.Q. in

charge of us, and Micholovitch never drew a sober breath the entire time. Our Colonel said that we should not be too anxious to get back to America, that we should be patient and grateful for what the Poles were feeding us, adding, "Eighty percent of the officers here are mentally ill from prison. We don't know what reception we will have in America. There will be much feeling against us, because we quit and gave up to the Germans."

When day after day passed, and Micholovitch remained drunk, we became uneasy and wanted to move. We complained to the Colonel who then shouted at us, calling us "goddamn silly kids" and told us to keep our "goddamn mouths shut" because he was running the post. He repeated his warning that if any of us departed, we would face court martial in America. Shortly after this flare-up, two pistol shots came through the ceiling of the red and white drawing room of the castle, but no one was hit. Two Russian officers were upstairs in the Colonel's room drinking vodka, and they had shot through the floor to let off a bit of steam.

We dug latrines outside in the ice and snow. The sides of the straddle trenches were slippery and it was not uncommon to land in the latrine with one foot. In addition, a blizzard was blowing and it was difficult to see and catch your breath in the cold, sharp wind and snow. We remained indoors as much as possible. Chaplain Scott playing popular pieces on the piano was our amusement.

A second announcement came to us from Max on the sixth day. The following day we would move in trucks seventy miles to Kutnow where we would be given medical attention, clothing, and taken from there to Moscow by train. We heard nothing more for several days.

In the meantime we watched organized Russian foraging parties arrive at the dairy and take livestock and vegetables for the Red Army. Amazed that we had not killed the animals ourselves, they would give our group pigs and cows from the stock. These Russians volunteered the information that after Berlin was kaput they would go after Japan. We would ask them where they were going with the food, and they would jerk a thumb toward the West and the answer was always the same—"Berlin." Odd Russians from private to major who dropped in were ushered politely to our Colonel who enjoyed a few drinks of vodka with them, and we would give cigars to the Red soldiers. They gave us some of their bread, which was coarser, darker, and grittier than Pole or Jerry bread. We would perhaps get nips of vodka from the Russians with the inevitable toasts to Roosevelt, Stalin, Churchill, and Studebaker. Some of the Russians were surprised that we were *Amerikanski* and at first believed that this was the junction of the American and Russian Armies which was to take place on the Elbe three months later. When we said we were prisoners, they were disappointed. These groups, unlike the first elements, had little or no tobacco, though their officers had plenty, which they rolled with newspaper in to cigarettes.

Their discipline was good. They were lax on saluting, and officers were very democratic with the men. But the respect was there. An officer would sleep on the bed in a room with his men on the floor around him. The next morning an orderly would hold the shaving water for the officer and help him on with his boots. Red officers had servants to shift their luggage.

Russians living for a night or two in the Polish homes around the castle ate well—fresh chickens and beef. They had canned lend-lease food, but their practice was to keep this for emergency rations and live off the land. This is the reverse of the American and British system. Our orders were strictly not to deprive the local people so long as we had our own supplies.

We had made a hospital flag out of a red hockey jersey and white sheet, which we flew in front of the castle. There was no medical aid for the Poles in the area, and our doctors delivered a few babies, attended sick Poles, and patched up Russian wounded who had been in a patrol fight with a small, by-passed pocket of Jerries eight kilometers from us.

The Poles who visited us from Exin told stories of Russian treatment of German civilians caught in the area. The Russians looked and acted like a conquering army and expected to be treated as such. For instance, a Russian private went to the house of a German in Exin, one of the few who did not leave for Germany. He asked for a bed and got it, but the German was a bit haughty. The next day, the Russian who had slept in the house gathered a few of his comrades and hung the entire family. This sort of thing did not disturb the Poles, as the family had arrived in Exin with the Nazis five years previously and moved in to the Polish house—keeping the owner and his wife in the basement as slave servants. There was not a Jew left in Exin after the Nazi occupation. They had been killed or moved to unknown destinations.

A Polish underground man who had repaired electric wires in our Szubin camp for eighteen months said he had not once been contacted by Americans in the camp as to methods of escape and the attitude of the Poles in the vicinity. He did not dare to broach the subject inside the barbed wire. He said when we were marching through Exin under guard of the Germans they were waiting for us to make a break and we could have taken over the small German force. He told us about the Polish girl who had passed our Oflag, waved to us, was sighted by the Germans, and given nine months' imprisonment.

The Army trucks making their way back from the front were loaded with captured German equipment such as anti-tank guns and motorcycles which the Russians repaired and used. In the Western Armies, these returning trucks would be loaded with prisoners. There did not seem to be the stress in the Russian Army on the maintenance of vehicles such as our officers were always concerned about. As long as the machinery would run, that was what was important. Russian drivers, for example, shifted gears in a grind that could be heard many meters.

Several of our American officers who had marched on with the column returned to the dairy with news of the prisoners. After leaving the dairy, they marched that day thirty kilometers. That night, the German guard commander, Captain Meinner, dismissed the guard company. The next morning our men were free, but the orders were for none of the men to evacuate the area as they could be more easily administered to in a group instead of running all over Poland. An organization was set up to get food, Command Post signs printed, and a staff organized. Thirteen hours after the guard company left, new young, tough guards arrived with Schmeissers and gave our column a half-hour to get on the road and start before they would shoot. It was a shocking, heartbreaking situation, but sixty officers had enough presence of mind to hide out or scamper away before the twenty-five guards marched the eleven hundred officers on the way to Germany. It was their last opportunity to escape until on the other side of Germany, General Patton sent a tank column to their new prison in an aborted rescue.

It was not clear who owned the animals on the dairy farm, but there were cows to be milked and chickens to be fed, and the former slaves continued their work after a three-day celebration of their freedom. When the Russians took the animals, the Poles did not protest but assumed an indifferent attitude. One of our favorite amusements if the weather was favorable was watching the dairy boar service the sows on the ice of the yard. It was a difficult operation, as pigs' feet are not made for proceedings on a hard, slippery surface.

On the twelfth day of freedom, we received another message from the Russian liaison officer who was with our group back in the Oflag. The American Government had set up an Embassy in Warsaw, and had had contacted the families of the Americans who were free. The United States had recognized the Lublin Government, our main column of prisoners had been overtaken by the Russians and were up the road, the Big Three were meeting in Warsaw. The final sentence was, "The American government will move the prisoners but at the present there is no time for it as the Government has other things to do."

Gloom fell on us. We thought that perhaps the Colonel had given us the right information about being in disgrace because we had surrendered to Nazis. There were more than three hundred of us loose, but United States would get around to us eventually. We received the news of the daring Ranger raid in the Phillippines that liberated five hundred prisoners of the Japs miles behind the lines, and we could not understand why we were not moved by our Government when it would not even involve a raid. We were there for the asking.

Later we knew the Big Three were meeting in Yalta, that there was no Warsaw Embassy, that we were not in disgrace, that our families had not been notified despite the information we gave the

Russians, that United States had not recognized the Lublin Government, that our prison column had not been overtaken by the Russians, and that the American Government had not been notified that any of us were free.

That twelfth day we learned we had picked up lice in the pigpen and moved to the stables where we slept for two nights on horse manure covered with hay. It was warmer than the pigpen, but the steam from the manure made our bodies and clothing damp.

The fourteenth day, some Polish men and women came in a cart and offered to take thirty of us to Jurgensburg, two miles away, and feed, house and clothe us. The four of us got our names on the list and marched to Jurgensburg, a community of forty-five families that had been working for Baron Hans von Rosen. Von Rosen had received Jurgensburg from Hitler as his pearl in the three billion dollar booty of Poland. Von Rosen had done excellent work in undermining Poland for the Nazi invasion and had left with the retreat of the German Army, taking only his family, jewels, and automobiles. The thirty of us moved in to the overseer's house. Then we invaded Grocholin, Baron von Rosen's home that was just as he suddenly left it. Half-filled wine glasses were on the dining room table. I got a long lounge for a bed, a pillow, a chair, a rug, and two bottles of rhubarb wine. Wiley snatched some ashtrays, a silver dinner bell, and a cot.

The rest of the officers also ran wild in the house, taking what they needed for comfort. We decorated our rooms in the overseer's house with oil paintings and valuable steel engravings from the Baron. I got the Barons top hat and silver riding crop and velvet dinner jacket which we took turns wearing. We picked up some of the grandchildren's toys to play with—such things as a perfect miniature, mechanical sewing machine complete in every detail, cannons whose wheels and adjustments except for size were the same as on big guns, and parlor games concerning the bombing of cardboard cities.

We spent hours looking at the Baron's postcard collection of Junker heroes and Nazi party leaders that we found in the den. The von Rosens were Hitler fanatics and had many of the Fuehrer's reproduced drawings framed on the walls—drawings that weren't at all as terrible as might be expected. One drawer of the Baron's desk was crammed with souvenirs of the 1936 Berlin Olympic Games. The gold-tooled leather-bound propaganda books showed Eleanor Roosevelt's picture touched to make her look as though she had Negro blood, while Franklin Roosevelt's photographs had his teeth blacked out, and he had been given definite Semitic characteristics. Captions under Fiorello La Guardia marked him as a Jew. Pictures of sobbing Poles taken during the 1939 invasion explained that they were not Polish people, but Spanish, Swedish, and American—that the Poles were happy Germany had entered their country. Unless seen, the tremendous amount of false propaganda turned out for all classes of the Reich is unbelievable—propaganda delivered while France, Britain, and America were internationally asleep. The elaborate genealogy book that traced the von Rosen title to the thirteenth century we used for toilet paper.

The friendly Polish women gave us one big greasy meal a day, and two meals of bread, lard, and warm milk. Yadwiga was in charge of the kitchen, an intelligent, pretty girl whose schooling had been stopped by Jerry. She said that the Poles liked Americans and would do anything for us, that they all hoped the Americans would be stationed in Poland, and that by having us in Jurgensburg, they would not have to have Russians around. At night, the Polish men with long, ancient rifles guarded our house while we slept. In the evenings, we could hear the Russian artillery pounding Posen.

Just before the von Rosens left their home in flight, they splashed in red paint on the living room wall, "We are coming again in 1945." Some Russians who dropped in rubbed out "1945" and put in "1975," and departed with Oriental and Persian rugs for the bottoms of their wagons. While I was searching for a shaving mirror in the Baron's bedroom, a Pole came in looking for loot, and saw a handsome photograph of von Rosen as a colonel in the Kaiser's army. He started—and grabbed the picture and smashed it in to a corner, leaving the room muttering as though he had seen a ghost. In the backyard was the Christmas tree lying in the snow—used only a few weeks before when von Rosen and his grandchildren were living handsomely.

Two days after we arrived at von Rosen's, Russians announced that twenty Poles from the locality must move toward Germany and take over German farms, where Nazis were to work for them as slaves just as they had worked for the Nazis. Some of the Poles did not want to leave. They had seen enough of slavery not to want any part of it, they explained to us. Also, they said, they could not be sure they would own these farms and that it might be a system of collective farming under supervision of the Russians. They did not want to work for the state. Yadwiga was one of the women selected, but she did not wish to leave her father who was a small Exin businessman before 1939 and had spent the following five years shoveling manure for von Rosen. The Russians permitted her to remain behind as she was taking care of us. These Russians who dropped in would ask us for some of our rapidly disappearing cigarettes. When we offered them one, flipping it half way out of the pack, they would take the entire package. As a result, we had to have one supply on us for ourselves, and another package with two or three cigarettes in it that we would bring out for Russians. The Poles usually refused our cigarettes as they knew we had few, or they might offer us some of theirs if they had any, which they usually didn't.

One evening a jolly Russian tank major dropped in, and we talked with him through two of our officers who spoke Polish. Said the major, "We'll go after Japan when Berlin falls. I don't know anything about politics and economics. I have no quarrel with anybody. But my business is soldiering. There is nothing for our soldiers back in Russia. Their families and homes are destroyed. We don't worry about death. We don't want to die, naturally, but we don't give much thought to it one way or another. We like traveling West, because the more we go, the more we got. My business is fighting."

One of our boys borrowed a bicycle to ride to Szubin to learn what the colony there was planning to do. Just before he entered the gate, a Russian private with a sub-machine gun took the bike away from him, and our officer reported this to a Red Army sergeant. This man didn't bother with orders. He just went over to the private, grabbed him by the collar with one hand and waved a fist in his face. The private returned the bike. We learned that Max had moved the bulk of the sick and wounded from Szubin and had gone toward Warsaw—having told us nothing at von Rosen's. The same day two of our boys visited our dairy farm, returned saying, "That Micholivitch is still drunk, doesn't know where his headquarters are now, and is still toasting Studebaker and Stalin whenever you ask him about getting out of Poland. The Colonel is disgusted and has dissolved the post and says that if any of us want to take off on our own we may, and the court martial threat is no longer in order."

That's all we wanted to hear. That night we made overlays from maps we found in von Rosen's and decided to head for Odessa and try to get a boat through the Black Sea. One of the officers contacted the temporary mayor of Exin who said we should hang around the depot and maybe the Russians would let us on a train. He gave us passes to travel unmolested. Doc Parker decided to remain behind and take care of the Polish families in an epidemic of diphtheria and typhus that had broken out around the Baron's. Herr, Wiley, Ackerman, and I walked in to Exin the next noon after thanking the kind, generous Polish women for their cooking and cleaning of our quarters. One of my boots had no sole and I knew it would be a wet and cold trip.

In Exin, the Germans who were too poor to flee were being used as street cleaners working under armed Polish guards. One group of old German men carrying some wood was being whipped by some young Poles, and no one seemed to be taking notice of the incident. Many of the houses and stories had "Polak" printed on them so that the Russians would not loot them. Stores that did not have this sign were usually sacked, as it was assumed they were German-owned.

The four of us went in to the one-room depot filled with Poles and burlap bags tied in string with names written on the sides, most ending in "ski." There were about forty there and some had been waiting four days for a train. All were returning to their homes from where Jerry had moved them as forced labor. A few had blue tattoos marking them as slave laborers. Childish old women, sick children, pockmarked, thick-lipped, unshaven men sat in blankets, wearing the red and white Polish colors and the same clothes they had put on every day for five years. Outside were a few Russian transportation soldiers who showed no friendliness. That first night the Polish stationmaster took the four of us to a dairy where we had some milk for supper, and some of the people in the railroad station gave us black bread and some greasy concoction which they scraped out of tin cans. The room smelled of bodies unwashed for months, and all of us went to sleep on the floor. I had my spot by the door and all night long people were stepping on me. A woman two yards from me had hiccups for an hour. Waiting for each hiccup was like waiting for the periodical drop of water on the forehead that sends men crazy. Another woman kept saying prayers out loud all night, and along about midnight two of them had a fistfight over a blanket.

In the morning, we went to a house near the station and asked to clean up. The Poles were very obliging with smiles and nods—as our group of prisoners by this time was well known about Exin. When we finished washing, we had a cup of ersatz coffee. The door suddenly opened and in blustered a Russian who elbowed his way to the sink in the crowded kitchen, washed himself, dried his hands on the family towel, blew his nose in it, and stamped out again without saying yes, no, thank you, or boo to anyone. The Poles didn't comment. They were used to it, but we had a laugh out of the exhibition.

In the middle of the morning, the stationmaster called the four of us out and put us on a short flat-car train going to Gnesen. Two Russians came along and told us to get off. Our tactics were to be timidly polite, and we got off.

Chapter Twenty-Three

In the middle of the afternoon, another train arrived. The stationmaster beckoned us to the coach, the rest of the train being made up of flat-cars and boxcars. It was extremely cold and snowing. The displaced persons automatically went to the flat-cars and boxcars. Just before the train left, a Russian artillery captain told us to get out of the coach. The stationmaster explained we were "*Amerikanski* officers," but the Russian said through an interpreter, "Coaches are only for Russians."

In the coach were six Russian privates and the captain. With apologies to us, the stationmaster helped us on to a flat-car crowded with booted women, shawled old ladies, men in caps, babies sucking on black crusts of bread, and five pretty young girls who had worked in Jerry kitchens. We were cold on that ride, but all of us on the boxcar were in high spirits. We were going home.

At Gnesen, seven more American officers joined us, and while the train was parked, some Polish women gave us sauerkraut soup and two pieces of bread. The Russians there had never seen Americans before, and when word was passed that we were sitting on a flat-car mob after mob of them came and silently stared at us. A few of them offered us cigarettes, and asked about our dog tags and fingered them. They then showed us their identification, a scroll in a metal cylinder that they carried in their pockets.

In the modern Gnesen station on the main Posen-Warsaw line, the stationmaster tried to get us a freight train, but it was no use. We sat in the midst of the refugees, and a Pole gave us his half loaf of bread and some ersatz coffee he was carrying in a green bottle. Early in the morning, the stationmaster called us out and walked us half a mile to a caboose with a stove. Eighteen Serbs, recent prisoners of war, followed and climbed in the caboose with us. After a short run, we stopped in Liubriunet where we sat for exactly twenty hours. We had no food, but I was trying to get some of the lumps out of the hay on the floor for more comfort and discovered a gold mine—twenty-nine raw potatoes. We cooked these on the stove and they kept us going for two days. During the wait, the Serbs took off and all but six of us left the caboose. We had food, a stove, a soft place to lie, and that's about all any of us could hope for, so we could see no profit in leaving. A Polish officer joined our car, only twenty miles from where he hoped he would find his home and wife after sixty-four months a prisoner of the German Government. He could speak English, as could a surprising number of Poles. They had learned it during the long years of occupation secretly listening to the BBC broadcasts.

The next four days we rode and jerked around Poland in that car. On halts we went to the doors of Poles to beg bread and were never refused. On a stop ten kilometers from Lodz, we left the caboose and walked into the town. Hungarian box-mines and shattered German equipment from the recent fighting were still strewn about. Entering Lodz on a Sunday, we caused a sensation. "*Amerikanski! Amerikanski!*" the people shouted, blessing us, shaking our hands, following us.

We felt foolish. In our United Nations' uniforms, we looked little like American soldiers and were ashamed that we could not present a better appearance as the first Americans these people had seen since the occupation. Straw from the boxcar was hanging on our clothes, white china mugs dangled from our coats, and our blue and white rucksacks were slung over our shoulders. Our dirty faces were grinning, and blushing. It was a great day. The Poles of Lodz were going freely to church for the first time in more than five years. Russian red flags sporting the yellow hammer and sickle were flying from many buildings.

We watched a Communist parade. Lodz has a population of several hundred thousand and is Poland's second largest city, but there were less than one hundred people in this demonstration. Every fifth person carried some kind of propaganda banner, but all we could read were the exclamation marks. Apparently this was no terrific movement because the people on the sidewalks and in the buildings paid not the slightest attention to the parade.

Under a red flag, we entered a building, walked in to the office, dropped our sacks, said, "*Amerikanski. Essen. Warschau.*" If we had had sticks, we could have knocked off the eyes of the men and women in the room. When their eyes popped back in the sockets, we repeated the three words. We said we could speak German when we realized they did not know our nationality, that we wanted to eat, that we wanted directions to Warsaw. A German-speaking scrubwoman was brought in to us. But the only German we knew was the phrase that we knew how to speak it. We tried French. A man in a cap rattled French to us. Finally they understood, told us to sit down, and in a half hour sauerkraut soup, ersatz coffee, bread, and oleo was given us in the office. Where it came from, I don't know. The building turned out to be the Communist headquarters of Lodz—not a restaurant or information bureau. While we ate, the occupants continued their meeting, giving us wary glances.

Down the street from this headquarters, we met three British Tommies, captured at Dunkirk. We asked them about a place in Lodz to spend the night.

"The best thing for you blokes to do is get out of here. We arrived here three days ago and the Russki Gestapo looked us up. This is our first day out. We have to report back in two hours."

"Any way to get to Warsaw from here?"

"Try the station. Trains might be running now. But don't go to the Russki headquarters here for griff. That's what we did, and they now have us in the glass-house."

In the next block, we had a conversation with three Polish military police who had arrived from the East with the Red Army. Asking them directions for Warsaw, we were advised to leave Lodz at once or we would never reach the capitol for several weeks. Friendly, they stopped an American truck driven by Polish soldiers, ordering the driver to take us to the railroad station. There were many smiles and offers of cigarette-makings when they learned we were Amerikanski.

The station was jammed with displaced persons sitting on their belongings. We gibbered to the ticket agent about a pass to Warsaw, and he asked for money. We had none. Only Lublin currency was being accepted. Things looked dark for us and we looked around for tall N. K. V. D. Russians to tap us on the shoulder and march us away. An English-speaking youth came to us, asked us what we wanted.

"We want to get to Warsaw and to hell out of here," Herr said.

"One of you come with me. My father is the stationmaster here. This is the first day trains have been running since the Russians came through. But I think I can get you to Warsaw."

I went with the youth, whose name was Leonard, and met his father. We talked through Leonard. It turned out that we would have a private compartment to Warsaw and would leave on the first train and until that arrived, we were to stay with Leonard. He took the six of us to his apartment above the station and we talked.

"What is this Lublin and London Government fuss all about, Leonard?" one of us asked.

"It is not clear yet. But it will be straightened out. Most of the people are for the Lublin Government. The Lublin Government put my father here as stationmaster last week to replace the Nazi."

Leonard might have been right. But it was the first time in Poland that we heard anyone say he wanted the Lublin Government. The other Poles had volunteered the information to us that their real government was in London. They did not necessarily want the men of the London Government, but they wanted the ideal for which they stood—free elections. But the Lublin Government was on the scene and moved rapidly to each village and city as soon as it was liberated and set up their offices and ruled the populace.

We ate bread, cheese, and ersatz coffee with plenty of sugar and milk, and Leonard's sister made us sandwiches for the train. We talked. Leonard was studying engineering, but for the last five years had worked in the fields with his hands for the Nazis. The people of Lodz had to speak German, the city's name was changed to Litzmannstadt, and the schools had been closed.

"We saw a big, burned-out building on our way to the station. What was that?"

"Warsaw refugees were living there. Hundreds and hundreds of them. The Germans locked them all in and set fire to the building. The charred skeletons are still there. That was three weeks ago today, just before the Russians arrived."

His sister said in Polish, to Leonard, "English language sounds like German."

When he repeated this for us, we looked surprised. He thought we were insulted, and got us more ersatz coffee, apologized, said that the two languages were not similar, and not to pay any attention to his sister.

He told us that the Russian advance had been so swift that the electricity and water systems were not destroyed by the Germans and that even the Gestapo had been caught in a Lodz cellar and were quickly killed by the Russians.

The train arrived and people packed it, including riding on the roof. But we had our compartment and Leonard and his father sent us on our way with many handshakes and promises to write after the war. At Koluszki, we were told the train could go no farther that night, and we went in to a warm station room where there were many liberated Polish officers on their way home after five years. Far from our homes, we did not envy these men who in a few hours would be where they had said good-bye to their families in 1939. They were trying to spruce their worn uniforms for the reunion. They did not know if their homes were still standing or who in their family were still alive. I had a conversation with a Polish lieutenant about thirty-five years old.

"America, I insist you take this scarf of mine. We received Red Cross parcels from your Government, and it saved our lives. The little I can do is give you this scarf for your journey."

I took the scarf and asked him where he learned English. He had studied it in prison.

"When the Russians arrived," he said, "the German guards in our camp fought fiercely. Many of our men were killed, after waiting for freedom so long. I was with the group of men who killed the German commandant with our hands. We choked him and kicked him. He was a swine."

Two Polish officers who were resting under a table got up and gave the space to two of us for sleeping. It was out of the way, and people would not step on us. At midnight, Herr awakened me. We were to leave for Warsaw immediately. The Polish officers elbowed their way through the crowd, shouting in Polish, "Save seats for American officers!" And in an open, cold, crowded coach were six seats saved for us. We offered to take turns standing with the Poles but they would not allow this. One man gave us all his tobacco. It made us feel cheap to accept the generosity of these people from whom the Germans had taken almost everything except the earth and sky. It was impossible to refuse. A Russian engineer captain and his orderly told us to stay with him and he would take care of us. He was very friendly, cold sober, told us his home was in Vladivostok, and we hummed "Rose Marie" and "Volga Boatmen" with him. At Pruszkow, the train stopped for the night, and the Russian captain walked in to the stationmaster's room, while his twenty-three-year-old orderly with a billiard ball head pulled out a stick grenade, held it in his cocked arm, and told the Polish guards we were using the warm office for the night. The rest of the people on the train stayed outside on the cement and along the cold tracks.

The orderly made his captain comfortable on a bench and until daylight sat near him without closing his eyes, which shifted around like a faithful, fierce watchdog's. The orderly pulled out nearly a pint of vodka, drained it in one gulp, and slammed the empty bottle on the desk. Having been in the Russian Army since he was fourteen years old, he made no more of a face about the taste and burn than I would about a sip of pure tap water.

The captain took us to the Bolsheviki Kommandant in an effort to get us transportation to Warsaw. En route, the streets were lined with women selling white bread for fifty zlotychs a loaf—about a half- dollar. We had no money and thought of giving a pack of our few cigarettes for some but decided it would be better to get along on black bread which people were giving us free. The Kommandant was young, good-looking, well built, and he seemed to have had a hard night. His hair was down in his bloodshot eyes. We got him out of bed, but dressing was no trick for him. He had removed only his blouse, and he pulled that over his head. Ready for business, he told us we would have to make our own way to Moscow where Churchill and Roosevelt were meeting Stalin—which turned out to be wrong. He took down our names and brought out his situation map, showing us Zhukov's prong, and Rokossovksi's, and Konev's, piercing into Germany. With our arms and hands we made a pincer, said, "Russki, Amerikanski—Berlin!" He got this and laughed. He went in to his sleeping quarters and brought out a large can of lend-lease pork and fat. We thought he was just showing us this, but he indicated that we should keep it. It was the first and last lend-lease food from America that we got from the Russians. As soon as we were outside the house, we opened the can and the six of us dipped in and finished it right there.

Back at the station, a redheaded Polish man named Witold was waiting for us in the office. He asked us if we would care to come to his home for a wash and sleep. We walked three hundred yards to what was once a comfortable apartment house in a prosperous suburb of Warsaw. Inside, five and six people were sleeping in each room—all evacuees of Warsaw, which they said was totally destroyed. When others in the apartment heard that Americans were in Witold's rooms, they came flocking to stare and smile at us and go away contented that they had seen an American. We had a breakfast of bread, lard, and ersatz coffee, while Izabella, a girl in her twenties, explained in halting BBC English that they had heard there were six hungry and dirty American officers in the station and they wanted to do something for them. The atmosphere was friendly but tense, as we could not say much to each other. Suddenly, in rushed a striking-looking, vivacious, middle-aged woman who said, "Good morning, America! Anything we have is yours. Tell us what you want."

Herr, Wiley, Ackerman, and the rest of us buzzed immediately. The woman had once been a concert pianist in America. First she told us about Warsaw where most of the people in the apartments had once lived. The Germans had systematically and ruthlessly destroyed the city from house to house, dynamiting and burning—first ordering the people out of the cellars where they were hiding. The Germans would stand on the sidewalks taking what they wanted from the people as they came up the cellar steps to the sidewalks. One German had more than thirty wristwatches on his arms. But the people didn't care about their valuables as they expected to be shot. The recent Warsaw uprising of General Bor had taken place because "conditions under the Germans were no longer tolerable," and one hundred thousand civilians were killed in four weeks.

Questions were fired at us. They had a well-thumbed copy of a

May 1939 *LIFE* magazine containing many predictions and warnings about Hitler and Europe that came true and were well founded. They said except for the illegal radio, we were their first contact with the outside world for more than five years. "Does America know about us?" they asked. "Do your people know how fiercely we fought?" "When are the Americans coming to Poland?" "Does the world know that we are terrific patriots?" "Will America fight for us if it is necessary?" "Tell us about the fighting in France."

Some of these questions we did not or could not answer. Many of the questions we had no chance to answer before another was translated for us. They told us they were afraid of the Russians and that Poland was "caught between the devil and the witch," with Germany on one side and Russia on the other. When Russians stopped in for the night, they always took some of the household belongings with them. The night before, five Russian girls had slept in the apartment, and when asked where they were going, said, "Berlin! To cut, cut, cut!" They were well armed with sub-machine guns and knives, the pianist said, and we knew they were because we had seen the armed Russian girls.

Some of the ideas they expressed were out of tune as might be expected in such little contact with the social, economic and political forces loose in the world since 1939. It was a case of ". . . few virtues the Poles do not possess and few mistakes they have ever avoided."

Izabella had worked as a nurse in a hospital caring for Bor's wounded when the Germans set fire to the building, burning three hundred alive. Witold said that the Germans did not bother shooting Jewish babies, but just broke open their skulls on the sidewalks with their boot heels. They did not tell these things with exaggeration or try to impress us. Atrocities had been the rule, and almost normal to them, and they were surprised that we didn't know the details on the rape of Poland.

A pale, quiet Jewish boy of twenty arrived in the room—one of the eight hundred remaining Semitics who had once been among the thousands and thousands of Lodz. He had just come out of a concentration camp, set free by the Russians. We asked him what it was like, and he said he would rather not talk about it, and we were embarrassed for asking the question. We could see his answer was not for effect—such as a soldier might say about fighting at the front—but because to talk about it would send him to pieces.

One of us said that things would be all right now. The Germans had been driven away. But that started it all over again. "The Russians are just biding their time. They have let us open our churches and go about our business because they are fighting a war. But wait. Doesn't America know? Already they are setting up a Government we don't want. London is our Government."

A lady who was an American citizen, had married a Pole, and once was in the American Embassy society of Warsaw. She was living in the basement with her family and several refugees. "Can you boys help us? Get word to America that we need help in Poland. I have many friends in New York and Philadelphia where I lived. Will you see them for me?"

She talked for fifteen minutes and we listened. "They killed my maid when they burned my home in Warsaw. I don't know why they let me live. But they took all my jewels. The Germans there killed half of my intimate friends last autumn. Many of them were burned alive. They threw benzene into the cellars where they were hiding and put torches to the liquid. I don't know how we stood it.

I didn't go in to the cellars because I knew it was no use. When they came in our house I waited for them to shoot me. But they just set fire to the place, shot the maid, and I ran out the door.

"I can't understand the Germans. They were very polite and well dressed during the occupation. The officers and men always looked very neat. Boots well polished and so forth. Then they suddenly went crazy. Some of my friends were able to buy their lives from the soldiers. We all had money, of course. I made my way out of Warsaw by darting from house to house."

We stayed with Witold's family for two days, and they wanted us to remain the duration with them. But it gave us a funny feeling to take these people's beds while they slept on the floor and to eat their food of which they had so little. In addition, we wanted to push on, as we knew our families in America were worrying about us.

Our last meal with Witold was pork, potatoes, gravy, sauerkraut, butter, and a can of raspberries that they had been saving for five years. They brought out some pre-war hundred-proof cask-aged vodka and gave us each a tall glass of it. Witold then gave us a bottle of vodka that he said was not very good but that the Russians would not know the difference and we would need it to buy our way to Warsaw. We were instructed to wave it at the Russian truck drivers and they would stop, drink it, and give us a ride. The Russian drivers do not pick up people unless there is bait.

Off we started, waving that vodka bottle, but the only ride we got was a short one with some Polish boys of the Lublin Army. They were very friendly, giving us their seats in the back of the truck, and one lieutenant insisted that we take all his tobacco. After that we had to walk. Every four hundred yards was a buxom, long-haired Russian woman M. P. in a fur hat, knee length big coat, boots, and lend-lease sub-machine gun. They were big, healthy, rosy-cheeked, and rough—but healthy rough. We asked them to stop an empty truck for us and give us a ride to Warsaw. We all had holes in our shoes, and the road was snow and ice. But they only laughed at us. And we continued in the wandering columns of broken refugees.

Chapter Twenty-Four

Across the snow, we saw the skeleton of Warsaw rising. On the outskirts were wandering figures, dark against the white background, moving like ants after their anthill had been kicked over. Inside the once-proud capitol the buildings that were not flattened had been gutted by fire. The few people walking through Warsaw were silent. The entire atmosphere was one of eerie silence, and it was the most humbling sight I saw during the war. Not one building was habitable. On each wall was chalked the amount of explosive necessary to destroy the structure. The untrammeled snow added to the quiet of the deserted city. The twelfth-century cathedral, the eleventh-century castle, the monuments, and the museum pieces had been systematically destroyed by the Nazis in retribution for the people's uprising.

The ghetto by the river was wiped out, and we stood aghast at the brutishness that had been displayed in this city. We thought of the indifference of the Western world while this tragedy was playing and felt ashamed. Frozen, yellow bones jutted through the snow from unburied bodies dead six months—the beleaguered patriots of Bor's revolt who had fought the Nazis with their bare hands. Crude wooden crosses on the main street marked some of the bodies while other crosses identified a few dead lying in the rubble of what had once been shop display windows. Thousands of those dead were in cellars, and they did not smell because it was too cold.

As the six of us crawled through the white ribs of Warsaw, we heard people who were carrying wood for fuel from the ruins to their suburb shacks, say we were Italians, French, or British. Tired, we sat on some steps near a smashed streetcar stopped when the revolt broke out. We ate the bread Witold had given us. When a Pole called us French, we said we were *Amerkanski.* His eyes bugged out, and it was as though we had told him that Christmas was coming every day. He shook our hands, talked to us in his poor but understandable English. Looking up and down the street, his eyes came to rest on us and with a sweep of his arm he said with a bitter sneer and smoldering hate, "Pretty, isn't it? We have the German to thank."

Other people were stopped by the man and told we were Americans, and they stared and smiled at us. Soon there was quite a crowd. They kept repeating over and over again, "*Amerikanski, Amerikanski, Amerikanski*," as though they loved to say the word. Many of them were carrying important-looking business brief cases, which they opened, revealing only bread and cognac that they offered us. We explained over and over what our insignias of rank and branch of service on our collars represented. Our presence seemed to them a symbol of the end of five years of slavery. Some of the Poles there at first thought we were the advanced elements of the American Army, and they were disappointed when we told them that we had been prisoners and that we did not know of any United States units coming to Poland.

One woman said, "We are not free yet. We can wear our colors and fly our flag, but we wear the red and white upside down. The Russians do not know this."

We could believe the Russians did not know whether the white should be on top or bottom of the Polish colors, because they did not recognize the American flag a few of us were wearing on our arms. Many times Red Army men asked what it was.

Loving their country fiercely, zealous patriots, great nationalists, they told us that the Curson Line was robbing the Poles of their own cities, and predominately Polish-populated land would go to Russia East of the Line. We could see this group of people represented the spirit and determination of the country to rise again. I noticed the high color in their cheeks as they talked. They had lived an outdoor life, but at the same time they were pinched and drawn, and though they looked harder than the six of us, they were not as much at ease.

We presented none of our own opinions, asked them few questions. They told us stories of the sack of Warsaw, which were unbelievable if they had not been presented in such a calm, matter-of-fact way such as many Americans might describe a lopsided football game. It seemed as though these people were beyond the sense of horror.

On the other side of the Vistula was Praga, and we reached it by walking across the frozen, white river on a muddy pontoon bridge in the midst of hundreds of displaced persons. The twisted wreckage of powerful, beautiful bridges lay in the Vistula. By this time we had learned to keep our watches, fountain pens, or any valuable personal items well hidden. Russian soldiers never searched us for articles, but if they saw a wristwatch, for example, on any of the escaped American prisoners, they politely and firmly took it—with an air of friendliness. They believed that the victor deserved the spoils and they didn't care who they spoiled. As fighting soldiers they would have greater use for the watch than the escapee, they courteously explained. The Russians' great weakness for wristwatches is comparable to the weakness of the American soldier for good German cameras. Americans and Russians have stopped at nothing to get both. The Red Army took many things the Germans had allowed our men to keep from them.

The Russians occupying troops in France did not have the theory that to maintain prestige with the people, they must be well groomed. American troops cannot enter villages well behind the lines unless they have the prescribed uniform of neckties and leggings and hats. British troops must have their boots shined and a clean uniform. German occupation troops maintain a smooth, soldierly appearance, and the people cannot say they are rabble. The hundreds of Polish soldiers who had been released in the Russian drive after four years of prison were neat—clothes brushed, patched boots shined with a bit of paper or rag, hats at the proper angle.

The quilted gray and brown Red Army uniforms were dirty and the wearers often drunk—not vomiting, but boisterous. Their submachine guns impressed the local people, and that was enough. There were many pictures of Stalin in Praga—none of the heads of the British or American States. Posters were plastered about of good-looking, well-dressed, advertisement soldiers saying with big smiles to the Polish civilians, "We are friends." The Russians in the posters wore steel helmets, but we never saw a Red Army man in one at the front or in the rear.

Soldiers of the Lublin Polish Army which had advanced with the Russians were in Praga, and while they were on good terms with the Russians, we never saw them mingling or drunk together. They were friendly to us, and I could see no difference between them and the Poles who had fought with us in Italy under Anders. Except that these Poles were well stocked with Lublin paper zlotychs, whereas Anders' men had been poor.

From Exin to Praga we had seen much of the Red Army. The secret, we felt, of its great record was in the skill of the engineers to rapidly repair railroads to bring up supplies, making short hauls by trucks to the front; in Allied bombing and Allied lend-lease, particularly American; in its abundant use of automatic weapons; in its hordes of people unitedly determined to push on and maul the guts out of the German Army which had wreaked such havoc in Russia; in the fact that the farther West it traveled, the more fun it had; in the ability to live off the land as it advanced.

On the outskirts of Praga, we asked some questions on directions from Russian military police parked in a light American truck. They said that we should give up trying to go farther East and join an assembly camp for allied officers at Rembertow ten miles distant. It sounded fine to us, and they offered to drive us there. Dropped on the edge of Rembertow, we met some British soldiers. "What kind of a set-up is this assembly camp?" Herr asked them. They looked at each other and grinned.

"Some of the blokes are nipping off already," one man replied. "We advise you to do the same. Don't sign in. Once you sign in, you have to stay."

"What's the matter with it?" Wiley asked.

"One meal a day. Some kind of wallpaper paste they call '*kosha*,' and tea. The tea's all right. Sweet, anyway. Plenty of bread, but it's hard on the teeth."

"No place to go to the latrine except out in the yard with all the women. No trenches for the latrine. It's just an area. You'll be there and some woman will come up and be right there with you," said another.

We were tired, wet, dirty, and hungry, and we decided to at least look at the place and maybe stay one night. In the village, we met some of the American officers from the Oflag. "What are you doing with those clothes under your arm?" Ackerman asked.

"It's the only way you can eat," a captain said. "We go in once a day and sell some of our clothes and buy bread and bologna. The Russkies give you something to eat, but it's only a tin can of rice and horsemeat gravy."

"Any word of moving to America from here?" Herr asked, thinking about his baby he had never seen.

"No definite plans. That Russki Lieutenant Max is here, and he says our Moscow Embassy knows about us but isn't ready to move us yet. Max brought the wounded and sick group from Szubin here three weeks ago."

"We wondered what became of Max. He gave us a lot of talk about going to Moscow back at Exin, and then we never heard or saw him again," said Lieutenant John O'Neil, Medford, Massachusetts.

The fenced-in assembly camp was no better than our information on it. There was one large building in the center which years before had housed the cadets of the Polish West Point. Inside the building was a stinging smell of sex, dirty bodies, poor food, bad cooking, and defecation. Including the two hundred American officers more than twenty-five hundred refugees were packed in the filthy, unsanitary establishment. More than half the people there were soldiers, but they had lost all their military bearing. The remainder was back wash of war—Lithuanians, Russians, Czechs, Norwegians, Italians, Jews, Serbs, and French. Even ten Italian generals complete with service ribbons were pigging it like everybody else. That made most of us feel better about the place, even though they were Italian generals.

After watching a wild, shouting fistfight between an Italian and a Lithuanian over a piece of bread, the six of us signed in with the Ranger captain in charge of American billeting. We were assigned space on the floor.

"I'll show you where we eat," said Bob Breazele who had arrived with the Szubin crowd. "The Russians are running it, so that means we eat any time from seven o'clock in the morning to midnight."

The room had no light except that which came from the kitchen. We watched the dregs of Europe fighting for places at the tables. Russian girls threw wooden spoons and American tin cans fitted with wire handles on the tables. The cans contained kosha, which was boiled barley. After fifteen or twenty minutes arrived small cups of sweetened tea. Due to the crowded conditions and lack of organization there was no chance to wash the tin cans. Our turn to eat those first twenty-four hours was at one in the morning.

The trouble with the mess was organization. One day we would get a can of soup—the next day two cans of kosha. But if our turn to eat came at three in the morning, many of us would miss the meal. Finally we Americans asked permission from the Russians to organize the service for all the nations. Our NCOs volunteered to replace the Russian girls on KP and as waiters. The Russians agreed, and after that everyone ate twice a day during hours of light. The tin cans were washed regularly, each nationality was seated together, and though the quality of the food was the same, we at least knew we would eat. We had meat occasionally in our rice or barley, and it was horse flesh.

We had little incentive and less water to keep clean. On the fourth day, I got three inches of shaving water in a cup for Wiley, George, and me. Delousing of the inhabitants was carried on daily, and men and women went through the process at the same time. However, we Americans were deloused separately. When Polish families of Rembertow and Praga asked to house the Americans until transport was arranged, the Russians refused. Why, we never knew. Possibly they were suspicious of us. If so, they probably had a right to feel that way. In the years between the wars, America and the world did not cooperate full time with Russia.

Colonel Drury was in command of us, and each morning he had an inspection of our floor space. When our officers complained about our living conditions and the danger of typhus and the mild dysentery we were suffering, he said, "Don't look at the forest. Look at the trees. This experience will separate the men from the boys."

Lieutenant Max said to him, "I don't know why you have not been moved from here. But there is so much that goes on behind the political screen."

Colonel Drury replied, "In my humble way, I will await your orders."

When Max assured us that our families had been notified of our release from the Germans, we did not believe him. Later we saw magazines and newspapers of this period in United States stating that no Americans or British had managed to escape during the Russian drive to the Oder and that the Nazis had been successful in moving all their captives from Poland to Germany.

During certain hours of the day we were allowed out of the enclosure guarded by girls and Red Army men. Breazele, Wiley, Herr, and I alternated on selling our clothing to local Poles. Wiley sold his extra pants for eight hundred zlotychs, or about eight dollars on the flexible market. George traded his shirt for eight loaves of white bread, and I parted with my battle jacket for five hundred zlotychs. We bought bread, sausage, onions, and marmalade. Sometimes we splurged and purchased small pastries, but they were fifty cents each and almost prohibitive as we needed a few clothes. Some of the small shops had American lend-lease food for sale. The prices on this were high, but some of our officers bought Russian-sold American butter from the shopkeepers with zlotychs gained from the Poles who bought our clothing, which might be British material or French cloth captured by the Germans. It was a merry-go-round of international finance.

At first it was humiliating, embarrassing, and degrading for our American officers to haggle with Poles over the price of dirty clothing. But we soon got used to it, and it was almost fun. Field officers, company-grade officers, and enlisted men all participated. There was a brisk market for our goods. The best prices were paid by Poles from miles around who were trying to collect complete American uniforms including the insignias with hopes of leaving Poland as a United States soldier and joining their army under General Anders in Italy. Some Poles asked our field officers to get them out of Poland disguised as Americans in order to reach their London-controlled army. But, of course, we could not do this.

British, French, and American NCOs began streaming in from Eastern Germany, and we found they agreed with most of us—that the advance Red Army tank and artillery units were crack troops, but that behind them followed a shambling rabble with orders that must have read, "Fall out in Warsaw, fall in at Berlin."

The large American NCO contingent from Stalag 111 C on the Oder arrived. Charley Feig and Jim Krohn of my old G Company were among them. The first day Krohn sold the underwear in which he was captured for tobacco.

Charley said, "We had quite a time getting here. Three weeks ago the Russians arrived just as Jerry was moving us farther in to Germany. About twenty of the American POWs were killed in the fight. The Russians jumped off the tanks and started firing in to our column before they realized we were Americans. Then they wiped out the German guard company. The Jerries—all last war veterans—would plead for their lives and the Russkies would just let a burst go in to their bellies. Or they might tell the Germans to start running, and then they just cut them down as they ran. They killed everyone. They had no time to fool with prisoners.

"We stayed around the Stalag a week waiting for instructions from the Russians, and we ate the hogs running about there. When we saw the hogs were eating the dead Jerry guards, we decided it was time to move out. Coming out of Germany, we saw the bodies of German civilians piled all around the villages. The first Russian waves were shooting everybody in sight."

"When we hit the road, I stayed at a farm house for a few days and got acquainted with the daughter," Krohn said. "She was pretty and had spent most of 1943 in one of those German soldiers' rest homes which seem to be the Nazi version of our rehabilitation camps—with Jerry innovations. The girl was proud of having been selected for one of these places. She said the rooms were comfortable, the food good, and that it was an honor to sleep with the

Fuehrer's soldiers. She had to pass a strict physical before being accepted and said that most of the girls had babies there, but she didn't happen to."

Krohn said that a few Russians moved in just before he left the farm. "I was in the main room with the Russki officer. He had a lot of maps and papers on the table and was working on them. Right in the next room there was a hell of a scuffle going on, and the mother of this girl was crying. Two Russki G. I.s were in there with her. There's rape now and then in all armies, I know. But we try to do something about it. This officer paid no attention to the situation and kept right on with his paper work. I'm glad those Russians are with us and not against us."

One night there was a German air raid near our area and over the Vistula near Warsaw. The Russian ack-ack defenses were capable. Jerry failed to break up the ice on the Vistula and smash the pontoon bridges. During the raid, one of our Russian guards became excited and for some strange reason threw a grenade which wounded one of our American NCOs outside watching the aerial display. The Russians put him in their hospital and gave him excellent care.

Eight thousand letters for our Oflag were brought by the sick and wounded from Szubin. They had been discovered across the street in the German headquarters and purposely not delivered while we were prisoners. Some of the letters had been received at the camp six months before Jerry marched us out. I searched through the stack but found no word from home.

One day, Lieutenant Max told us that we would have to remain in Rembertow for at least another month, but that in two weeks we would be allowed to write a letter home. And the next day we received information by telegram that Marshall Zhukov had ordered the immediate transportation of all American, British, and French troops to a Russian port for shipment to their countries. Wiley, Breazele, Herr, and I took a gamble that the message was correct and sold all our spare clothes for fourteen-hundred zlotychs, buying two pounds of sausage, eight loaves of bread for the train trip, and several pastries and cups of tea for immediate consumption. The Russians got us soap and tobacco, including twenty-two cigars each, which had been captured in a German warehouse.

The Colonel who was in command of us at the dairy near Exin appeared, having been hiding in Praga to avoid the filth of the assembly camp.

The night before we left the building, the Russians unplugged a barrel of strong wine for the British and Americans, giving each of us a full cup. We had toasts—to Allied victory, to Stalin, Roosevelt, Churchill, to the fighting armies of the United Nations. The dapper CCNY graduate, Lieutenant Max, standing on a table in his boots, uniform, and Sam Browne, gave the last toast. He raised his china mug to the ceiling, said, "Here is to the millions of dollars which Russia owes America!"

We cheered, because we were happy to be once again on the move, and it was one of the few times we had heard any Russians mention lend-lease. We all raised our cups. Max finished with a snap, "And here's to the millions of liters of blood America owes Russia!"

Chapter Twenty-Five

Seven hundred British and Americans made that trip to Odessa on the Black Sea—thirty-seven to a boxcar, one young Russian tommy-gunner guard to each car, our field officers, Russian officers, and Red Army women in the lone coach. No more than four of us from each car were allowed out for the latrine at any one time. Food consisted of two cups of soup daily. The soup was thin with large chunks of pork fat with bristles and the yellow rind floating on top. We were always hoping for some of the lend-lease supply of canned goods but were informed that we could not have any until we had consumed the fifteen-days' ration of soup. The weather was bitter cold, but the Russians had given us a stove for each car and we scrounged wood along the route. By sleeping in shifts all twenty-four hours, we managed to stretch out full length. Our orders from the Russians were to buy no food from the Poles or Russ peasants selling food along the tracks. We would be put in jail at the termination of our journey if we violated these orders. Some of the men, however, entered the market at Rowna during a long halt and sold clothing for bread. When it was discovered the Anglo-Americans did not know the value of the ruble, the price on bread trebled in fifteen minutes.

At Brest-Litovsk we cheered when we glimpsed ten packed boxcars of German prisoners looking stonily out of the small windows—more crowded accommodations than they had provided for any of us on our worst days. At Katuska in the Ukraine we saw Russian men and women smartly marching in the same ranks carrying weapons and singing stirring, martial airs with serious expressions—a far cry from the light or bawdy songs with which our troops usually relax on the march. Parked for eighteen hours in a light blizzard at Komel, we had a conversation with our young, friendly guard. Those of our officers who could speak Polish were able to converse with Russians. We were asked, "Do you have trains in America?"

He was apparently rather proud of the boxcar caravan and hoped we would say we had trains but nothing as good as that on which we were making the peregrination to Odessa. Though he was obviously ignorant of United States standards, he could name all the American possessions—which most of us in our car could not. For eight days, the guard was shooting his sub-machine gun at fence posts or birds as we bumped along. We asked for a few shots, but he refused politely.

The morning of my thirty-fourth night in a boxcar during the war, we arrived in Odessa and our strange group walked silently through the muddy, devastated city with its Turkish, onion-shaped roofs. Russians stood on the curbs and watched us. We knew only by their presence that they were curious about Americans. They were silent, as we were. In a park in the center of the town was a fresh graveyard of heroes of the Soviet who had distinguished themselves in the Odessa fighting. On each tombstone was the picture of the dead soldier. We saw two beggars, which was a surprise to us as we had understood that Communism and the war had done away with that class. Great and small pictures of Stalin looked down at us from every vantage point.

Russian women, some very pretty, passed opposite us on the road, carrying bundles of sticks, sacks, or baskets of scrap-iron. They were shoddy in dress, paid no attention to us, and we outwardly ignored them. Their faces, heavily rouged and well made up with lipstick and other cosmetics, seemed out of place with the rest of their appearance.

A mile outside the city, we entered a large yard surrounded by a stone wall capped with barbed wire and guarded by young Red Army men with fixed bayonets. In the yard was the gaudy old Italian Consulate building, two hundred yards from the Black Sea. The American officers were quartered there, and the enlisted men lived farther down the road in better accommodations, but also fenced in. Thirty of us slept in the large reception room, and after five days the Russians installed electric lights and produced shaving mirrors. Our diet was fish-heads or tails, kosha, and black bread. All but 15 percent of us had starvation dysentery, which was not serious.

Our wounded were taken to a Soviet hospital where they were well cared for, but the Red Army was adamant about no visiting hours. I had a mild case of influenza and was attended by a pretty female doctor who had spent fifteen years in the Red Army and was guarded by an armed male orderly.

We were warned not to leave the grounds. Three American officers got out undetected and walked in to Odessa where they were thrown in jail for several hours. They were returned, but we were informed that if it happened again, the Russian courts would handle the offenders. Walking four hundred yards down the street to the delousing chambers, we were allowed to go only with a Russian "guide," and there was no opportunity to talk to Soviet civilians. Forty of us at a time stood naked in the shower room of the delousing process. Pleasant White Russian women in white dresses handled the administration of the delousing, and though this embarrassed us somewhat, we had grown accustomed to almost anything. A buxom girl came up to one of our men and gave him a firm slap on the bare buttocks. We laughed loudly. The smitten one took it pleasantly with bright blushes and smiles. The recipient of the woman's vigorous humor was a chaplain.

Two American destroyers that had been on hand for the Yalta conference heard about our food situation. They immediately sent us C rations, bacon, pancake mix, coffee, condensed milk, gum, and cigarettes. I don't think any of us will forget the first two cups of Blue Ribbon coffee. An English ship, the *Moreton Bay*, which had just arrived with a boatload of Russian prisoners liberated in Normandy, gave us socks, shoes, tooth powder, soap, cigarettes, and chocolate. The Russian cook-sergeant stole some of our food, but we did not care, as our stomachs were comfortable for the first time since being taken prisoner. The Russians came through with Red Army boots, hats, overcoats, shirts, and trousers.

We gave our old clothes to our Red guards who took them quickly, with no thanks, stuffed them in their coats while looking around to see if any other Russians had seen them, and quickly disappeared. Evidently they were not supposed to have extra clothing in the Communist state at war. At any rate, we could not understand their actions over discarded uniforms.

A Major Hall, Cornell University '42 and a member of the

American Moscow Military Mission, arrived from the United States Embassy. He had flown from Moscow, said that our Government had no word that any of us were free until the day we left Rembertow, and that there were plenty of clothes in Moscow for us—as this situation had been anticipated. But he could not get the clothing to us on such short notice. The Russians had said that we were to remain in Odessa at least thirty more days, but Hall had different ideas and arranged for us to leave almost immediately on the British boat. He took our names and serial numbers and promised that our families would know within forty-eight hours that we were no longer in the hands of the Germans. We doubted this as the Russians had asked for this information five times in two months, and nothing had been done about it. I learned later that Barbara knew I was free twenty-four hours after Hall arrived, and until then had been worrying about me being inside the fast-crumbling Reich. It was the same in all our cases.

As we had gone east through Poland and into Russia, two things had amazed us. One, the much-vaunted Russian Army did not keep its personal weapons clean. Rifles and sub-machine guns slung on the backs of the soldiers were often rusty and dirty—an unforgivable crime in the Western Armies. Two, Red Army soldiers were young in both rear area and front line jobs. Russia had not scraped the bottom of its barrel for combat men. Non-combat administrative positions in the German, British, and to a lesser extent American Armies, were all handled by older men.

Immediately prior to leaving for the boat, a lieutenant colonel from Texas addressed us, saying that most of us would be returned almost immediately to the fighting in France. This was after we had visions of home in a few weeks. But we did not believe him. It was the same officer who had said to his men in the barracks in Szubin the night before we left the Oflag, "This march will be tough. When the Germans run a bayonet through you on the road tomorrow, die like a man." We knew him as a kill-joy.

A Red Army band marched at the head of our column through the streets of Odessa to the docks. A few civilians silently watched us. The band played over and over, "Roll Out the Barrel," apparently the only Anglo-American tune they knew. The British, all captured at Dunkirk sang on their own, "We'll Hang Out Our Washing on the Seigfried Line"—for the news from the West was good, and it was right and fitting to revive the song of the dark days. In between the "Beer Barrel Polka" numbers, we Americans sang "Pistol Packing Mama." The entire column joined in "Rolling Home" as we sighted the British and American boats in the harbor.

We were packed into the *Moreton Bay* every which way, and I slept in the potato hold with Wiley—happier than I had ever been in my life or probably ever will be again. The *Moreton Bay* was the first United Nations vessel to go south through the Bosporus as Turkey had just entered the war. We stayed two days in Istanbul taking on oil and water, which was not furnished in Odessa. It was the prettiest sea port I saw during the war—Asia on one side, Europe on the other, the channel five hundred yards wide, high hills lapped by the sea, snow-capped mountains in the distance. The houses of the modern city were clean and white in Roman and Turkish architecture. Nestled in the gray of the ancient section of Constantinople was St. Sophia where Mohammed II struck his blow at Christianity.

The Sea of Marmara, the Dardanelles, Gallipoli, the Aegean Sea past Crete, the Nile Delta, and then our first whiff of genuine freedom—Port Said in the Suez. The United States Government gave us uniforms, another delousing, beer, and blankets. We began to look and feel like soldiers once again.

Efficiency, cleanliness, friendliness, magazines, cigarettes, candy bars, camp beds, ENSA and USO shows, and sending a cable home created such a ball of happiness in my stomach that it hurt terribly—like pain, love, or hunger. Every meal was like a Christmas dinner, and we felt guilty when we thought of the prisoners of Oflag 64 who were still in Europe. Of the fourteen hundred in our camp, about two hundred had escaped, two hundred were left sick and wounded by the Germans, and about one thousand had been marched in to the Reich.

We were given back pay of one hundred dollars each, and few restrictions were placed on us. Blow-some-steam-and-get-it-out-of-your-systems was the attitude of our commanding officers. The morning after that first night in Port Said, ex-Kriegies had huge heads and black eyes from dimly remembered brawls in perhaps the world's roughest city. Another hundred dollars was paid us, and we bought presents for our families and friends. At night was the smell of Africa and the fresh sea wind—clean and enchanting.

In a few days, once again we were on the move, and as British boat *Samaria* pulled out, the 7th Hussars Band played for us, and the American flag was run up over Cox and Kings. The Mediterranean was blue and warm, and we had double rations for our mild malnutrition. On board, there were fifty-three much sought after women who grew prettier, as always, as the voyage continued. There was much kissing in the corridors of the crowded boat and no one objected or took undue notice. British, French, Americans, Yugoslavs, Norwegians—all once prisoners of the Nazis—made up the passenger list. Three wealthy Polish women who had escaped their country to join the London Colony were riding with us. They had come in to Russia and down to Egypt as the wives of British Tommies who had married them on the journey for the convenience of both parties. The Tommies gained wives for a short period, and the women could leave the country.

At Naples, the Red Cross met us with survivors' kits, sweaters, and doughnuts. We lived on a racetrack near some sulfur baths used by Romans and Greeks—and more recently by King Albert, Kaiser Wilhelm, Mussolini, General Nobile, King Gustave, and Ciano, for sixty cents a plunge. Near the baths was the "Dog Grotto" where canines were put to death for the amusement of spectators before the war.

I had not heard from Barbara for nine months. I sent her an airmail letter telling her to come east from Iowa and meet me on the Bucks County farm, and the next day we sailed for the last lap on the *Mariposa*. In Germany, the last round was on and this time there was to be no gong. The ship seemed to be riding in the clouds, and during the nights I was so excited I could not sleep. I thought over the last forty-three months while smoking in the dark of the quiet cabin.

War: Separation and unnecessary worry were the two worst parts of it. It was worth fighting if it had cost many times the lives and dollars it eventually totaled.

Russia: It is wise not to get too excited with that country, but to talk back when necessary. We must not be obsequious with her, and it will be prudent to call her bluff on future occasions. Russians are childlike, blunt, pushing, and naive, and we must make a tremendous universal effort to cope with them and understand them. Russia must let us get information in to their country, and take information out of the Soviet Union to the world. Only in this way can understanding be reached and the roots of well-founded suspicions among Russia, Great Britain, and America destroyed. Statesmen, reporters, and military observers have seen little of Russia except Moscow, and our problems with Russia are largely unknown and mostly suspected. If we continue movements to create buffer states against Red Russia, naturally the U.S.S.R. will be security-conscious to a high degree. What we permit Russia to do and see, they must permit us to do and see. If we sincerely work for this, we will keep the "Beat Russia" rooters in the five-cent seats where they would sit if we had a third World War anyway.

England: More than one out of every ten soldiers returning from overseas thinks that we will have armed hostilities against England sooner or later. We won't.

England fears the hidden, deadly, dormant germ of isolationism, which she knows is in America. She fears it will come out of its abeyance in post-war disillusionment. To protect herself, therefore, she might build a bloc of nations which would only lead to a rival alliance. She does not realize that America does not realize that for England to exist at all she must be in some sort of form of Empire.

I liked the English—as differentiated from the British—personally. But it took me many months of very close contact with them to arrive at this absolute conclusion. Many Allied soldiers did not see or comprehend England's easy, pleasant way of life. It was not apparent at a glance. Because the United Kingdom's plumbing is not as good as America's, it is no criterion on which to base the statement, "Those people do not know how to live."

Poland: Like most of America, I never thought much about the Poles one way or another—until I was in their country. Their internal situation for centuries has been a chronic ulcer in the world. Poles are the first to admit when they are to blame, and they do not exonerate themselves in all their troubles. But they have not been entirely at fault. If we do not remove the basic economic flaws which have embroiled Poland in all its bondage and fighting, the country will be the birthplace of World War III— which will be the first of its type, as World War II was the last of its type.

The Poles individually are well educated, possess a sense of humor and pristine courage, and are the kindest, most generous people I have ever met—possibly because they have suffered so much themselves.

Germany: Because they have lost two wars in succession, the Germans have not given up hope. A strong country and people in defeat, they must be policed for at least forty years and placed in long-term restraint after our soldiers leave. We should not do this because we seek revenge for the Nazi effort to demoralize the entire world, but because Germany is capable of a quick renaissance and it will then be they who seek revenge. Many pressures and views, some natural and some fostered by Germany itself, will be loose in America and the world and difficult to resist. Sob sisters who wish to point to the evils of the Versailles Treaty might examine the armistice agreements the Reich forced on its defeated European neighbors. Those who were in Germany before the defeat of its armies know that not only did the headline Nazi gang believe that man has no rights, only duties, but also the people were solidly behind the evil doctrines. With few exceptions, the German people were all for Hitler and enjoyed without objections the fruits of the early Nazi victories. Granted that the Germans were badly led, the fact remains that they followed gladly and the ideas of that leadership will exist in people's minds for two generations.

America: Having seen many nations and tongues in the last years, I realized we are still a nation of children. We have the violent, unreasoning prejudices of children. We have the willfulness and boastfulness of children, but we are more fresh and alive and infinitely more fun than other peoples and countries.

To remain the greatest country in the world, we need honest leaders in all our departments who will put the public interest above personal political ambitions. We must mature quickly, before it is too late. We who have suffered so little and have so much cannot, in the flush of victory, forsake the countries and ideals for which we fought—disregarding the political, economic, and social interpretations and causes for the war. I remember a hill we had taken along the Moselle, and after the battle we adopted the attitude of thank-the-Lord-this-is-over. We had not made immediate and proper preparations for a counter-attack, and when the Nazis came at us, we lost the objective for which we had shed blood. Active living and thinking by all America is now our responsibility—so that we do not lose our objective.

If our individual thinking is wrong, no matter; the important thing is that our people think. And out of the mass thought will come peace that is more than an armistice. We do not want United States to be the world's Father Christmas, and we can avoid this by using the kind of sound judgment, which founded our country—judgment which was not colored by preconceived opinions and ridiculous demands. Unless we meet its requirements more high-mindedly, we shall lose our world—the world we almost lost this time.

America will be tired mentally and physically when the proceedings are closed. The people will realize there is no immediate danger of war. We will quickly depart from the martial tang in our reading, thinking, and actions. We will relax and have a building boom and more babies. It will be difficult to keep awake and have our long-term international policies constantly in front of us. Therein lies the danger for the next generation.

Soldiers: Those of all nations were scared when facing a capable enemy. The few at the front who were not afraid were not normal. Well-trained soldiers of all the Allies were about the same in action. As a nationality, there was no great superiority of one over another. Untrained soldiers or soldiers who had received confusing orders from higher headquarters were more pusillanimous in the face of the enemy than those who knew why we were in the war and had received clear-cut instructions on the mission. There were a few men in all the armies who were not mentally fit for combat duty but did excellent work in rear echelon jobs. Combat qualities are ones that can not be determined until the man actually is faced by the enemy—and most men found that they were mentally fit for action, much to their own surprise as they admitted later.

Very few soldiers, in comparison to civilians, criticized the Allies' top commanders. Any criticism they had to offer among themselves was reserved for officers they knew and could see. And there was not much of this in the front line, as all of us were new to war and had few new solutions of our own to offer. Any criticizing was usually done after the Hun was at a safe distance.

Nearly half the soldiers returning from overseas have the philosophy of despair—that there will be another war within twenty-five years. About one in ten believes that there won't be another World War for fifty years. The majority of soldiers who actually had fought the enemy were caught in the draft and ordered to a line outfit, and there was nothing they could do to change the circumstances. The minority of the soldiers who came through the war without serious wounds feels their country owes them a living. Those who were up there for a severe, long whack are so thankful it is over for them that they will gladly take civilian jobs with less glamour and responsibility. Soldiers will, after an initial six months, readjust themselves to civilian life as easily as they did after the more vigorous change, which came in to their lives when they joined the forces. However, life had assumed a great meaning and a terrific purpose during the war, and when this is suddenly taken away from an individual by peace, it creates a vacuum in his existence—a vacuum which is filled by nostalgia and depression. Life is apparently without a great purpose. The close companionship most soldiers found in the army will perhaps never again enter their lives, and so we are bound to have a certain amount of the "lost generation" attitude. But for the most part it will be an attempt by pseudo-heroes to glamorize the war or use it as an excuse for idleness.

Our soldiers talk of keeping the peace and making a better world and they have an interest in what is going on. Broadened, this same age group before the war would have devoted more time to discussions on larger refrigerators, the Cardinals and the Cubs, and what Jane said to Nancy about Jimmy. Full reality of the war hits the soldiers when they meet the gold star parents—who are the most tragic of all the aftermaths of war. Only then does the big meaning of those deaths in actions strike home. For the man who died, it was usually a sudden death and no pain. For the man who watched him die, it was just one of those things on which one did not dwell. But meeting the parents is different.

The soldier in civilian life will stew a while about the kind of future he will have and then he will take up his work. He will gradually forget about many things except when he annually joins the parade of old-timers on Armistice Day—a parade which will form at Jackson Park, follow down Main Street to Fourth, go west on Fourth to Locust, and disband at the Elks Club. Then, for a few hours, he will be faithful to old memories, old turns of expression, old associations.

Myself: Many things had happened since that 60th Rifles sergeant had given me the first command, "By the right, quick march!" I had come to know myself—where I was a failure and on what points I was weak. I would be generous in the overseas way—such as we were when the going was the roughest. I would avoid having the perpetual, nervous ball in the stomach, because I had learned it was not worth it. I would avoid this ball by distinguishing between what is important and what is not important. The important would thrash itself out without suffering the tortures of the damned. I would be tolerant and not jealous. I would spend often but not foolishly—because I had been caught on buying worthless trinkets in foreign countries. In civilian pursuits I would live an easy pleasant life, seeking natural contentment rather than momentary happiness. Life was short, but there was plenty of time for everything—and I would not rush. I would take for granted that 90 percent of the people are wholly sincere and genuine until proven otherwise. I would not be a war bore. I would settle for an occasional remembrance of something that was good and fine and—such is the alchemy of memory—forget what was sordid, filthy, and foul.

I knew that these were all simple truths, but that they had been said so many times they had lost all their meanings in platitudes and in the months of Arbuthnots. But I thought in forty-three months I had learned how to live.

Chapter Twenty-Six

The *Mariposa* was nearing Boston, and we could see the red and white night skyline. It was a moment I can't explain. But I knew it happened only once in a lifetime, and this was it. There was cheering as we tied in at the port, but inside we were subdued, quiet, and thankful. As the first full boatload of prisoners to return to America and with Europe in its last heaves of the war, we were treated as heroes. We knew we were not heroes—but just lucky.

Bewildered, happy, nervous, we looked at the signs—"Dine, Dance, Variety," "Drugs," "Johnny Walker." The next day we made the anxious telephone calls. All was well. Barbara was waiting for me at the farm. We talked for twenty minutes. She had waited thirteen weeks after the "missing-in-action" telegram before the arrival of news that I was a prisoner. Braden had become an assistant Military Attaché in the London Embassy and later joined the Office of Strategic Services in Italy. Alsop had jumped in France and fought with the Maquis. He and Tish had married in England. Danielson had transferred to the American Army. Fowler was with the 60th Rifles in Greece. Thomson had gone to China with the O. S. S.

Going down the New England Coast by train, we were unaccustomed to railroad tracks that were not ripped and twisted, houses that were not caved in from fighting, shelling, and bombing, and store windows that were not empty or smashed. Headlines of newspapers jumped out at us, and it was strange to see them after the conservative ones of Europe.

I met Barbara in the living room, and she said I looked like an excited little boy. For an hour we asked questions and talked fast. And then we went upstairs to our room and she handed me the letter that I've included in the front of this book.

I took her in my arms and everything was as I had dreamed.

Glossary

AEF: Australian Expeditionary Force.

Alamein: The Battle of El Alamein, Egypt, then a British colony. El Alamein was a strategic command post, which later played a crucial role in the Allied attack on Libya, eventually heading north into Italy.

Arbuthnots: A reference to British soldiers.

Army Specialized Training Program (ASTP): A short-lived program that recruited college students and hastily prepared them for a specialized job in the army. Most of these skills were normal professional skills, such as medicine, dentistry, psychology, linguistics, and engineering.

Aski Mark: A form of German currency that was used during the period between the world wars. The aski could only be used within the German borders to purchase German goods. The value was often manipulated by the German Reichsbank and could not be converted into foreign currency. Because of these restrictions, it was worth much less than the standard form of German currency, the Reichsmark.

Baronet: A hereditary title of British nobility, ranking higher than a knight, but lower than a baron.

Battle of Britain: July 10, 1940–October 31, 1940. The German onslaught of Great Britain, first by way of the English Channel, then the British Royal Air Force fields, and finally the city of London, resulting in huge numbers of civilian casualties. The battle was a series of firsts: history's first war battle fought entirely in the air, the first use of radar as a means to track the location of aircraft, and the first German military defeat of the war, resulting in Winston Churchill's proclamation of Britain's "finest hour."

Beveridge Plan: The 1942 plan of Sir William Beveridge, laying out Britain's postwar plans for the establishment of a welfare state, social security, and a national health service.

The Big Parade: A 1925 silent movie comedy/romance about an American soldier's experience in World War I.

Boche: French slang for "rascal," originally used during World War I as a pejorative term for a German. The British soon adopted it as their own colloquialism.

Boston: The Douglas DB-7 light bombing attack airplane.

Bren Gun: The Bren Gun was a portable, lightweight machine gun used primarily by British soldiers during and after World War II. It was originally a Czech design and its name is derived from the city of Brno and the "en" of Enfield.

Burp Gun: A Russian machine gun that used a circular magazine to load its rounds. The Germans were known to have been very impressed with this weapon and took any that they could find.

Cripps' Mission to India: In 1942, Richard Stafford Cripps traveled to India (then a British colony) to garner Indian support for the Allied efforts. For decades, Indian dissidents had been rallying for independence. The mission failed to secure the support that Cripps had sought.

Curson Line: The border between Poland and the Soviet Union, settled at Versailles and drawn in 1919 by Lord Curzon, the British foreign minister. The border was drawn not according to ethnic boundaries, but according to diplomatic and historical ones. As compensation for the loss of ethnic territories to the Soviets in the east, some territory was ceded from Germany in the west.

Darlan Arrangement: The appointment of Francois Darlan as the head administrator of the French colonies after the fall of Vichy France to the Germans.

Dornier: German bomber

DSO: Distinguished Service Officer, a British award for bravery in battle.

FA: Field Artillery

Free French: This term refers to the exiled government seated in Vichy, southern France, after the fall of Paris to the Germans in 1940.

German Junkers Ju 88: An airborne bomber often used during blitzkrieg raids, known for its speed and range.

Halifax: A British bomber.

Jerboa: A small, nocturnal, leaping rodent indigenous to North Africa.

KP: Kitchen Police.

K-Ration: Ration of food issued to U.S. troops. The package was lightweight and contained enough food for one day (three meals). Originally praised for its usefulness, it eventually was criticized because of overuse, sometimes forcing the troops to eat the same meal every day for months at a time.

Kriegie: Abbreviation for Kriegsgefangener, German for "prisoner of war."

"Lala:" Lala Andersen was a Swedish big-band singer during the 1930s and 1940s. Her signature song was "Lilli Marlene," a German tune about a girl who fancies men in uniform. It became wildly popular among Nazi soldiers.

Lance-Jack: British slang for a Lance-Corporal.

Lee-Enfield Rifle: This was a World War I era bolt-action rifle, Britain's main infantry firearm. Both the Bren Gun and the Lee-Enfield Rifle used the same ammunition.

Lend-lease: An agreement between the U.S. and the Allies to supply American-made war goods to the British and Soviets. Under this arrangement, the U.S. would send supplies to the Allies, with the recipient repaying the goods at the end of the war, with interest. The plan began nine months before Pearl Harbor and lasted until just after the Japanese surrender.

Lublin: City in southeastern Poland; in 1944, the Soviets "liberated" this city and established the first post-war Polish government there. The following year, the capital was moved to Warsaw as a puppet communist government.

Mark IV: A model of Sherman Tank

Naffy: British slang for N.A.A.F.I. (Navy, Army, and Air Force Institutes), the catering services for the British Armed forces widely mocked for serving awful food.

OCTU: Officer Cadet Training Unit

Old Monty: Bernard Montgomery, British army officer who, as lieutenant-general, commanded the Allied forces at El Alamein, defeating Rommel's German forces.

Pescara: Italian city on the Adriatic coast where Allied bombers landed in 1943. Ninety percent of this city was destroyed in the raids.

St. Nazaire raid: The 1942 British mission to destroy the loading docks at St. Nazaire, in Normandy, France, a key port used by the Germans to gain access to the Atlantic Ocean.

Schmeisser: The German MP40 submachine gun, known for its low production costs, sharp accuracy, small size, and light recoil.

Schutzstaffel: Elite Nazi paramilitary guard, commonly referred to as the SS. They had uniforms, rank, and organization separate from the regular army.

Sherman: The Sherman tank, named in honor of Civil War General William T. Sherman. Many Shermans were sent to the British as a result of the lend-lease program.

Square-bashing: A military drill practiced on a barracks square.

Stinger: a heat-seeking surface-to-air missile launcher that rested on a soldier's shoulder.

Ulio: Major James Ulio, commander of the U.S. 29th infantry division during World War II.

The 34th Red Bull Division: This was the first division of the U.S. Army to fight alongside British troops in World War II. They landed at Salerno, Italy, on September 19th 1943; the casualty results were disastrous.

Touhy gang: Chicago mafia outfit, led by Roger Touhy.

War Debts: During the First World War, Great Britain financed its war production, in part, through loans from the United States. At the outbreak of World War II, Britain had not yet repaid its debt to the U.S. and eventually borrowed even more money to finance their participation in the second world war.

Yalta Conference: The conference held in Yalta, in southern Ukraine, in February 1945 between the "big three" Allied leaders: Winston Churchill of the United Kingdom, Joseph Stalin of the Soviet Union, and Franklin Delano Roosevelt of the United States. The conference laid out the postwar occupation of Germany, which was to be divided into four occupation zones (one for each country present, plus France), as well as a quadripartite occupation of Berlin. These partitions eventually became East and West Germany and Berlin.

Acknowledgements

We would like to thank Elizabeth Alsop Winthrop, whose guidance and encouragement were invaluable, and Peter Carry for believing in the legacy of this story. We are deeply grateful to Thunder's Mouth Press, and especially to Johnny Saunders and John Oakes who shared our vision of this book. Dad inspired others to help bring his story to the public, including Tom Braden, Tom Stoner, Lavonne Ellsworth, Bill Donlon, Karl Zobell, and Richard Speaks.

Index

Y

Z